CU00690653

BUILDING BRAND COMMUNITIES

ALSO BY CHARLES H. VOGL

The Art of Community: 7 Principles for Belonging
Storytelling for Leadership: Creating Authentic Connection

BUILDING BRAND COMMUNITIES

HOW ORGANIZATIONS SUCCEED BY CREATING BELONGING

CARRIE MELISSA JONES
CHARLES H. VOGL

BK®

Berrett–Koehler Publishers, Inc.

Berrett-Koehler Publishers, Inc.
1333 Broadway, Suite 1000
Oakland, CA 94612–1921
Tel: (510) 817-2277   Fax: (510) 817-2278 www.bkconnection.com

Ordering Information

Quantity sales. Special discounts are available on quantity purchases by corporations, associations, and others. For details, contact the "Special Sales Department" at the Berrett-Koehler address above.

Individual sales. Berrett-Koehler publications are available through most bookstores. They can also be ordered directly from Berrett-Koehler: Tel: (800) 929-2929   Fax: (802) 864-7626; www.bkconnection.com

Orders for college textbook/course adoption use. Please contact Berrett-Koehler: Tel: (800) 929-2929; Fax: (802) 864-7626.

Distributed to the U.S. trade and internationally by Penguin Random House Publisher Services.

Berrett-Koehler and the BK logo are registered trademarks of Berrett-Koehler Publishers, Inc.

Printed in the United States of America

Berrett-Koehler books are printed on long-lasting acid-free paper. When it is available, we choose paper that has been manufactured by environmentally responsible processes. These may include using trees grown in sustainable forests, incorporating recycled paper, minimizing chlorine in bleaching, or recycling the energy produced at the paper mill.

Library of Congress Cataloging-in-Publication Data
Names: Jones, Carrie Melissa, author. | Vogl, Charles H., author.
Title: Building brand communities: how organizations succeed by creating belonging /
    Carrie Melissa Jones and Charles H. Vogl.
Description: First edition. | Oakland, CA: Berrett-Koehler Publishers, [2020] |
    Includes bibliographical references and index.
Identifiers: LCCN 2019054295 | ISBN 9781523086610 (hardcover) |
    ISBN 9781523086627 (pdf) | ISBN 9781523086634 (epub)
Subjects: LCSH: Branding (Marketing) | Brand loyalty. | Customer relations.
Classification: LCC HF5415.1255 .J655 2020 | DDC 658.8/27—dc23
LC record available at https://lccn.loc.gov/2019054295

FIRST EDITION
26 25 24 23 22 21 20   10 9 8 7 6 5 4 3 2 1

Production manager: Susan Geraghty
Cover design: Nola Burger
Interior design and composition: Westchester Publishing Services
Copyeditor: Michele D. Jones
Proofreader: Cathy Mallon
Indexer: Rebecca Plunkett
Author photos: Ruby Somera [Carrie Melissa Jones]; Tony Deifell [Charles Vogl]
Illustrations: Dianna Brosius

From Charles to Kep.
In whatever way is yours,
may you bind others with purpose
in ways that both inspire and heal them.

From Carrie to Marcella.
Your mother taught me everything
about connection. Follow her
and you will always remain near to hugs,
a table full of friends,
and a community to guide you.

CONTENTS

We have all known the long loneliness and we have learned that the only solution is love and that love comes with community.

—**Dorothy Day**

The most daring thing is to create stable communities in which the terrible disease of loneliness can be cured.

—**Kurt Vonnegut**

PREFACE

A Note from Charles

Readers of my book *The Art of Community* know that my journey toward community expertise began with my own lonely years wondering if I'd ever create the friendships that I wanted or find a place where I knew that I belonged. It took many years and travel through several time zones in Africa and Asia to get to a place where those thoughts no longer distract me. On the journey, the miles were less important than the wise words from mentors, examples from my now heroes, and too many embarrassing experiments to remember.

The journey never ends. It's a daily practice to remain connected to the people I love, reach out to the people I want to know better, and ensure that I'm supporting people important to me. My personal community is a dynamic creature that needs attention, feeding, hugs, and occasionally a shoulder to cry on. This of course is normal and the best-case scenario.

It's been a pleasure and a privilege to learn that the principles distilled in *The Art of Community* have inspired dinners, rituals, retreats, family reunions, heartfelt speeches, and long deep conversations across continents. Thank God for you who gather people you care about.

When starting this book, we aspired to write a guide that would speak equally to and embolden leaders in nonprofits, businesses, civic agencies, faith organizations, and political movements. Indeed, we believe nearly every principle discussed will serve all of these leaders equally.

We educate and encourage leaders to invest in authentic brand communities that both serve organizational goals and also enrich, support, and even heal participants. In our aspiration, this will replace misguided, shortsighted, and exploitative efforts.

As we developed this book, it grew apparent that the language of business and nonprofit leadership is different enough from that of social, cultural, faith, and political movements that we could not write a single book that speaks to both audiences equally well. This is disappointing.

This book speaks directly to businesses and nonprofit leadership in applicable language because they will continue to invest astounding resources to both connect to and gather people for the foreseeable future. In fact, we personally consult with organizations that collectively touch far more than one billion people, and their influence grows daily. Such investments will accelerate as organizations adapt to our growing "experience economy"[1] in which customers seek appealing experiences that connect them with brands.

For those considering this resource to support movements making our era safer, more welcome, honest, and connected, please take what serves you. It's here for you, and our hearts go with you.

This little book is an offering to help everyone working toward more connection, healing, generosity, love, safety, and joy in a time that really needs it. We promise it is the best we could do at the time.

May all of us who pick up these ideas teach the next generation to conquer the loneliness and disconnection of our time.

Go get them and Godspeed.

Charles Vogl, M.Div.
Beautiful Oakland, CA

A Note from Carrie

When I was ten years old, a teacher asked my mom if I was mute, and my hand shook when I raised it in class. Speaking up was painful.

Yet my silence hid a deep hunger for connection. I wanted someone to ask me, "How are you?" and then wait the five minutes I needed to offer an answer. I both wished for and feared what might happen if others knew my inner world, so I kept my mouth shut.

But when I turned fourteen years old, my father set up a hand-me-down computer in my bedroom. Little did he know that plugging in those cables sparked a career that would lead me to one day connect people around the world—employees, customers, and innovators—and would eventually lead to this book.

At that time, emo (emotional) music—filled with screaming about unrequited love—offered me a safe container for my angst and loneliness. At first, I listened alone in my room. With that "new" computer, I discovered that I could listen with others. I found forums sponsored by my favorite musicians. They felt magical to me: a place where I could find my voice. We talked about music, but more often, we talked about our lives. I dropped my emotional armor online and, for the first time, felt confident that I could speak up and be known.

The forums helped me connect to both my favorite musicians and others around the world. My online friends lived in the Philippines, Florida, England, and New York. We chatted until the wee hours and made phone calls when tragedy struck. These friends taught me how to accept and be accepted. But only from a distance, online.

One night, my childhood friend Samantha called. I listened to her cry before a word came out. Gasping, she asked to meet outside my house. This was the first time someone asked for me in a crisis. Outside, she fell into my arms and then, on my street curb, she shared the painful and vulnerable hurt inside. Just as I shared with others online. I knew to sit and listen.

She then asked if I was OK. For the first time in my life, I answered honestly. I shared feeling alone and broken, forgotten and invisible. I hadn't yet processed personal family tragedies or my own loneliness with anyone face-to-face. Then I too cried. And she too remained and held me.

Our friendship, cemented that night, got me through high school safely.

Only as an adult do I now recognize my teenage depression, anxiety, and traumatic stress. Then, I saw only a dark pit of loneliness before experiencing being held and accepted. Those musicians, those fans, those concerts, and those forums connected us as lifelong enthusiasts. They taught me how to create community online and then to extend it into my neighborhood and school. I now recognize that we made a life-changing brand community.

So, with hard-won lessons, I now choose to be in connection. Even when (especially when) it hurts. I recognize the importance of a place, online or physical, where fans, friends, colleagues, neighbors, classmates, or anyone else can discover that someone cares. That someone will remain.

Now I help others create this within organizations around the world. There is no cause too small to gather around. Playing with makeup, mobilizing a social movement, and resurrecting a rural school are all great reasons to join together.

Many mistakenly assume that strong community always looks "touchy-feely," like emotional blathering and directionless wandering. In real-world practice, community is a key to unlocking many critical outcomes, such as innovation, crisis response, and policy change.

Measurable outcomes and relationship building are not opposite ends of a spectrum. They're connected. Most people just don't know how to connect them. I hope that through this book you will discover what many are missing.

Welcome.

Carrie Melissa Jones
Seattle, WA

INTRODUCTION

If you're reading this now, it's likely that you want to bring people together in a new or more powerful way. Kudos to you. The world needs more people like you. We wrote this book to make you more effective, become a stronger community leader, and help you avoid bad and potentially hurtful mistakes.

Over years, miles, and time zones, many people have approached us seeking help to build communities for their organizations. This includes numerous schools, political advocacy groups, professional collectives, religious organizations, and, of course, for-profit companies spanning the globe. All want to invest in bringing together the people important to them. These include employees, customers, colleagues, political and artistic collaborators, and volunteers. These leaders all aspire to build a community that serves both their organization and the envisioned members. Doing this in a way that honestly enriches members and delivers organizational benefits looks like mystical enchantment to many.

Many professional community managers have also shared their longing for something that articulates what they already do and for wisdom to make them better.

Both the words *community* and *brand* lack singular definitions in leadership writing. Although several definitions may be useful in differing contexts, the discrepancies create much confusion. We use our own working definitions in this book.

We define a **community** as a group of people who share mutual concern for one another. A **brand** is any identifiable organization that promises value, no matter its size or mission. A brand can serve for-profit, nonprofit, political, social, artistic, faith-based (or any other) purposes.

It follows that a **brand community** is any (real) community that aspires to serve both members and (at least one) organizational goal.[1] They're often started by, inspired by, or managed by an established organization, but not necessarily so.

Although brand communities will (1) look and feel very different from one another, (2) work toward different goals, and (3) address different maturity stages, *many core principles remain the same* no matter where or who makes them, or what their purpose. You will recognize these principles by the end of this book.

Many aspiring leaders don't even know how to articulate the ways imagined communities will serve their organization. They often assume that community is (probably) better than no community. It's also often hard for them to articulate how their community will enrich members within it.

We'll discuss the most common ways authentic communities serve organizational goals and thus warrant meaningful investment:

- *Innovation:* creating *new* value for stakeholders
- *Customer and stakeholder retention:* keeping customers and stakeholders involved with the organization and providing value to the brand
- *Marketing:* informing the market of offered value
- *Customer service:* helping customers/users with the brand service or products
- *Talent recruitment and retention:* attracting and retaining the people your organization needs for success
- *Advancing movements:* creating a fundamental shift in the culture or business
- *Community forum:* making the brand a destination for a specific community

Building Community (versus Promotion and Mobilizing)

We use the term **building community** to mean *facilitating, accelerating, and supporting the individual relationships that together form a community.* Authentic community building is a pointillistic endeavor. A community exists as a network of relationships made up of participant pairs feeling trust and appreciation between them. Each relationship is like a "point" in our bigger view of community. If we facilitate enough authentic interconnected relationships and nurture them over time, we create a community. We think of this metaphorically as growing relationship threads that knit together into community. (See figure I.1.)

Some resources use the term *building community* to refer to promoting events or mobilizing groups. This includes instructing organizations in what social media platforms to leverage, posts to write, and photos to share (promotion), and how to leverage established connections to coordinate action (mobilize). Although both promotion and mobilization can be compatible with community building, and are often important, we make a distinction between each activity, for several reasons.

First, tools and strategies for promoting are well known and accessible. Please use the best honest tools to promote your events and community programs.

Second, you can both promote many events and mobilize thousands of people while building little or no community. Film screenings, park concerts, and trash pickup days do this all the time, with no criticism from us. For

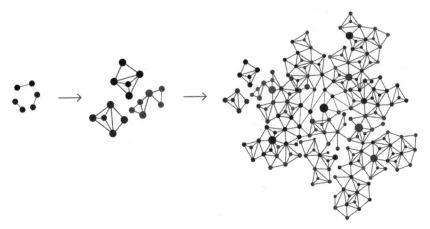

FIGURE I.1. The Network of Connections

community builders, focusing too much on promotion or calls to action can mean overlooking the principles that grow connections when and where people show up.

Third, believe it or not, public promotion isn't always necessary for a successful brand community. Many robust communities don't need to promote or even grow membership. We know of brand communities that remain invitation-only and keep the admission process secret. They know that size and intimacy are inversely related, and they want a tight-knit, effective, dare we say "elite" membership.

Unfortunately, many mistakenly believe that if you just bring people together (e.g., at a concert or bar), enduring relationships naturally form. Although you may get lucky, this rarely happens without proper supporting principles at play.

Our Lonely Era

Research indicates that you (and everyone you know) live in the loneliest era in American history. Nearly *half* of Americans report sometimes or always feeling alone. One in four Americans *rarely or never* feel as though there are people who understand them. And two in five Americans sometimes or always feel that *their relationships are not meaningful* and that they're isolated from others.[2]

This isolation trend has been getting worse.[3] Teens in the US today are now "less likely to get together with friends in person, go to parties, go out with friends, date, ride in cars for fun, go to shopping malls, or go to the movies" than the generations before them. To be clear, teens do gather differently, but they are more isolated overall than seemingly ever before.[4]

The trend is sharply affecting mortality rates. When we look at large populations, there is a positive relationship between loneliness (disconnection) and suicide.[5] Said bluntly, the more loneliness, the more suicide. Teenage suicides are at an all-time high.[6] In fact, the number-two cause of teenage death in the US is suicide. The number-one cause is accidents, which includes all car, firearm, drowning, and poisoning events combined.[7] The rising rate of suicide, although affecting certain groups and intersections of groups more than others, is occurring across gender, class, and ethnic categories. We live in a time when the wealthy city of Palo Alto, California, must create a Track Watch program to hire patrolling security guards to prevent teenage suicides along rail lines.[8]

Loneliness at Work

The growing loneliness trend doesn't apply just to our teenagers. We Americans spend more time at work than with our families. Yet loneliness at work is such a crisis that the *Harvard Business Review* has published a front-page article with the unsubtle title "Work and the Loneliness Epidemic: Reducing Isolation at Work Is Good for Business," by former US surgeon general Dr. Vivek Murthy. Research indicates that "strong social connections at work make employees more likely to be engaged with their jobs and produce higher-quality work, and less likely to fall sick or be injured. Without strong social connections, these gains become losses."[9]

Research also indicates that there is a link between loneliness and low organizational commitment among professionals in fields as diverse as hospitality, education, and medicine.[10] Lonely people disengage, and such disengagement costs organizations of all types in many ways, including "almost 37% higher absenteeism, 49% more accidents, 16% lower profitability, and a 65% lower share price over time."[11]

Our work-based communities are disintegrating. Among non-self-employed Americans, the number of those who regularly work at home has more than doubled since 2005, and these workers frequently state loneliness is a major concern.[12]

Moreover, loneliness has profound health effects. Loneliness is as bad for your body as smoking as many as fifteen cigarettes a day.[13] It causes stress and thus elevation of the stress hormone cortisol, which at high levels is connected to inflammation, heart disease, digestive problems, and sleep regulation problems, among many others. Loneliness can erode our thinking, including our analytical ability, concentration, memory, decision-making skills, and emotional regulation.[14] So if you care about the people you work with (socially, professionally, politically, philanthropically) remaining emotionally, mentally, and physically capable, then attending to how connected your teams grow is important to you too.

Technical and Digital Context

Despite this reality, when we speak to Americans, most mistakenly think that we're in a more connected era because of the new digital tools for reaching others. The truth is, we're all far less connected and way more distracted. Distraction caused by digital devices is so powerful that just putting our digital devices in our view distracts us from full enjoyment in social interactions.[15]

Research indicates that even using digital devices for conveniences (such as Googling walking directions rather than asking a stranger) reduces social connection.[16]

Those who turn to digitally connected communities for relationships experience at least two shortcomings that often go unresolved. The first is that most social media "connections" are, at best, only weak ties. And every minute spent entertaining weak ties is possible time taken away from creating or deepening strong ties. Over years, the distraction of social media–based weak ties radically changes the number of strong friendships we can turn to when we need friends most. These needs range from pet-sitting to shoulders to cry on.

Charles, for example, has more than fifteen hundred "friends" on one social media account. Far fewer than one hundred showed up to help him move across the country. He's not confused about the difference between real and social media friends.

There are many well-intentioned organizations that "connect" citizens and neighbors to share information such as local crime incidents, town hall events, and civic alerts. They serve real needs and provide convenient, even lifesaving information. But let's recognize that past generations received similar information from friends and neighbors in regular conversations. They met new neighbors by knocking on their doors. Although new technology offers a lot of information, relying on these tools doesn't grow the relationships that used to form among citizens and neighbors.[17] Either we learn to invest differently in such relationships, or they won't form.

Organizations Want to Invest

Smart for-profit and nonprofit organizations recognize that there is a widespread hunger for connection and are investing to address it. Many seek a way to profit by addressing the new isolation.[18] We don't object. We do object to the amount of rhetoric about community compared to actual community building.

Marketing departments and C-suites continue to use the term *community* to label wide-ranging organizational investments, including neighborhood events, charity partnerships, online forums, and even simple email lists. But a closer look reveals that most (and sometimes all) of the community-building measures are superficial or even irrelevant to real community.

In fact, the term *community* has been used by brands to refer to so many ideas over the past twenty years that the word has lost whatever shared meaning it once had—a loss for the organizations as well as the individuals within these so-called communities. We call these so-called communities **mirage communities**: groups that organizations may label as communities, but that a trained eye can recognize are not. (We will discuss mirage communities further in chapter 1.)

When we ask individuals inside organizations how they define community and how they understand its importance for their roles, most are hard pressed to define the term for their work. Often the best they can come up with is, "Community is good for people." The answer is hollow at best and meaningless at worst.

Although brand communities do not and will not totally resolve this era's isolation crisis, they can address many hungers:

- How individuals grow and form friendships that support one another

- How we grow beyond our own individual and team limitations

- How we restore feelings of agency and efficacy

- How we gather to form meaningful relationships

- How we set up future generations to avoid our era's loneliness

Although successful brand communities must serve organizational goals, to build an effective brand community, you must begin by rejecting the premise that everything an organization does or offers must serve profit or exist in a transaction. Real communities are made up of relationships. Always. Relationships exist in the realm of personal experience, and although they may include transactions, they are never purely transactional. They include some generosity, at least the kind where we help others without calculating the return on investment (ROI) for sending a card, answering a timely question, or holding a door open for a stranger coming in from the cold. Said differently, community relationships transcend transaction.

People don't commit to, feel safe in, or extend themselves for relationships that only serve a person (or brand) "getting" something as cheaply and easily as possible. We commit to relationships where we believe that others care about our success too.

In real community, members help one another become who they want to be. This can include sharing information, skills, hard-won lessons, and, very often, attentive friendship. When a brand can offer this to members (customers, users, staff, colleagues, volunteers), then something much richer and more rewarding can develop.

Brand Communities in the World

Let's consider some real-world examples of brand communities that made a difference for organizations that invested in connecting people important for their success.

Twitch

Twitch is the largest online gathering space for people to watch and stream live digital video broadcasts. Over two hundred million people visit it each month to see over one million broadcasters.

Twitch's business depends on a two-sided marketplace. That is, the brand needs successful broadcasters to use the Twitch platform to reach audiences, and Twitch needs many more viewers to return to the platform for content. Marcus Graham, Twitch's director of creator development, understands that to make the business work, both broadcasters and viewers need to understand and feel that they belong in the Twitch community. In fact, helping them recognize that Twitch provides supportive and responsive relationships is Twitch's competitive advantage over other broadcasting platforms. Twitch therefore invests in big events and countless small actions so that users feel seen by and connected to one another and to Twitch staff.

The brand hosts two annual conventions, called TwitchCon, which bring together tens of thousands of users into a shared space. As Marcus put it, "TwitchCon ensures what is transactional online can grow into moments of connection and belonging. It's a physical manifestation of our online world. When flesh and blood is pulled out of the internet and into a physical location, something magical happens" (personal communication with Marcus Graham, July 2019).

At a TwitchCon presentation in 2018, the company shared the importance of collaboration for the whole brand and how Twitch broadcasters (media creators) collaborate in rich ways: "Twitch is a place where broadcasters aren't competition; they're collaborators."

Twitch's Erin Wayne explained that Twitch needed to ensure that members accurately see themselves as part of the organization. Representing them had to be accurate in terms of both information and tone. She noted that it was a challenge to highlight and celebrate member collaborations authentically in the context of a corporate voice (personal communication with Erin Wayne, October 2019).

To meet this challenge, Twitch turned to broadcasters 88bitmusic and BanzaiBaby to lead a creative project to celebrate and highlight Twitch collaboration. In four weeks, the members gathered costume designers, musicians, composers, camera operators, and all the needed talent for a professional-grade video celebrating collaboration in the Twitch community.[19] The volunteers even created a brand-new game for all to play at TwitchCon. At the end of the video, each member of the collaboration was highlighted for their role. The creative work and quality stunned Twitch leadership, and Twitch was able to share media with a truly authentic message.

Twitch leaders discovered that members were "ecstatic to contribute," and the project opened their eyes to the possibility of using members rather than outside agencies to address the growing company's creative needs. They saw that no outsider could better understand and share what makes Twitch special than their own present community.

Twitch helps us understand how an organization can tap into and return to unique resources by binding together members who gather around shared values.

The United Religions Initiative

The United Religions Initiative (URI) is a global interfaith network of organizations and individuals promoting interfaith cooperation to end religiously motivated violence.[20] Twenty years old, the organization includes more than a thousand Cooperation Circles (member groups) in over one hundred countries. URI-connected projects touch on leadership development, environmental protection, justice, and interreligious harmony. URI provides a support network to local grassroots leaders. These leaders often work in places with deadly interfaith conflict.

Sister Sabina Rifat, URI coordinator for women in Pakistan, was invited to lead an interfaith program for both Muslim and Christian women in the Mirpur Mangla province within the Kashmir region. She wanted to empower and educate local women there in several ways: (1) by teaching them skills to grow as area leaders even though they live mostly within their homes; (2) by inspiring and demonstrating interfaith harmony; (3) by encouraging them to "struggle" for their daughters to get better educations than they got for themselves; and (4) by practicing the freedom to work together with Christians, Muslims, Hindus, and other sects and castes.

But the event was a five-hour drive from her home in Lahore and was in an area with ongoing religious conflict. Sr. Sabina feared the trip both as a single woman traveler and as a Christian woman visiting a majority-Muslim province to encourage women's leadership.

Then Ahmad Hussain, chair of the Inter-Cultural Youth Council, Islamabad, another URI group in Pakistan, came to her assistance. He learned about Sr. Sabina's invitation and security concerns through another member of the URI community. He then offered to accompany her as a supportive Muslim man and remain with her as she traveled within the province. Sr. Sabina accepted this offer, which made her visit with the Mangla women possible. The URI community also connected her with a local Kashmir family who fed her in their home in daytime even during their own Ramadan fasting. The reliable connection among members of the URI community in Pakistan gave Sr. Sabina security and confidence, and it enabled her outreach to women in a remote part of Pakistan. Sr. Sabina reported that approximately one hundred Muslim and Christian local women participated in that first gathering bringing them together.[21]

Her experience is a fantastic example of individuals and an organization growing more powerful in pursuing a goal when members are connected by far more than a quid pro quo or transactional relationship.

Harley-Davidson Motorcycles

The Harley-Davidson motorcycle company was founded in 1903. In 1969, it came close to bankruptcy. New investors moved Harley's production from Wisconsin to Pennsylvania, fired employees, and neglected both product development and quality control.[22] The company couldn't compete with new Japanese products, and Harley had used an unreliable "shovel-head engine" that disappointed customers.[23] By 1981, the company hadn't rebounded much, controlling less than 5 percent market share. That's when internal executives bought the company back because no other buyers wanted the firm.[24]

On January 1, 1983, just after inking the buyback deal, Harley executives rode together to return the company headquarters from Pennsylvania to Milwaukee, Wisconsin. Along the way, they invited Harley customers to meet them. Some consider this trip the first ride of the Harley Owners Group (HOG) program. Former vice president of business development Clyde

Fessler would later say of HOG aspirations, "We thought we'd get about 25,000 people nationwide, sell a few patches, sell a few pins and have a good time."[25] He was wrong.

In the first year alone, more than thirty thousand members joined a HOG chapter.[26] Literally tens of thousands of riders connected with others longing to get out on a Harley bike, meet new friends, and enjoy the freedom of the road. The nascent group offered group rides, HOG "Fly & Ride" privileges that allowed members to rent and ride a Harley on distant vacations, a HOG magazine, and pins, patches, and collectibles.[27]

The next year, 1984, Harley launched the first HOG rallies in Nevada and Tennessee, with combined attendance of about three thousand. A year later, in 1985, HOG exceeded sixty thousand members in forty-nine chapters.[28] It quickly became the world's largest motorcycle club.

Harley dealers around the world live and die by customer enthusiasm for Harley gear. All could see that Harley indeed had a robust, excited, and accessible following.

In 2003, the formerly almost bankrupt company earned a record profit of $1 billion. By 2006, the company held a 65 percent market share, more than four times that of its next-biggest competitor, Honda.[29] In 2012, HOG reached over one million members in one hundred countries. Former Harley CEO Rich Teerlink would go on to report that "perhaps the most significant program was—and continues to be—the Harley Owners Group (HOG)."[30]

Harley built a community of customers who wanted to find one another for support, fun, and growth and were perhaps waiting for someone to invite them in. When the company built relationships with these customers, it had access to the very people who wanted to help it innovate in its field and share the brand's excitement worldwide. Harley-Davidson helps us recognize that even struggling brands may have much goodwill available to them if they can bring fans together in relationship.

Part

1

BRAND COMMUNITY FOUNDATIONS

There's a place where we don't have to feel unknown
And every time that you call out
You're a little less alone
If you only say the word
From across the silence
Your voice is heard.
—Benj Pasek and Justin Paul

1

RECOGNIZING COMMUNITY, BRAND COMMUNITY, AND BELONGING

This chapter will clarify the relevant terms we all need in order to recognize and support community building. As we distill the terms, we provide a list of elements that must be incorporated for success. Just knowing the terms provides all with a stronger vision to recognize and discern effective brand communities.

As we stated in the introduction, we define a community as a group of people who share mutual concern for one another. (Hereafter in this book, we will refer to "mutual concern for one another" as "mutual concern.") Communities convene around at least one shared value, usually more.

In his book *The Art of Community*, Charles shares fundamental wisdom about how communities come together and create belonging using principles tested over the course of more than a thousand years. It's available if you need to understand community fundamentals. In that book, Charles distills seven principles used to bring people together:

1. *Boundary:* the line between members and outsiders

2. *Initiation:* the activities that mark a new member

3. *Rituals:* the things we do that have meaning

4. *Temple:* a place set aside to find our community

5. *Stories:* what we share that allows others and ourselves to know our values

6. *Symbols:* the things that represent ideas that are important to us

7. *Inner rings:* subgroups in a community that together present a path to growth as we participate

We will dig deeper into specific kinds of communities, so let's recap: Communities almost always share some values, identity, and moral prescriptions (how people should act).

This definition may seem unfinished to you. You may argue that you know of a collection of people who share values, identity, and moral prescriptions, but don't feel like a community. You're right! For example, Charles still identifies as a returned Peace Corps volunteer. Charles also still values international travel, cultural sharing, and serendipitous adventure. And he thinks that there are moral and respectful ways to explore foreign cultures, as do most Peace Corps volunteers. However, given that his Peace Corps service ended years ago, he is not active in a Peace Corps group that shares mutual concern between himself and other returned volunteers. There is such a community in the world, but he is just not a part of it now.

He considers his relationship to other Peace Corps volunteers as tribal. This means that they share some values and identity, yet he is not organized, active, or even in communication with other volunteers. If someone collects names of returned Peace Corps volunteers living in California, he will become part of a list. That list doesn't make the people on it a community. Without mutual concern, whatever Charles is included in is not a community but a group. (And this is OK.)

By contrast, Carrie is a part of a Seattle yoga community in which members gather for yoga classes and workshops. She recognizes that friendships have formed among members so that they care for one another even outside class time. This makes her experience as a community member far richer and more fun than just showing up for poses in a group.

There's nothing wrong with groups. Most of us are involved with lots of groups. An advocacy campaign (say, advocating for clean Oakland streets)

may never develop into a community, but as a group, it can serve a rich and powerful role for Oakland. The danger comes when we can't distinguish between groups and communities and we expect more from a group than it can ever deliver. Or we fail to invest in a group to grow a community (say, an Oakland streets cleanup community) and then despair at the failure.

In 2014, an activity known as the ALS Ice Bucket Challenge inspired people to create and post more than two million videos online.[1] The challenge was an effort to raise both awareness and research funding for amyotrophic lateral sclerosis (also known as ALS or Lou Gehrig's disease). In each video, participants were doused with a bucket of ice water, and they then challenged others they knew to do the same. This mobilization campaign served a deep need to activate people into a conversation about a disease and to raise money. It did not knit participants into a community where members cared about one another. Now, growing an important conversation and fundraising for a cause can be a very satisfying outcome. It's just not a community-building effort. It's mobilizing a group.

This book speaks to a broad spectrum of organization types because fundamental principles apply broadly. So, for this book, **organization** refers to people participating in an agreed order, including at least one element of membership, hierarchy, rules, monitoring, and sanctions.[2] The following organization types, although very different from one from another, all count:

- *Business:* working for financial profit
- *Nonprofit:* humanitarian motivated and acting to relieve suffering, advocate for the poor, protect the environment, provide social services, and more[3]
- *Religious or spiritual organization:* offering spiritual growth and education
- *Community-based organization:* serving needs within a particular geographical area
- *Association:* connecting people to benefit from one another professionally
- *Ephemeral organization:* formed in extreme and disaster environments for rescue and relief[4]
- *Political organization:* working toward political change
- *Movement:* working for cultural change

In this book, a **brand** refers to any identifiable organization (whether for-profit, nonprofit, political, or otherwise cause-driven) that offers value to others. The brand uses a distinguishing name.

Brand *communities* are often inspired, created, or influenced by an already established brand, but not necessarily. For example, enthusiasts (such as camping, music, or video game fans) can start an identifiable community (e.g., the Oakland Adventure Club, California Dragon Boat Association), and the organization itself operates as a brand community.

For ease of communication, we'll use the terms *organization, company,* and *brand* interchangeably.

Brand Community

A brand community is a special kind of community. *All brand communities we're discussing aspire to serve both (1) members and (2) at least one organizational (brand) goal.*

In this discussion, an authentic brand community includes *all* these elements:

- Members who share a mutual concern for one another's welfare
- Members who share a connected identity founded in shared core value(s) and purpose[5]
- Members who participate in shared experiences reflecting the shared value(s) and purpose

This working definition is purposefully broad. Many principles for building different kinds of brand communities apply across the board.

As we have explained, successful brand communities serve both members' and the organization's goals. If a community fails to serve one or the other, you'll have trouble inspiring one or the other to participate as soon as it figures that out. Building brand communities takes work, and there's no reason to do the work unless there's a benefit to all involved.

When a community is connected to an established organization, it's important that the community's and organization's goals overlap, align, or complement one another. For example, Yelp is a crowdsourced review forum for local businesses. Today it attracts more than seventy million people a month through its mobile app and website.[6] Yelp's purpose is to guide readers to helpful resources including reviews. Yelp Elite members (a brand community) want to connect with other review writers to share friendship, experiences, and grow better at writing reviews. All intentions are aligned.

The same is true for the Harley-Davidson Motorcycle Company and the Harley Owners Group (HOG). Riders want to ride, and Harley wants to sell motorcycles, merchandise, and accessories. In both cases, no one wins by holding back the other side.

If the organization's goals are not in alignment with those of members, then there is a real question whether the organization can offer genuine value to members.

When a brand community stands alone as an organization (e.g., the Oakland Adventure Club), then typically there's no conflict between the purposes of the organization and those of the members.

For the sake of clarity, we offer a few examples of brand communities to at least scratch the surface of what's out there:

- *Activist community.* The United Religions Initiative (URI) connects individuals promoting interfaith cooperation and ending religiously motivated violence.

- *Celebrity fan community.* World-famous performer Lady Gaga created the Little Monsters fan community to connect and support her global fans.

- *Collaborator community.* Google gathers invited thought leaders together in "Labs" to collaborate on an envisioned future and influence Google investments and spending.

- *Customer community.* Online streaming platform Twitch created the Community Meetups program to connect their users in cities around the world.

- *Employee community.* Home builder True Homes invests in many events and activities to connect all its employees in satisfying ways.

- *Enthusiasts community.* HOG chapters connect brand enthusiasts who own Harleys or are invited guests of Harley owners.

- *Professional community.* The New York State Association of Independent Schools connects education professionals to support one another across their region.

- *Sports community.* The California Dragon Boat Association connects boat paddlers.

- *Volunteer community.* Global software company Salesforce created the Trailblazer Community made up of users who volunteer to support other users.

How do brand communities succeed in serving both members and the organization? Consider this example.

SEPHORA DISCOVERS OPPORTUNITY

Sephora is one of the largest beauty retailers in the world, with twenty-five hundred stores in thirty-two countries.[7] For years, the company hosted an online forum that drew approximately twenty thousand customers who were "the most hard core beauty lovers" (personal communication with Shira Levine, April 2019). It was little more than an online forum, with a single full-time community leader, one part-time moderator, and an engineer ensuring that it didn't collapse.

Then Sephora leaders noticed a competitor successfully stealing market share. They decided to invest in building a makeup enthusiast community that was both accessible on mobile devices and integrated into the shopping experience.

Inside the community, customers could and did discuss a variety of beauty products and methods, regardless of whether they were related to Sephora products or not. In the community, members could gain access to beauty techniques and product information, engage with beauty company founders, and experience an affirming space with others who love the fun, play, and transformation of makeup.

The community grew to over 1.6 million members. By participating in the members' discussions, brand managers, buyers, and product scouts could and did learn what customers wanted and what beauty trends were growing.

Involving this huge community with business decisions taught Sephora's team that strong measures in five areas guarantee success for new products:

- Social proofing (seeing others happy with the product)
- Fear of missing out (FOMO)
- Adorable photos of customers testing products
- Honest reviews
- Involving "hard-core" category loyalists

For instance, some years ago Sephora leaders noticed significant discussions about "strobing" and "highlighting." These were new ways to make faces sparkle and glow. Industry research also indicated that many customers were dissatisfied with makeup largely made for Caucasian skin. Sephora's team noticed that only hard-to-find brands that served hard-core enthusiasts were catering to the trend.

Beauty enthusiasts may have noticed that soon after the community investment, Sephora launched several products that delivered to the unmet demand.

Participation

Here, a **participant** is anyone who freely takes action to participate in a community in some way. This is intentionally a very broad definition. All brand communities include participants who share mutual concern. Discovering participants is one way to recognize a community.

In time it will be important for you to understand the differences between types of participants, such as novices, members, elders, principal elders, and allies. For simplicity in this discussion, *participants* refers to anyone participating, including both visitors and members in general.

A **visitor** is someone who seeks to learn more about your community. Typically, this individual discovers your community (reads about it, visits the website, sees a video, or visits an event for the first time) and then can grow more interested.

A **member** is someone who returns to connect with members, considers themselves a regular participant, and ideally has experienced some kind of opt-in initiation. The initiation gives them reason to see themselves as a member. Without a recognized initiation, members are difficult to distinguish from visitors. Even if the initiation experience isn't dramatic, there should always be some discernible difference between members and visitors.

Very often, we want to create community events that draw the right visitors—those who will return and grow into members.

Consider an Oakland Miata drivers' community. Members go on drives together, visit races, and share meals where they discuss fixing and improving Miatas. Anyone who discovers the community via website, video, or flier can participate in virtually all the planned events. But just showing up, even registering online for a drive, doesn't make someone a member. When someone shows up to learn more and experience the community, that person is a visitor. What do we mean? Anyone visiting your house is not instantly a part of your family just because they walked in. There is a process that makes someone a family member. (It may include marriage.)

Visitors participate, but participation alone doesn't make them members. Visitors may even visit a community several times. Membership results when someone crosses a boundary into the community. The boundary is always monitored by at least one elder, someone with history and at least informal authority in the community. When an elder handles this role, we call them a gatekeeper; there can be many gatekeepers in a community. Communities have different ways of determining when and how a visitor appropriately becomes a member. In many cases, there is a "novice" or "probationary" stage (which can go under many different names). The important lesson is that visiting participants should make an informed choice to cross the boundary into membership.

In the Miata community, crossing the boundary may include paying membership dues and participating regularly in planned activities. In other communities, the standards may be much higher.

In all real communities, not all participants are members, but all members are participants.

Participation Conditions

Participants show up, participate, and then return because at least three conditions are in place for any activity or invitation.[8] If any one of these is missing, then the participant generally won't meaningfully engage. The three conditions are as follows:

1. *Choice:* the ability to say yes or no to membership and participation

2. *Connection:* forming relationships with other people

3. *Progress:* advancement toward a purpose

Protect choice. If members "must" participate in a community, they're usually coerced into taking part. This means they're fulfilling a transaction to avoid bad outcomes. This is the opposite of community connection.

It's OK to have requirements for membership (e.g., dues). But if you require members to pay and they cannot opt out of membership, then building a real community is difficult, if not impossible. You'll largely remain a group because members lack choice.

Support connection. Members want to be recognized by others and accepted for who they are. This includes being appreciated for shared values and commitments.

Ensure progress. People want to experience progress toward some purpose. This might mean progress toward mastery of an art, skill, or field. We often refer to this progress as a form of growth toward "being." People want to *be* a support, change maker, friend, cook, dancer, firefighter, or anything else.

When you consider brand communities that once interested you but from which you drifted away, you may now recognize that the community did not meet one of these three conditions.

Mutual Concern

When building any community, mutual concern among members remains both fundamental and critical. Without it, there is no authentic community to support an organization. This is why mutual concern is often missing in what we call "mirage communities" (more about these later in this chapter).

For example, if you have a newsletter reading list, subscribers may respond back and forth to your emails. That's great. But if those subscribers don't yet care about one another's welfare, there isn't a community (yet).

What you have is a list of readers or followers, and there's nothing wrong with this. Community building takes different and far more investment toward creating something richer and more powerful, and offering different possibilities.

From your own experience, you can undoubtedly think of groups to which you've belonged where the participants cared about one another, and groups where they didn't. Once you look for them, the differences are obvious.

Feeling Camaraderie

Nurturing a group into a brand community requires at least two commonalities among its members:

- Shared values (at least one)
- Shared purpose

In our favorite description of *camaraderie,* we say that we feel camaraderie when we learn that others *share our common value(s) and purpose(s).* Sharing only one of the two is never enough. (These ideas are based on personal communication with Aram Fischer, April 2019.)

If visitors share both common values and common purposes, we call this being "compatible" or a right "fit." It's important that visitors learn quickly whether they are compatible. Compatible visitors will know whether they want to return and explore fuller participation.

If a visitor doesn't share common values and purposes, then they're unfortunately incompatible or a wrong fit. This doesn't mean that a brand community is doing something wrong. In fact, it's important that not every individual *will* fit with every brand community: Many motorcycle riders won't fit in HOG.

The key here is that *participants need to learn the relevant shared value(s) and purpose(s) so that they can experience camaraderie.*

If you have doubts about your values and purpose, then it will be hard for visitors to feel or recognize whether they have camaraderie. If you try to bend values and purpose to whoever finds you, then you can never offer consistent value to members.

Part of creating a strong brand community is choosing what values and purpose your organization will commit to, and encouraging only the right people. You can't be all things to all people. In fact, drawing a strong boundary for the right people is always an important part of creating a resilient and effective brand community.

When we invite compatible people inside based on values and purpose, we call this an invitation to "cross the community boundary." The boundary creates an **inner ring** for members where they feel safe inside to explore the shared values and purpose (camaraderie). (For more on the boundary principle, you can refer to *The Art of Community*.)

If members are in fact incompatible, then community integrity is eroded. Imagine attending a HOG event and someone who loves motorcycles joins to discuss sourcing 2004 Mazda Miata parts. Too much of this will pull away from the brand community purpose. It really doesn't matter that we all like twisty roads and the wind in our hair.

Please note that selecting members based on values and purpose is a morally neutral idea. The distinction can be used to create really strong and supportive communities, and it can be used to create the opposite. Anyone can create a community or inner ring based on vile and hurtful values and purpose. (We know of too many.) This can even happen inadvertently when we choose people who "just feel right" for membership. "Just feel right" often really means "people who look and act like me" and the others will never belong.

We encourage you to do something far more powerful: Create a brand community with clear core values and purpose so that you can welcome a broad range of people who are compatible with an enriching purpose, instead of adhering to a vague notion of who belongs and who doesn't.

For example, we admire the efforts by Nish Nadaraja to ensure that the Yelp Elite originally connected people to "share what's great about their city" as opposed to write a lot of reviews for a website.

Every successful community has leaders (formal or informal) who keep the community inside safe enough. "Safe enough" means there is the possibility of vulnerable conversations and the avoidance of "wreckage." (See more on inside safety in part 3.) Vulnerable conversations make feeling connection possible.

We also admire Etsy's efforts to gather and celebrate artists and their craft beyond working to sell goods. Etsy is an online commerce website that focuses on handmade and vintage items. The site hosts over two million sellers, many of them craft artists who call themselves "makers." Over thirty-four million customers now buy on the Etsy platform.[9]

Danielle Maveal was a founding Etsy team member and Etsy's twelfth employee. She helped build the Etsy Community team and soon after launched and managed the Seller Education team.

Every day in Etsy's Virtual Labs, Danielle shared that members met to share their craft work during critique sessions. Danielle knows that sharing work for criticism includes real vulnerability for makers. So an Etsy team member or community leader (elder) developed ground rules and modeled acceptable behavior when sharing both positive and negative feedback. Then all participants were invited to share positive and critical thoughts, moderated by the elder. For sharing their vulnerability, makers were rewarded in growth for their work and business (personal communication with Danielle Maveal, August 2019).

Vulnerable conversations are necessary to develop connected relationships. Here *vulnerability* means uncertainty, risk, and emotional exposure. This includes anything that participants fear will cause others to possibly reject them if revealed. Often this includes any evidence of weakness, failure, inadequacy, and some feelings (such as fear, loneliness, or even unbridled delight).[10]

Although "safe" looks different among, say, Army Special Forces operatives and Oakland hospital chaplains, the principle is the same. All need to believe they can share something vulnerable within the community and remain connected. Even leaders in the toughened special forces community ensure consequences for those who make their community unsafe.

For example, former Army Special Forces operative Eric Paul explained that everyone in his team had to stay with a "battle buddy." This helped protect all on a mission and avoided the need for searching for a lone lost soldier. When someone broke the rule, "mass punishment" was assigned for the whole team so that the rule would be respected in the future. Eric shared further about how master sergeants made "after-action reviews" a conversation where real and helpful criticism could be shared safely among soldiers (personal communication with Eric Paul, August 2019).

When people (including us) exhibit vulnerability, they're uncertain about how others will react. They seek empathy but fear they'll be negatively judged. We agree with Brené Brown when she asserts, "Vulnerability is about sharing our feelings and experiences with people who have earned the right to hear them. Vulnerability is based on mutuality and requires boundaries and trust. It's not oversharing, it's not purging, it's not indiscriminate disclosure."[11]

Others must earn our vulnerability over time, as happens in communities with safe (enough) spaces. As leaders, we must understand that without a space for possible vulnerability, real connection will never develop.

Feeling Belonging

Belonging is a feeling. None of us wants to participate in a community where we don't feel good, welcome, or appreciated. We certainly won't stay and invest. Of course, what makes us feel in particular ways differs from person to person.

When possible, people leave places where they don't feel belonging. They proactively move to where they do feel belonging. At the end of the day, we want to create a feeling of belonging among participants. Otherwise, community never works. At best, you'll just get grouping.

Research indicates that **belonging** shows up when we experience two feelings:[12]

1. Feeling valued (or needed) by the entire group or some part of it

2. Feeling that we are a fit for what is needed in the community and the environment that has been created

Reflecting on the past twenty years of research and practitioners' experience, we say that the feeling of belonging usually arises when participants experience some collection of the following feelings *at some level*:

- Accepted

- Welcome

- Valued

- Cared for (mutual concern)

- Appreciated

- Possessing insider (esoteric) understanding

To create these feelings, the community must provide an experience where participants can *notice* they are accepted, welcome, valued, cared for, appreciated, and in possession of insider understanding.

Notice that successful leaders generate positive feelings in participants, which inspires participants to return and become members. Though this can sound like a magical task to some, after you've learned principles that make communities work, it will sound more achievable.

As a feeling, belonging is experienced internally as a first-person experience. These experiences are difficult for a third-person observer to measure, but that difficulty makes the experience no less critical.

Many first-person experiences important in relationships (and the world) don't lend themselves to quantified measuring, such as a mother's love or the trust in your neighbor. Measuring belonging is similar to measuring a mother's love.

A critical takeaway here is that creating community involves far more than offering a trade or a transactional relationship. It includes offering a space (digital or physical) and experiences that inspire feelings. If you forget that— or worse, never understand this—you'll waste a lot of time.

Insider Understanding

Successful communities grow stronger the more members share **insider (esoteric) understanding**. By *esoteric*, we don't mean something weird; we are just referring to things insiders understand that outsiders do not or cannot.

Melissa Allen is a retired firefighter captain. She shared how much she appreciates spending time among other firefighters in her community because they understand the complexity, pressure, and passion that often come with the role. They share much never-spoken understanding and compassion for one another. This is so strong that she notices that if a firefighter spouse joins the group, the conversation changes. This isn't because spouses aren't welcome or loved. It's because they simply never share the insider understanding that career firefighters gain.

Usually when we seek out people who have shared an experience similar to our own (fighting cancer, living overseas, running a marathon), we seek others for shared insider understanding.

In a very different kind of example, within the Lady Gaga fan community Little Monsters, Elena (last name withheld on request; interviewed April 2019) volunteered as one of the first moderators. As a new Gaga fan, she had posted Gaga photos and videos on social media, and her friends considered it spam. They didn't share her enthusiasm and identification with Gaga. She noticed that the first time she posted similar media on the Little Monsters platform, she immediately saw forty-five "likes." Others reached out to her with warm comments and "followed" her profile. The Little Monsters members also reached out to her on other social media platforms so that they could connect further. She had found other insiders who understood her feelings and identification with Gaga.

Jeremy Ross cofounded an online platform called Honeycommb, which builds and hosts fan communities for many brands, including Lady Gaga, Manchester United USA Supporters, and North American Tribal Leaders of Sovereign Nations. He told us that brands often want at least one private online space for fans because brands have learned that their fans often get ignored and ridiculed when sharing their enthusiasm in public. The fans are excited and relieved to participate in a space where their enthusiasm is both understood and appreciated. Twitch's Marcus Graham believes that the stigma associated with video gamers is an important factor in explaining why Twitch grew into a global gathering space for gamers. For many, Twitch was perhaps the only place they could express their enthusiasm safely to others who understood and empathized.

When an organization convenes a community, participants are drawn in because they share some values more intensely than do outsiders. *We want to feel understood by the people who share our values.* We want to see that the people inside understand this more than the people outside our community. This is one reason why a community can't succeed if it accepts anyone, anytime, with any values.

Shared Experiences

All brand communities share experiences. These are often planned events, but they don't have to be. They could be extemporaneous outings (e.g., rock climbers meeting at a cliff base) or emergencies (e.g., firefighters convening at a call). For real communities, there must be many experiences where participants can and do return.[13] If there are too few shared experiences or they're not enriching enough for participants to return, then the relationships that knit participants into a community don't get built.

A **shared experience** is an event for a community that articulates, references, or reinforces the shared values of that group. In a brand community, the brand's values must agree with the relevant member values. Brand community shared experiences include particular elements:

- *Reinforcement of values.* The experience reflects and reinforces insiders' (members') important values. Participants should feel the attraction to and appreciation for the specific experience more than outsiders do. In other words, the experience doesn't appeal to just about everyone everywhere.

- *Time boundaries.* There is a beginning and an end to the experience; that is, others cannot go back in time to share the experience when it is over.

- *Space boundaries.* Participants must go to a specific place (physical or digital) to share the experience. This means that no one can "send" them the experience. Typically, this also means that participants must be invited, or learn about the event from an insider, "in the know" person. Invitations are typical, but not always necessary.

Understanding how shared experiences work for a community calls for more nuance and thought than simply doing something fun. (We're totally supportive of fun.) Even for advanced community builders, it's important to regularly assess the purpose and form of your community's shared experiences. You can find much more on creating successful shared experiences in chapter 8, Creating Shared Experiences and Space.

Empty versus Meaningful Engagement

When we build an authentic community, participants (visitors and members) will engage. What do we mean by *engage*? We've seen the term *engagement* used to refer to, well, just about everything, from reading a blog post to tattooing a logo on one's body, visiting a single meeting, leading a regional subgroup, and replying to a social media post. We're going to use the term more specifically.

Meaningful community engagement *is any action by a participant that supports that participant in (1) caring about the welfare of other community members and/or (2) feeling connected to the community as a whole.*

Meaningful engagement is experienced only by members, not organizations. Only members can decide what is in fact meaningful; when they find it, it inspires them to remain connected. This enriches and strengthens a brand community.

You may now wonder how to determine or measure the depth or meaningfulness of engagement.

As we noted earlier, quantitatively measuring "engagement meaningfulness," like measuring maternal love or mutual concern, may be nearly impossible. And like maternal love, meaningfulness still matters a lot for most of us.

There are detailed and nuanced ways to explain the difference between quantitative and qualitative measurements. For simplicity and practicality here, *quantitative* means objectively measurable by an outside observer. *Qualitative* here refers to a description of a first-person experience. We can quantitatively measure how many gifts your mother sends you. We can only seek to understand how much your mother feels love for you qualitatively by asking her to describe it (personal communication with Gabriel Grant, PhD, October 2019).

Because quantitative measurement is straightforward, we often see organizations default to measuring behaviors that contain actions (clicks, visits, views), but that never tell them whether people feel more connected or caring. When leaders can't measure quality, they default to measuring quantity, which usually fails and misleads without informed discernment (Grant interview). In chapter 11 we will discuss this measurement problem called *surrogation*.

Empty engagement is engagement for engagement's sake. It eats up time and mind space. It also disregards emotional connection or serving needs. For example, imagine that we post cute photographs of ourselves in our online community, living a picture-perfect life in a tropical wonderland. There's nothing wrong with cute pictures. But this is empty engagement if we're hiding our true selves, challenges, and longings while hoping to fool others with our posturing. No matter whether participants do this knowingly or not, we call this *avataring*. We know it's empty because no one is growing a closer understanding or mutual concern with such activity. Communities that confuse avataring with connecting will not grow real, meaningful connections.

We see this frequently in social media groups and other mirage communities, where the engagement includes posting memes and selfies that never speak to the group's values or goals. To be clear, there's nothing wrong with pretty photos, selfies, and memes. They can add important diversity to daily life's sobriety and challenges, but let's not conflate avataring with authentic community-enriching engagement. We will discuss helpful content principles in part 3.

Meaningful engagements relate to the community's core values and purpose. The engagement also grows or demonstrates mutual concern.

It may be difficult as leaders to distinguish what's meaningful and what isn't. There will always be a gray zone where some participants consider an engagement empty and others consider it meaningful. It's important that you can distinguish engagement types at least in broad ways, because the distractions of empty engagement will lead to a community's stagnation or decline.

Empty engagement means almost nothing for community enrichment. It can gain attention (promotion), but that's not the same as growing something durable. Consider grocery brands that reward customers with a gas card. The brands get lots of grocery lists and gas purchase locations. Every purchase *can* get counted as an engagement, but none of it builds connection or community.

To help us distinguish between meaningful and empty engagement, imagine that we're planning a pizza party in the Frank Ogawa Plaza in downtown Oakland for the Oakland Public Works (OPW) Department. OPW is an identifiable organization (brand) that supports volunteer trash pickers, among many other volunteers. Imagine an OPW manager named Michael who would love volunteers to feel more connected and to remain vigilant, and he always appreciates new volunteers making Oakland cleaner. (Yes, we know: A pizza party is probably not the best community-building investment possible for OPW. Just roll with us for now.)

There are any number of ways to throw a pizza party, from flying in Italian masters to arranging Maltese dogs for pizza-lunch cuddling.

The first imagined event will take place this Wednesday. We'll hire University of California, Berkeley undergraduates to

1. Hang a banner that reads "Thank You Oakland Volunteers."

2. Hand out free pizza to anyone nearby with a "Thank you for making Oakland amazing" greeting.

3. Hand out an OPW volunteer registration card with each pizza slice.

4. Offer a free soda for every social media posting tagged "Oakland Public Works Amazing."

We can measure at least four kinds of engagement:

- How many times a pizza slice was taken

- How many people took pizza

- How many social media posts resulted

- How many people drank soda

We're confident that we'll rack up big engagement numbers as long as the pizza flows. And you already instinctively know how poorly the measured engagements will reflect the current or future community of OPW volunteers and stakeholders. Although the event may build brand awareness for OPW, it will do little else except spend OPW funds.

Giving away pizza (or tacos, beer, T-shirts, etc.) will not build a pizza community or any other kind. It's *never* the pizza alone. We'll discuss effective elements in chapter 10.

If Michael at OPW really wants to connect current volunteers for retention and also recruit new responsible volunteers, we can consider how to make an event connect with the community values and purpose.

We will do at least three things differently:

1. Use language in invitations and activities on-site that connect directly to the community values

2. Create a shared space for relationship building inspired by the values

3. Ensure that participants have access to an intimate "campfire experience" when they attend

This second event will require significantly more preparation to establish intention and venue:

1. Send an invitation to past volunteers explicitly acknowledging their part in making Oakland safer and cleaner. Invite them to a bounded space to meet other invited volunteers and learn how they all make a difference in Oakland.

2. Allow each volunteer to bring two friends interested in getting involved with Oakland volunteering for a safer and cleaner city.

3. Share that volunteers will get an opportunity to learn how OPW can support new projects.

4. Introduce volunteers within neighborhoods to learn how they contribute. They'll sit together in "intimate spaces" where they can talk.

5. Give Michael the space and time to share what inspires him to support OPW, and invite participants to share their inspiration with one another.

6. Explain that we'll serve pizza from Oakland's own Bare Knuckle Pizza so that we can celebrate our commitment and friendship within the city together.

YELP MEANINGFUL ENGAGEMENT

Nish Nadaraja served both as Yelp's brand director and as its editorial director in its early days. Yelp faced a classic chicken-and-egg problem: The brand was only helpful after it attracted enough useful reviews for new visitors, but it would only attract enough reviews and reviewers when it was seen to be helpful. And the critical mass had to be built in every area in which Yelp would be relevant.

This meant that Yelp needed to encourage the right people to review local businesses and go out to discover new and uncelebrated jewels in each city. Nish knew that paying or trading for reviews would never get Yelp to a sustainable place. There would never be enough revenue to pay for enough reviews, and Yelp would start a bidding war for the best writers across cities. Yelp needed to tap into internally motivated reviewers already present in each city and provide a venue for them to share what they were already excited about. (See more on internal motivation in part 3.)

Nish and Yelp did many things right. That's why it is a global billion-dollar public company now, with over $940 million in revenue last year.[14] In the beginning, it was just a vision.

Nish wanted to find people who loved their own city (value) and who wanted to share what their area offers (purpose). He did this by reaching out to people who met a particular profile. They already wrote about their geographical area online, loved sharing opinions, and highlighted their favorite places. Yelp offered to support their purpose using the Yelp platform.

Nish's team sought the most active reviewers and experience-recommenders. Then they reviewed these people's work to select some for an invitation-only Yelp Elite membership (boundary). Nish then intentionally supported them in developing an authentic community. Although there is much more to the program than events, we will discuss how Nish ensured that members experienced his events both as meaningful and as supportive of relationships.

First, Nish knew that the membership and the benefits could never be transactional or earned by a points metric. Some people would then dump many easy reviews onto the site. Instead the reviews were evaluated and judged for quality, considering the depth and nuance in the writing.

The membership and its many benefits offered a higher status for reviewers. In short, membership made them Yelp insiders. Membership wasn't earned one point at a time. It always remained an acknowledgment of evaluated commitment, participation, support, and sharing of good taste.

Yelp created at least one Elite event each month, and local community managers additionally created at least another event per month. This meant that Elite members had at least two exclusive events each month, always free to them, at which they could connect with other Elite members. Nish ensured that each event had a "host" who would introduce members, and he announced out loud that "there are no strangers here; only friends we haven't met." In this way, he always made it clear that the time was meant for connecting with friends far more than for enjoying drinks and food.

During these events, members could and did build friendships that grew over time, seeing one another many times and privately messaging on the Yelp platform. When they found one another on the online platform, they were each identified with an Elite badge. Because he wanted real connections formed, not simply bigger events, Nish kept the Elite events to between 50 and 150 attendees. As Yelp grew, intimacy and member connection remained a priority.

Further, Nish created a members-only private calendar so that Elite members could plan to reconnect at the next event and message one another using Yelp's platform. Lastly, Nish worked directly with Yelp creative director Michael Ernst to create a special brand identity for Yelp Elite. Yelp used the identity for carefully thought-out Elite-branded "swag." Each item then served as an exclusive token of membership. Nish explained that each swag item needed the Yelp brand to shine through, so they were designed to be cute, fun, and cool so as to become keepsakes for members. Our favorite examples include a custom-made metal Yelp lunch box with a thermos in a retro Flash Gordon theme and, separately, a baby bib with the words "Oops! I Yelped in my pants!" The latter was given to new parents within the Yelp community.

The repeated intimate experiences within a boundary and in comfortable venues, with access to Yelp community managers and staff and a clear purpose for the event (relationship building), helped forge member relationships. Nish knew that the events were working exactly as he had hoped when members created many gatherings in addition to the Yelp events because they wanted both to see one another and to discover new experiences together even without Yelp (personal communication with Nish Nadaraja, August 2019).

This second imaginary event is by no means an ideal experience. As with all new things, we'll discover how effective it is by experimenting. The imaginary example reveals how structuring an experience can lean toward growing relationships and mutual concern and support. It will remain hard to know how meaningful the participant connections, conversations, and memories will become. This is the nature of creating something qualitatively important and then measuring it quantitatively. Participant numbers and length of stay help us a little bit, but not very much. The success will largely be measured through qualitative study—asking participants about their experience. (See part 3 for more on measuring success.)

Given that the second event invites participants to connect with their values and with others who share them, you have an idea how much more that event can enrich the community.

As an experiment, imagine yourself invited to the second pizza party, except swap "making Oakland safer and cleaner" to something you care about more (women's education, refugee safety, fun in school, etc.) and consider whether you'd like to experience such an event.

Mirage Community

Now that you understand what a community is, you will notice many instances in which so-called communities fall short. When we look closely at communities managed or labeled by an organization, we often find what we call a *mirage community*. A mirage community may look like a community to outsiders and the untrained. But those who are close to it can easily see that it's not the real thing. Mirage communities lack fundamental infrastructure and deliver none of a community's powerful outcomes for members or organizations.

A **mirage community** is a group that aspires to form community, and may even call itself a community, but lacks fundamental elements that constitute a community. As a result, mirage communities fail to deliver positive community and organizational benefits.

Many times, you can recognize them because participants will miss *at least one* of the three conditions that support meaningful and returning engagement:

1. Freedom to say no to participation or membership

2. Connection to other people

3. Progress toward a purpose

The fastest way to make a community building effort create only a mirage community is to neglect participant freedom. **Coercion** occurs when someone uses fear and threats to get people to do (or not do) something that the coercer wants done (or not done). We know of company leaders who think they are "leading" an employee brand community when in reality they're coercing. In fact, we know a nationally recognized professional association that used to "voluntell" members how they would participate and contribute. "Voluntelling" was a euphemism for threatening members' credentials if they didn't give what the leadership wanted. Unsurprisingly, the association's members were deeply dissatisfied at every level. There was no actual community. At best, there was community theater (members acting as though community existed), a classic mirage community.

When people try to build "community" with coercion, they're always creating a mirage community at best. We recognize this right away when we hear language like this:

How do we *make* people . . .

>Show up to our event?

>Post more?

>Engage more?

>Give us . . . ?

Authentic community leadership asks such questions in a far more collaborative, caring, and connected way. This sounds more like

How do we encourage members to . . . ?

How do we make clear that . . . ?

How do we share that . . . ?

How do we invite them to . . . ?

How do we make it safe for people to . . . ?

How do we better model . . . ?

How do we grow awareness about . . . ?

There will come a time when leadership must share instruction, requests, and requirements. If any of these needs are contextualized outside a conversation of serving, enriching, emboldening, supporting, or protecting the inside, then it's likely to be coercion.

With coercion, as soon as people can get away from you, they will. That's why it isn't community. By the way, as soon as they get away from you, they'll tell anyone who will listen that their experience was terrible.

Remember that research indicates that Americans everywhere report that they tell more people about poor service than they do about good experiences.[15] So when your participants see that you're manipulating with coercion, they may do a better job sharing about your harmful mirage community than they ever would about a positive community experience.

2

SUPPORTING ORGANIZATIONAL GOALS

This chapter articulates problems that brand communities often address for organizations and the ways communities support the organizations investing in them. The distinctions discussed here will help leaders recognize why and when to invest. If you're already confident that your brand community does or will warrant attention and investment for meeting your organizational goals, then you may prefer to skip to part 2, where we jump right into discussing building a brand community from the beginning.

Successful brand communities address many ongoing challenges that brands face. The seven organizational goals discussed in this chapter and the deeper discussion in appendix A collectively address these challenges (inspired by personal communication with Scott Forgey and Bobby Scarnewman, September 2019).

RELEVANCE

- Revising stagnant product and services growth
- Innovating content for the marketplace and field

- Connecting new developments with customers
- Predicting market demand

TEAM

- Attracting the most talented and effective team
- Finding and recruiting critical talent with passion and purpose
- Inspiring collaboration among team members and partnership with both customers and colleagues

GROWTH

- Reducing customer turnover in dynamic and increasingly competitive marketplaces
- Getting the attention of the marketplace ("cutting through the noise")
- Connecting the most important messages to the customers who need to hear them
- Creating fundamental shifts in industries and markets

The good news is that properly gathered brand communities can both dramatically and uniquely address these challenges. As we noted earlier, the seven most common ways that a brand community can serve an organization include enhancing and supporting the following goals:

Innovation: creating new value for stakeholders

Talent recruitment and retention: attracting and retaining the people your organization needs for success

Customer retention: keeping customers and stakeholders involved with the organization and providing value to the brand

Marketing: informing the market of offered value

Customer service: helping customers/users with the brand service or products

Advancing movements: creating a fundamental shift in the culture or business

Community forum: making the brand a destination for a specific community

If you don't yet know how (or even if!) your brand community serves your organization, then start by focusing on only *one* organizational goal. Experiment there, and find what failures point you in the right direction. All the other goals will remain for you to grow into when you're ready. Aiming for too many goals at once will only distract your efforts, and when some things fail—as they will—it will be much harder to discern what went wrong and how to correct it.

Each one of the organizational goals we've described refers to whole professional fields in and of themselves. Obviously this book is limited in the wisdom we can share here. You can find critical principles important to support each goal in appendix A: Brand Goals Practices.

Innovation

In this context, we define innovation as creating *new* value for stakeholders. In many fields, the demand for faster and richer innovation is so great that the only way leadership can know where to develop is by listening to stakeholders or customers. In fact, after surveying more than two thousand companies for their research, business scholars Tim Kastelle, Nilofer Merchant, and Martie-Louise Verreynne declare that "community and purpose are the new sources of advantage."[1]

Innovating from feedback is an impossible task if handled one email at a time. Many times, the importance of a brand community includes accessing and curating insightful ideas in a fast-changing marketplace.

Such innovation can address many areas, including improving customer experience, operational efficiency, or even design. To build a community to support innovation, leaders must pick a specific innovation area (e.g., customer experience *or* operational efficiency).

Innovation Areas

Consider focusing on one of the three areas described here. Confuse or conflate areas and you will confuse members and stakeholders.

NEW PRODUCTS OR SERVICES

Earlier we mentioned that worldwide beauty retailer Sephora hosts and manages a customer community called Beauty Insiders where members can discuss beauty topics even if those topics are unrelated to Sephora. The community conversations showed Sephora a specific market opportunity none of its competitors were filling.

Former Sephora head of community Shira Levine confirmed that "community conversations definitely influence product creation across Sephora" (personal communication, April 2019). Within scant years of starting the community, Sephora served as the exclusive launch retailer for the Fenty Beauty by Rihanna product lines, largely designed for women of color. The ninety new products launched included "shimmer" sticks that allowed dramatic highlighting for more skin tones. The line sold $140 million in its first forty days and was named by *Time* magazine as among the best inventions of the year.[2] The innovation has shifted the entire market.

CUSTOMER EXPERIENCE DESIGN

Brand communities can improve how customers interact with a brand at any or even all stages in the customer journey.

Airbnb hosts summits around the world for its hosts so that those who choose to can grow as hosts in a supportive community. Access to the community helps Airbnb support them as the market and online platform constantly change. Airbnb company engineers have learned that it's important to spend time with the host community because even in brief conversations, engineers and designers can learn what the most active members seek, and concept-test imagined improvements. This allows Airbnb's teams to make faster and more relevant improvements than any competitor can.

INTERNAL COLLABORATION

Brand communities can improve the way work gets done.

Airbnb's Louise Beryl told us (interview, July 2019) that staff noticed a growing conversation among Australian hosts. Many were seeking information on how to better host Chinese guests. The Australian market was shifting to more Chinese tourists, and their different preferences, customs, and expectations were a surprise to many members. Australian hosts suggested providing a wider variety of kitchen utensils and appliances to meet the needs of Chinese guests. Several Chinese guests and hosts applauded the thoughtfulness.

Louise noted two profound things worth celebrating for Airbnb. The first was that hosts, who were in some ways competing for guests, were also showing how much they were willing to ask for and offer help among members. The second was that these members helped the Airbnb team recognize that there was an opportunity to support and train hosts in the changing market.

Ways to Reduce Innovation Investment Risk

A brand community reduces innovation investment risk in three ways:

• A community already interested in and attentive to innovation development provides *diverse perspectives*, which highlight unknown or unpredicted opportunities, uses, and problems.

Both Sephora's attention to unserved makeup demand and Airbnb's discovery of Australian host challenges are fantastic examples of diverse perspectives highlighting something new.

• *Community cocreation creates buy-in* (i.e., reduces rejection of change). When stakeholders understand and feel connected to change, even see opportunities to inform change, they're more willing to accept it.

You can recognize the importance of community buy-in most clearly when considering what happens when a brand launches an innovation *without* such buy-in. Digg was an online news-sharing and discussion platform with over thirty-five million users a month.[3] In 2010, Digg launched a redesign without inviting member input. The changes included a new interface, story popularity algorithm, and user rating system. Within weeks, 34 percent of UK users and 25 percent of US users abandoned the site.[4] Had Digg cooperated with even a small percentage of members in the redesign, the platform would have been much more likely to avoid the community abandonment. Some speculate that Digg might have grown into a household brand name. Instead, it was sold in 2012 for $500,000. Four years before, Google had reportedly offered $200 million.[5] Ignoring the opportunity to innovate with community buy-in may have led the brand to lose over $199 million.

• *A community can provide faster feedback for iteration.* Designers get pertinent feedback from stakeholders familiar with the problem and interested in a solution.

Salesforce is a customer relationship management (CRM) software company with over 150,000 client companies, more than thirty thousand employees, and annual revenue of over $13 billion.[6] Jennifer Sacks, Salesforce's senior director of customer and market insights (personal communication, October 2019), explained that in the company's early days, executives learned that they could never adequately understand what users wanted changed or redesigned simply by reading individual customer service tickets. In response to this issue, Salesforce created the IdeaExchange community, made up of customers.

IdeaExchange gives product developers ready access to those who understand how the product is used in the real world. Sacks says that over three thousand implemented features have been sourced from the community, helping Salesforce grow a fast-improving machine. (See more on innovation and Salesforce in appendix A.)

When stakeholders experience cocreation and brand responsiveness, they can grow more loyal to both the brand and the people involved. This loyalty is measured in customer retention and lifetime value. In other words, involving your brand community in innovation also strengthens many critical relationships.

PATAGONIA CHANGING THE WHOLE MARKET

Patagonia is now one of the best-known outdoor clothing brands in the world. It was founded by rock climber Yvon Chouinard in 1973 and remains privately held. Recent sales exceeded $700 million a year.[7] It didn't start that way.

Yvon started his outdoor retailing by selling rock-climbing hardware. This included ice axes and pitons, the spikes that climbers hammered into cliffs to attach safety ropes. The company was then called Chouinard Equipment. Yvon and the friends who helped start the venture understood that if any one of their products failed, it was entirely likely that one of their friends, or someone connected to their friends, would die or be seriously injured.

Rock climbers make an exceptional market. They're a specially connected community of people who trust one another in partnership as they hang dozens, hundreds, or thousands of feet from cliff bases.

Yvon and his colleague Tom Frost recognized that every time a climber drove a piton into the rock face, a crack was widened. It fundamentally harmed the rock's integrity, which meant that every future climber would find the rock in worse condition. Around the world, climbers were destroying the very resource that gave them so much joy. Chouinard Equipment didn't just need an innovation, Yvon and his colleagues realized: The whole industry needed to change to protect the future.

Yvon knew of little metal nuts called "chocks" in Britain that allow climbers to secure themselves in cracks without damaging the rock. He wanted to shift his own production and sales toward chocks. But American climbers weren't familiar with the product.

As a world-class climber and provider of lifesaving equipment, Yvon was well connected within the community. In Yvon's 1972 catalog for the then renamed Great Pacific Iron Works company, he included an essay by another important climber, Doug Robinson, explaining the importance of protecting rock faces with "cleaner" gear.

In the nine months after the catalog and included essay were released, the Iron Works business shifted to 70 percent chocks. As Vincent Stanley, who worked with Yvon at the Iron Works put it, "The essay was discussed at the base of every route and in every climbing club in the country." Yvon and his team learned that if they spoke to customers not just as consumers but as friends and equals about necessary evolution they could bring about remarkable change (personal communication with Vincent Stanley, June 2019).

One lesson we may glean from the company's influence is that when leaders communicated with a whole sporting community about shared values (going beyond self-promotion), they could inspire something revolutionary. Within a year, the company started an industry trend that still protects the natural world a generation later.

Talent Recruitment and Retention

The term *talent recruitment and retention* refers to the efforts made by an organization to bring in people crucial for meeting organizational goals and to keep them involved. Talent can include employees, investors, vendors, volunteers, and collaborators. If you want these people to care about one another, then you want a strong brand community. We've heard about the profound difference this makes from employees at premiere brands including Patagonia, REI, and IDEO.

Every community needs to pay attention to member retention. This is non-negotiable. Without attracting the right members and keeping them involved, no community can work.

When your staff and members feel seen, understood, and cared for, they'll generate referrals that are important for your success. And, just as important: Highly skilled staff want to stay where they feel belonging, connection, and support. If you're in an industry where competition can steal your best people at any time, then nurturing a community where they want to stay is crucially important and a gigantic competitive advantage.

Work engagement—employees' participation at work—can be measured in terms of output. According to Gallup research, "85% of employees are not engaged or [are] actively disengaged at work. The economic consequences of this global 'norm' are approximately $7 trillion in lost productivity."[8]

Yale researchers Emma Seppälä and Marissa King wrote in the *Harvard Business Review* that *lonely people disengage,* and this disengagement costs organizations in several ways, including "almost 37% higher absenteeism, 49% more accidents, 16% lower profitability, and a 65% lower share price over time."[9] This means that many executives have a lot to gain by helping teams connect more.

Seppälä and King write that 50 percent of people across professions and corporate hierarchies are burned out. This is a costly problem. Further, "50% of people say they are often or always exhausted due to work . . . [T]here is a significant correlation between feeling lonely and work exhaustion: The more people are exhausted, the lonelier they feel."[10] These authors suggest that exhaustion's link to loneliness means that more human connection at work may be critical to addressing widespread burnout.

Leadership author David Burkus reports on recent research indicating that positive social relationships with coworkers may be the *most important factor* in work happiness and that *having friends at work makes us far more productive.*[11] Research firm Gallup found that "close work friendships boost employee satisfaction by 50% and [that] *people with a best friend at work are seven times more likely to engage fully in their work*" (emphasis added).[12]

Work friends help productivity by giving us people to approach for help when we need it and by sharing information through informal networks when formal systems work poorly or not at all. These may be reasons why belonging is connected to better retention, productivity, and well-being.[13]

The concept of belonging also takes the contemporary focus on diversity and inclusion to a higher level, helping employees go beyond "fitting in" (which, according to University of Texas social researcher Brené Brown, is "the opposite of belonging") to feeling belonging as who they are, to their team and organization.[14]

Belonging doesn't happen by accident. People create it intentionally, using a variety of soft skills, including listening, empathizing, and applying emotional intelligence. In short, when there is a context for community to grow, organizations experience incredible outcomes.

It seems obvious that when we feel connected to people at work, when we believe that we share values and that colleagues care about us, we will grow our engagement. It's a shame so many managers never understand this.

Customer Retention

Customer retention means keeping customers who get value from the brand. If they ask to participate in the brand community, this almost always means that they already believe the brand can help them achieve or become what they aspire to. Participants believe they share some values with the brand, and participants want to grow in some way.

There are many ways to retain customers without community. Strong customer service, high-touch account management, and just plain better products are all worthy investments. An enriching community is just another offering (one difficult for others to copy) but not right for every brand.

Customers who only want a product or a service are not good candidates for a brand community. You want customers who want to grow, learn, contribute, and connect. For example, Harley-Davidson has invested internationally in forming HOGs. Why? Anyone with enough money can buy a motorcycle and take it out.

Members participate because some want to learn with, grow among, and contribute to others like them (Harley riders). In this way, the community offers additional value *beyond* the products. Harley-Davidson offers safety classes, scheduled rides with Harley owners, and access to more experienced long-distance riders.

Organizations can offer ways to grow and experience fun with four key principles:

- *Active engagement.* Active engagement means you're inviting participants (customers) to experience something through membership (e.g., riding their motorcycles), as opposed to strictly passive engagement (receiving company announcements or watching videos of others riding). If your brand isn't inviting participants to actually participate in something fun that helps them grow, then you almost certainly don't have a true community.

We spoke with a San Francisco cultural arts institution executive who oversaw a performance series that cost hundreds of thousands of dollars to produce. The hope was that, after attracting many new visitors with the series, the institution would build a stronger support base for ongoing programming. The executive shared with us that, in retrospect, she now recognizes that there was no effort or investment to connect new visitors with one another or the institution staff. New audiences came for fun events, saw them, and then left with no relationship to develop. Without participation that builds community, all the new introductions turned into lost opportunities.

• *Keeping the brand top of mind, but not making the brand priority 1 in all communication.* All communication should offer value to customers that will help them grow further into who they want to be. They can do this without having to buy more product all the time. This is true for Harley riders, who can participate in HOG events without buying yet another motorcycle.

Many brand communities struggle with allowing competitors or disconnected brands to post in their community, and members to post about competitors. Both Sephora and Little Monsters confront this today. The wise choice is that these posts absolutely should be allowed if the information, opportunity, experience, or anything else helps members grow as they aspire.

Your brand and members live in a much larger ecosystem than your community. For example, Harley-Davidson riders obviously already know about other brands and part makers. Members feel connected and committed to brand communities because these communities help them grow. If you censor anything helpful but competitive, then you're seeding distrust. When you show that you'll support anything that will help members grow, your members' trust, respect, and enthusiasm will increase because you demonstrate real commitment to their success beyond marketing manipulation.

You do need boundaries to ensure that participants are enriched by their experience and never distracted from what they seek. Competitors freely promoting products can distract from the community purpose. Consistent with keeping the inside safe, all spam and superficial marketing must be moderated so that the inside remains a place for enrichment and connection instead of a space mostly for marketing.

- *Using shared experiences to grow trust.* If customers don't have access to shared experiences, they aren't connecting often or well. Brands must offer events and spaces to encourage shared experiences that can build empathy and trust. (See the discussion of the campfire principle in part 3.) These experiences can take place in physical or digital space, ideally both. If there are too few shared experiences (or none), the community connections will stagnate or never form. For many brands, the lack of shared experiences means they only have mirage communities.

Etsy addressed this by offering daily "newbie chats" where new members were invited to digitally connect in a chat room with elders and the Etsy team. New users noticed that they were welcomed and introduced to community, the various segments, and to each other. Their new arrival was celebrated, and new sellers began to trust others who joined these chats (personal communication with Danielle Maveal, August 2019).

- *Creating safety so that customers return to participate.* If you want customers to keep returning, then the brand must ensure (as much as possible) that the space is safe for participants. If they are going to get teased, harassed, or hazed, the community will not succeed. We double-down on this point because even though it should be obvious, we've met several brand leaders who don't understand it. They assume that a neutral stance—let participants "work it out"—is the best policy. If you do that, you'll lose the people who want to participate but gave up because of the hassle.

There are many examples of brands doing a great job investing in making brand communities safe. Our favorite example: Harley-Davidson provides members with riding safety clinics, group-leader training to handle unruly members and legal challenges, and even *insurance* for the group rides. Even when its customers dress as the toughest people in their county, Harley-Davidson understands that making the events safe is critical for the company's international success.

In another example, within the early Lady Gaga Little Monster's fan community, moderators discovered that, without enforceable guidelines, some members got harassed and felt unsafe. Nude photographs and hateful comments showed up. This led to strict guidelines to foster a kind and compassionate space. Moderator Elena personally responded to every conduct flag even when they reached an average of twenty reported each hour. She and the volunteer moderators ensured that members felt safe enough to stay.

Marketing

Marketing refers to the efforts to inform the marketplace of the value offered by your brand. To understand how community and marketing work together, we must first understand a powerful principle: That "How can I build a community to sell more stuff?" is a community-destroying conversation starter.

It's OK to sell stuff.

It's OK to want to sell more.

It's OK to reach out to people who want your stuff.

But if you're building a community *only* to sell stuff, you're at best building a mirage community. And you'll look like a manipulative jerk.

This is because the relationship you have with someone as a customer and the relationship you have with that person as a community member, though not mutually exclusive, are distinctively different. Twitch, for example, has millions of customers who are also active community members.

Customers overwhelmingly seek a transactional relationship. As Twitch's Bobby Scarnewman put it, "The relationship with community members and strict customers is totally different. When someone is only a customer, we're constantly competing for their attention and dangling shiny objects to get it. Customers seek maximum value for minimum cost" (personal communication with Bobby Scarnewman, August 2019).

Community members return because they're growing (progressing) in a way they want, and they seek to both connect and contribute to others on the journey. Bobby notes, "Community members seek to add value so that they can be seen as valuable by other members, and show others that they care." In fact, in contrast to customers in a strict transactional relationship, community members can appear to outsiders to be contributing far more than they get. Their contribution can help them connect and grow, experiences they feel on the inside. This is the way that many of Twitch's city group leaders relate to their community volunteering around the world.

The foundation of community building is always helping members grow into who they want to be.

If you're a community builder with a marketing goal, ask questions like these:

How can we help people feel more connected (less isolated) in some way?

How can we help people grow toward what they want to be with others?

What kind of marketing opportunity would become available if we could do this?

The final point here is so important that we will risk repeating it in slightly different words:

You can market without building a community.

You can build community without selling stuff.

You cannot build a community *only* to sell stuff. The community will fail.

LULULEMON CHOOSES AMBASSADORS WHO SUPPORT OTHERS

Lululemon, the Canadian yoga-inspired athletic apparel company, builds community among a wide variety of ambassadors—professional athletes as well as small-town yoga instructors—through its ambassador program. The company has built the program for over five years, and its growth remains robust.[15]

These brand ambassadors both represent Lululemon in the marketplace and *actually serve* others. This is to say they care about the community members with whom they share experience. They live according to the health values they advocate in the community. It's no surprise that by offering access to and association with such a community, Lululemon is a hot brand among yoga enthusiasts.

Robyn Alazraqui is a CrossFit fitness coach who was named a Lululemon brand ambassador for a one-year term. She was totally shocked when the company selected her for ambassadorship. She said the company selects ambassadors who authentically care about their own health and fitness *and* about supporting others in achieving healthy lifestyles. She noted that if Lululemon just wanted attractive and popular people, they could have picked from many younger and slimmer coaches with what she called "yoga bodies." Instead, in her own words, they picked an "old mom coach"—in this case, a mom coach working to support middle-aged athletes every day (personal communication with Robyn Alazraqui, September 2019).

Robyn also felt connected to the brand through mutual care. She said that the Lululemon team didn't just give her the store credit that comes with the role. Reflecting back on the time, she says: "They really cared about my career, and they were great to me."

HARLEY-DAVIDSON CUSTOMERS REPRESENT

Motorcycle manufacturer and lifestyle brand Harley-Davidson is transparent about the HOG community's value to its marketing and sales outcomes. The more that members ride bikes with other members, the sooner the bikes wear out—thus more sales for new Harley bikes. Further, the more involved that members grow in the Harley community, the more that owners spend on Harley gear.

Imagine seeing thousands of Harley riders touring roads around the world. People who see the groups decked out in leather Harley gear get a brand impression that attracts some and repels others. Either way, Harley gains visibility.

HOG members also know that participation in the community leads to lifelong memories with friends, traveling to places they otherwise would never visit, and feeling free from everyday responsibilities on the open road.

How, exactly, can a brand community support marketing without primarily focusing on selling? By following the *watering hole principle.*

Imagine you're on a photo safari. If you're trying to find rhinos, giraffes, and lions for great shots, you'll soon learn that they all go to watering holes. They need water; watering holes have water. If you find the watering holes, you'll find the wildlife.

So if you create a good watering hole, you'll get access to wildlife. Wildlife return to watering holes because they get what they want, and water helps them survive another hot day and grow into mature animals. They do not come to pose for photographs.

If you forget the water element in your watering-hole strategy (because you focused on lighting and tripod arrangements), we can safely predict how well your photo safari is going to go.

Authentic brand communities, like watering holes, offer what visitors seek for their health, needs, and growth. The more you deliver enrichment, the more the wildlife comes. The bigger the watering hole, the more rhinos it will fit. Who doesn't want to connect with the best watering hole?

At some point, rhinos will defend their favorite watering hole. This is similar to how community serves marketing. When we deliver enough connection and enrichment, then members will defend the watering hole we've created. It will become "their" watering hole, meaning they'll feel ownership or entitlement. This can be a good thing when it's helpful, and a challenge when it's not. In a brand-building world, defending a watering hole ideally excludes aggression and violence. No matter how members show up, they'll also connect with us whenever they return to "their" watering hole.

As an example, consider how Harley's HOG members often defend the brand by responding to critics in person, on motorcycle forums, and in social media. This includes members defending Harley's electric motorcycle investment choices.[16] Former "HOG Captain" Robert Jones explained that in general, even when he feels critical of company decisions, he gives the brand the benefit of the doubt and remembers that Harley executives have a hard job (interview, October 2019). He gives Harley feedback and will defend the company because he's a proud Harley rider and member. Robert has never seen Harley train members in how to advocate for Harley. The company doesn't need to. Community pride fosters the protection.

Customer Service

Most organizations can, in principle, turn to their brand communities to have them help customers with the brand's services or products. But most brands haven't supported their nascent brand community enough to make it possible for members to provide as much support as they want to. In such cases, the customers feel mutual concern for one another, but do not have tools to offer meaningful support.

For clarity, customers help largely when there is an authentic community. We wince when thinking of brand leaders who claim they have a customer community when they really have a customer list.

When communities are well supported, the results can be stunning. Apple customers can get support twenty-four hours a day, every day, from other volunteer Apple customers. CRM software provider Salesforce's products help support customer relationship management; the company has built the Trailblazer Community to help customers (whom they call "trailblazers"). Sephora's Beauty Insiders community is a resource to any beauty product consumer seeking help, including appropriate product choices, on any day of the year.

When a brand community can support customers, the community provides three extraordinary brand benefits:

- *It externalizes customer support costs.* The community relieves the brand from having to staff a comprehensive help team for users everywhere at all times.

- *It's scalable.* A community that supports an increasingly diverse user base can organically grow to serve emerging customer types.

- *It provides an accessible touch point.* The community offers customers an easy way to become more involved with the brand values and purpose.

Warning: Just expecting brand enthusiasts to show up and help won't make that support happen. The product and brand must first grow compelling enough and important enough to customers that they want to support others with similar challenges and aspirations. As Joshua Zerkel, head of global community at project management software brand Asana put it, "The product must be truly loved."[17] If it isn't loved yet, then that issue has to be addressed first.

Advancing Movements

Movements refer to brands that create a fundamental shift in our culture, political policies, or ways of doing business. Recent for-profit examples include Airbnb and Lyft. We also see political movement–oriented brand communities. The most famous social movements in the US all included brand communities, among them the Student Nonviolent Coordinating Committee for civil rights advocacy, the National Woman Suffrage Association for women's rights, and the Japanese American Citizens League for post–World War II internment reparations.

True movements can take years (often generations) to achieve their goals, so they need *repeated engagement.* This often means coordinating volunteer work, sending communications, and representing a cause with volunteers' bodies (at rallies, protests, office visits, and the like). We wish it were obvious to more leaders that participants remain and return to movements over a long haul when they find connection, friendships, and shared identity there.

Although we can get nuanced and particular in parsing movement types, here we're simply discussing any movements that bring together people who care about one another. Said differently, participants make friends and look out for one another as they invest in social change. Although a great deal of communication, promotion, and organizing takes place online, at the end of the day, every movement where forming community is important relies on an active "ground game": real people meeting with one another, many times over. Repeated gathering builds the friendships that support participants through the hard work. The power and importance of these relationships is always the same.

Community Forum

Although brand communities are designed to serve members and brands, the primary purpose of some brands is to serve as a community forum. Certain conferences, summer camps, sports leagues, and professional associations can be described this way. All provide a space and context (digital or physical) for participants to connect and grow. Indeed, this is the primary purpose for these brands to exist.

Because of the very nature of what we call here "community forum" brands, all the principles discussed in this book apply to these organizations. We therefore will not dwell on how community serves this kind of brand because a strong community is existentially important to their success.

Before we move on, we can help leaders distinguish such brands. Let's consider two brand examples: Reddit and Stack Overflow. These sites are both community forums.

Reddit is an online news aggregator and discussion platform that organizes niche communities around the world on one giant platform. It hosts over one million subcommunities.[18] These segmented communities are interested in wide-ranging topics, from Zen meditation to cat ownership. Stack Overflow is an online platform that connects programmers from around the world. Both of these brands provide the spaces for interest-based communities to form. People had these interests before these communities existed, but finding similar others was difficult. These community forums bring people together as their raison d'etre. Both Reddit and Stack Overflow offer a place for niche (and growing) communities to connect for support and growth.

Online brands whose primary role is to provide a forum for connection do this at a scale that was historically impossible before the internet. Online brands are part of a technical development trend that democratizes tools for building online community.

Even within community forum brands, growth by itself does not necessarily mean community success. A large forum will fail if it does not provide a safe space and help members connect and meet goals. We've seen many brands conflate more people showing up or making a click visiting web pages with building a successful community. This typically happens when (accidentally) leaders focus on building a mirage community.

Part
2

BUILDING FROM THE BEGINNING

Great things are born out of chaos.
—Rev. Dr. Yvette Flunder

3

DISTINGUISHING COMMUNITY

Earlier, when we discussed mirage communities, we noted that many people use the term *community* to refer to many other things, most of which are not actual communities. So, now that we've discussed what makes a brand community and the ways that many communities support brand goals, for clarity, let's distinguish other things that leaders mistake for brand communities before.

Recognizing Platforms

We refer to a community **platform** as a technology that allows members to directly communicate, share, and discover one another and resources no matter where they are. A platform almost always involves software that enables participants to connect with shared information. It's a tool, which is never enough, by itself, for creating a community.

Evan Hamilton has spent years supporting and nurturing users' communities at Reddit, among other companies. He offered a helpful metaphor: "A *platform* is a restaurant where you meet friends weekly for noodles and dumplings. *The community is the group of friends*" (personal communication with

Evan Hamilton, April 2019; emphasis added). The community is durable and precious. Even if the restaurant closes, the relationships continue. Friends find another place to gather.

In other words, building a platform (even a really good one) does not guarantee that a community will form. If you build an oak dinner table, you can't assume that fantastic dinner parties will suddenly appear, complete with witty banter and delicate desserts. The parties are certainly possible, but a lot more and different work lies ahead.

Many mistakenly believe that technology alone (e.g., a new platform) will attract members and create connectedness. This is never the case. To go back to our dinner-table example: invitations, a warm welcome, generous eats, and the like will do more to create a fantastic dinner party than even the most beautiful table. In fact, if the other parts are right, the table can be perfectly ordinary.

Communities can change venues and platforms. What we set up, encourage, and invite others into so that they can grow connections is what eventually creates a community.

Remember that everyone who visits a community platform is not automatically part of a community, just as simply visiting a local sports field doesn't make you part of the circle of friends who meet there, although that may be a first step. Participants begin as visitors. We visit because someone is creating something (a basketball game?) that we want to experience.

We visit and join communities because we want to participate in the leadership's vision and mission that align with our own values and some growth aspiration. Sharing ourselves in intimate ways creates the relationships, which create community.

Recognizing Advocacy Campaigns

By **advocacy**, we mean any organizational effort to motivate individuals *outside* the organization to enact change. Advocacy work usually includes sharing a change message widely. With advocacy, an organization seeks to grow its influence. This growth can take place, for example, in the domain of political change, in the adoption of a for-profit company's technology, or in a nonprofit's involvement in promoting a social good.

It's important to understand that advocacy and community, though often related, remain distinct from each other.

Advocacy campaigns often seek to build community, and for good reason. Addressing the world's challenges takes many people working together over long periods of time. Sometimes, advocating organizations create community; sometimes, communities become advocating organizations. We (Carrie and Charles) both have participated in many advocacy actions. These have included standing among thousands we didn't know and leading dozens who all knew us.

When police pull some advocating activists aside and detain them, a larger group may not notice that someone is now missing, or who. In a community (of activists), it's far more difficult for someone to get lost, because members know and care for one another. This is especially important when there are others who want to make trouble for harassment's sake and when we're including vulnerable participants.

There are at least two types of organizational advocacy:

1. Brand advocacy, which promotes a brand

2. Political advocacy, which works for policy change

There is overlap in these categories: a political organization can brand-advocate by promoting its own brand (e.g., Black Lives Matter or Greenpeace), and a corporate brand can organize political advocacy (e.g., Patagonia's Open Rivers advocacy).

How Advocacy Differs from Community

Leadership must recognize that, strictly speaking, advocacy is distinct from both the brand community itself and the community-building work in at least five ways:

1. Advocacy can be a *one-time effort* (one day, one week, one event).

2. *Priorities are chosen top-down.*

   Members are told what will be advocated.

3. The top goal is *promoting something.*

   Mutual care among members is a lesser (perhaps even ignored) commitment.

4. Relationships trend toward the *transactional.*

   This can mean rewarding someone for taking an action (calling, speaking, or attending), in contrast to a generous commitment to one another to uphold fundamentally enriching relationships. Examples of tools used for transaction include swag, exclusive invitations, cross promotion, internal points rewards, badges, and labels.

5. Relationships trend toward a *"wagon wheel" structure.*

   Participants primarily connect with an authority and keep few or no relationships with peers. By contrast, authentic communities tend toward a web-like relationship structure whereby participants connect with peers.

There's nothing wrong with advocacy, advocacy campaigns, or gathering people in a group to make a difference together. In fact, we're big fans of all three, and we participate in many advocacy groups. You can do all of this effectively both in and outside community. The important lesson is to recognize that *focusing only on strict advocacy will never form a durable community.*

Community requires different attention. In fact, focusing exclusively on advocacy can harm community dynamics that may already naturally be in place. This shouldn't be surprising: Few of us want to remain connected with others who want us primarily to serve their agenda. You have to invest in a foundation of community first and *then* engage in advocacy.

For example, Charles joined a political phone-bank event to support ensuring access to health care for all Americans. The event was hosted in a downtown San Francisco office, and more than thirty professionals came in on a sunny Saturday to volunteer. Each participated because they cared about all Americans getting medical attention (value). They all wanted to support making this happen (purpose).

As volunteers arrived on-site, the organizing leader pointed to a URL on a whiteboard and told them to login and then start calling the numbers and use the talking points provided by online software.

The organizer didn't spend even five minutes encouraging volunteers or giving them introductions or time to connect with one another to find camaraderie. He didn't acknowledge that the volunteers' showing up was a reflection of commonly shared values or that all in the room shared a purpose. He also never acknowledged that this work was important if any change was to happen!

He did, however, give instructions to "get something done" (phone calls). That organizer treated all those volunteers merely as free labor for his organization.

To effect the change that all the volunteers worked toward that day could take years. It was, and is, vitally important that volunteers who showed their commitment on that sunny weekend return to do more. They'll only do this if the volunteer opportunities provide them an opportunity to feel connected and to participate toward a purpose. There was so much potential to start a community of people who could have enthusiastically worked together for years. All was missed by focusing on "getting something done."

Leaders of an advocacy community must distinguish between just a "group" volunteering on a Saturday and a potential community gathered to work together toward a purpose for possibly years. If your advocacy goals will take years and need ongoing support, we imagine that you'll always want both community and advocacy. If you ignore the community part, you'll always be left with fleeting participant manipulation.

All too often, people *assume that advocacy naturally builds community.* We hope that by this point in the discussion, you already understand that the opposite is true. Strict advocacy can impede community building because relationships remain transactional, and even the time needed to build connections goes missing.

People also too often *rely on fragile transactional relationships,* assuming that such relationships will eventually create an advocacy community. In reality, using a transaction strategy means a group's durability will end as soon as the leader (or the brand) stops offering transactions. When the rewards stop, the relationship stops. It's really that simple.

Our guess is that you almost never nurture relationships in which others only want to get something from you (e.g., your labor) each time you connect. We all know people like this, and we don't call them. They only call us to ask for stuff. They may think we're friends, but they're wrong.

Brand Advocacy

Many brands invest in advocacy efforts that misunderstand how and why members mobilize. Misguided leaders believe the myth that if people are already in their community, they'll advocate for the brand under any conditions.

Carrie worked with an online media company that learned this the hard way. The company helps over one million users contribute relevant media to several online platforms. (We've slightly altered this description to protect privacy.) At the time, the company managed more than five thousand members in a collaborative messaging platform. The leaders assumed that they could use these members to promote the company widely on social media platforms.

They decided to "empower" their customers to share sales promotions and feature announcements. The intention might have worked if the program had also helped members achieve their own goals. This was not the case.

The company invested in "ambassador management software" that allowed happy customers to post messages in exchange for points toward both Amazon and Starbucks gift cards (a transaction).

In the first six months, *only fifteen people* participated. Neither the director of marketing nor the community strategist could understand how more than 99.5 percent of their customers ignored the program. They wondered why loyal customers wouldn't love sharing messages for the company in exchange for coffee or other products.

Well, it's because no one loves sharing messages if doing so doesn't help them connect, become who they want to be, or progress toward an aspirational purpose. At no time did the company consider how it was supporting participants in connection or growth. Later research showed that the participants didn't want to get distracted from work tasks in order to promote the company. Essentially, the trade the company offered wasn't enough to "buy" the time and the help from participants. Therefore, participants ignored them.

By contrast, consider an organization that approached membership advocacy totally differently. In 2007, then Illinois senator Barack Obama ran for the US presidency. The Obama for President organization needed many people to join advocating for the senator. Yet the campaign didn't have the budget to pay for field organizers in every state. The campaign managers knew there were thousands of volunteers who wanted to get involved even when the campaign didn't have the bandwidth to organize them.

According to authors Elizabeth McKenna and Hahrie Han, who wrote the book *Groundbreakers* about Barack Obama's presidential campaigns, "Before the 2008 Obama campaign, many political operatives treated community organizing and electioneering as mutually exclusive endeavors . . . Neglecting the long-term base building that characterizes community organizing, most contemporary electoral campaigns focus on creating temporary voter turnout machines that disappear when the election is over. These campaigns win without investing in citizens' capacity to make change, or to be leaders in their communities . . . In such campaigns, volunteers, when available, do not have responsibility for any real outcomes and are sometimes viewed as a drain on resources rather than an asset."[1]

Inspired by Harvard Kennedy School professor Marshall Ganz, a campaign strategy was created to empower disconnected enthusiasts without a traditional centralized authority. The new strategy depended on building authentic community. The campaign built the online platform My.BarackObama.com which enabled supporters to both create and connect at grassroots local events, where they made friends among neighbors and colleagues.

Volunteers didn't create events and support the campaign in return for money, awards, or trades. They did so (1) freely, so that they could (2) connect with like-valued citizens and (3) advance toward electing a more progressive president (purpose). In other words, the campaign supported internal motivation to participate in community *in all three critical ways*. (We will discuss internal motivation more in part 3.) Past campaign strategies had neglected the importance of interpersonal connections for similarly motivated participants.

For the Obama campaign, many thousands of volunteers created local events where participants could and did share intimate experiences and discover how much they shared in both values and aspirations. Because event creation didn't depend on campaign headquarters, many more events were created than in the past. This meant that supporters could and did grow friendships connecting during *multiple events.* They also experienced shared delight and memories that they will carry with them for the rest of their lives. The intimacy and friendship building were a sharp contrast to past campaigning where volunteers were largely invited to tedious hours of phone banking, canvassing, and data entry.

Eventually, more than two million volunteers advocated for Obama's campaign, making it the largest volunteer-powered presidential campaign in history. The phone banking, canvassing, and data entry got done. According to early volunteers, the "secret ingredient" that inspired so much volunteer advocacy was the formation and deepening of personal relationships within the campaign. Volunteers in time considered themselves "family." Though Obama even considered the campaign a trial run in the beginning, the campaign powered by millions of volunteers across all states won him the US presidency.

Recognizing Social Media Management

Managing social media is as different from building a community as is running an advocacy campaign. This doesn't mean it's unimportant. As leaders, however, we must recognize the distinction between promotion and relationship development.

Social media can be fantastic for *promoting* a community or event(s). But it's lousy at knitting together relationships to create or deepen community—just as building a dining table doesn't make you a good cook and sharing menus doesn't make you a good dinner host. We must distinguish between furniture building (the platform), menu sharing (promotion), and actual dinner hosting.

Now, in our metaphor, guests may enthusiastically share the menu, dessert photos, and selfies with a chef on social media. This can be great for cataloging a lasting memory, attracting others to the next dinner, and just plain celebrating a successful dinner. However, at the end of the day, the events that deepen relationships overwhelmingly happen within intimate experiences (not on social media). This means that participants *joining* the dinner grow relationships that make a community. Everyone else just learns about it.

There are three key principles to understanding how social media management differs from the core work of building brand community.

1. *Conversations are prompted.* Many social media managers start conversations to get more "engagement" from customers. Although there's nothing wrong with this, in a mature brand community, leadership will see unplanned conversations start and grow without prompting or stoking.

2. *Brand promotion is the primary motive.* Most social media management holds its primary goal as promoting a brand, ideally deftly. The most important measurements then become "impressions" (number of people who "could have seen" a posting) and "clicks" (follow-up act from an impression). Clicks are measured as a CTR (click-through rate). In an authentic brand community, the quality of value delivered to participants and the relationships are far more important for community strength than any number of clicks.

3. *Communication is largely broadcast (one to many).* Most social media managers "push" content out to many, seeking impressions and clicks. This can be both effective and fun. It also builds an audience

(not a community). In authentic brand communities, we see group conversations in which the communication resembles people sitting in a group talking rather than a speaker presenting to an audience.

None of these conventions are necessarily bad. The danger lies in using them too much, thereby inhibiting the growth of an authentic brand community.

When leaders misunderstand social media's relationship to community, they often try leaning heavily on increasing branded postings and asking participants to promote (i.e., to act as a brand ambassador). An invitation to "brand ambassadorship" can be fun for members while it's novel (or if it distinguishes them within an inner ring), but by itself, ambassadorships never result in authentic community. This is always true if there is little (or likely no) opportunity for developing mutual concern among participants. Intimate shared experiences remain necessary for real connection.

To be effective leaders, we must distinguish between social media activity that *promotes events* and other meaningful engagement that *knits* community. Glossier did a good job focusing on promotion when appropriate and not pretending that its audiences make a community. Glossier is a billion-dollar beauty brand that focuses on products for millennials and Gen Z and millions of social media has followers.[2] The company often features customers in its brand Instagram stories along with almost daily photos of celebrity influencers using its products. The brand thus inspires customers to showcase their own looks on social media. Some customers also started their own Glossier Instagram profiles, such as Glossier Boys (for customers who are men) and Glossier on Brown Beauties (for customers who are people of color). The company's robust growth is in large part a result of encouraging customer fanaticism. Note that with this activity, *Glossier is not building community with its fans (yet), but is still effective in celebrating fans and driving business growth.* Their choice is both transparent and perfectly appropriate (and successful) for the brand.

Elsewhere in this book, we discuss Sephora's efforts to connect and provide meeting forums for customers both in stores and online. The company is growing a different kind of success with different investments. Investing differently just creates different outcomes.

4

STARTING AT THE BEGINNING

Just about everyone we speak to wants to work on supporting mature-stage communities. In this stage, friends meet up spontaneously, there are interesting and relevant activities going on year-round, there are insider jokes and funny stories that get recounted, and there is greater power in numbers than there ever was when members were just enthusiastic individuals. We know.

Unfortunately, for those of us who want to create great community, like everything else in life, things begin at the beginning. This is the part that so many want to skip because it's unglamorous, the results are uncertain, and progress moves more slowly than we want. It's often also scary because we might prove that we can't bring people together with our best efforts. This is normal.

Just like life in general, when we start with clarity, vision, and focus, whatever follows goes better (if never perfectly). Eventually, when we've created something that works, we get to laugh at the humble beginnings.

Clarifying Organizational Purpose

It's hard to make a good meal if you haven't decided what makes a good meal. Does it have to be hot, easily portable, eaten with the fingers, gluten free? No meal scores a perfect 10 on all possible measures of "good." Imagine preparing a meal without first choosing a menu: chicken fingers, banh mi sandwiches, or soup noodles? You may end with sandwiches stacked in noodle bowls and wonder why lunch just didn't "feel right." We see the community version of this very often. Leaders present options before they know what a good community will look like for members and the organization.

All too often, organizations decide to launch a brand community without first clarifying what they want their brand community to do for their organization (let alone for members). For any of this to work, you'll of course need to offer some enriching opportunity for members to grow.

The beginning is the right time to ensure that organization goals and member aspirations overlap, align, or complement one another. Explain at least to yourself how the organizational goals and the community purpose fit together. The beginning is not the time to choose *how much it delivers*, because you don't yet know how, if, or how much it will work.

In this chapter, we'll discuss understanding members' roles in different stages, how to choose your leadership team, and critical growth principles for a changing community.

Understanding Your Members

If you don't know who you're bringing together (or whether they even want to come together), you'll need a lot of luck to succeed. So to depend less on luck, *you must understand your prospective members as full human beings (beyond the brand relationship)*. With both care and consent, start conversations with prospective members about everywhere they go and everyone to whom they're connected. Remember, these efforts are all intended to discover ways they want to grow, not to manipulate them.

If we wanted to plan a perfect birthday party for you, we'd have to know what you eat, do, like, believe, and feel when it is *not* your birthday (and not dinnertime): Do you like big gatherings or small ones? Are you vegetarian? Are you a morning person or a night owl? Are ritual and tradition important to you, or do you prefer spontaneity? And so on.

This research is always tailored to the needs of prospective participants and the inquiring brand. Only you can discover all the areas helpful when considering the communities your participants want to find.

If you're feeling stuck when it comes to conducting such research, a good place to start is to consider asking about the following areas. (These categories were developed with assistance from Sarah Judd Welch in an interview, October 2019.)

Demographics: age, gender, location, job title, faith tradition, income, and number of children.

Technical fluency: knowledge of and comfort and familiarity with technology at work and home. This is important for knowing where and how you will find members. People who don't have social media accounts won't log in to a social media website.

Career: current work, goals, achievements, how time-consuming their work is, and how fulfilling.

Personal information: health, aspirations, political priorities, personal challenges, and cultural preferences. You will want to know, for example, whether participants are healthy and mobile enough to come to meetings and travel together.

Challenges: challenges members face related to this community; any other challenges.

Goals: any goals, aspirations, and fantasies related to your brand's purpose and value.

Current communities: where participants go to find and get connection now.

We've found that the best way to learn about people's lives after they've started a conversation about themselves is to encourage them to tell stories about their lived experiences and then ask about their feelings during those experiences. We like the nonjudgmental open prompt "Please tell me about a time when you . . ." Some examples:

. . . attended a professional development meeting

. . . volunteered for a community

. . . participated in a conversation about _____

Imagine you've been asked by a private school parents' group how to encourage new parents to get connected in school communities. What kind of questions might help you choose the kind of invitations to try?

We know of a parents' group that was confused as to why scholarship-recipient families didn't like attending charity auctions where, over several hours, guests watched others bid more than $10,000 each for ski vacations, theater tickets, and special-access dinners. We learned that no one had *ever* asked the new parents what kinds of events would make them feel most welcome.

The invitation–member mismatch can remain hidden until the work to understand members is done firsthand. For example, one of Carrie's financial services clients was confused about why its members didn't participate in live chats among themselves about their own retirement plans. Goodness knows they all wanted to retire comfortably! When the leaders then actually spoke with members, they learned that many *members didn't have retirement plans to talk about!* In fact, members had sought out the firm because they couldn't afford a personal financial planner for one-on-one help. When the company then included retirement-planning experts in online chats and forum threads, the members showed up with rich questions.

The "best" and most powerful forms of research are, in descending order:

1. In-person, one-on-one conversations

2. Video calls

3. Surveys

Never confuse these options as equivalent research tools.

TWITCH

A few years ago, Twitch's research team showed solid usage numbers reflecting how archived video was consumed on the platform. To help new content show more prominently, one August the team set a new two-hour limit for video length on the site. Twitch believed that this change would get new videos more views.

Then, hours after the limit went into effect, Marcus Graham, then Twitch's director of creative development, received an angry message from a prominent member, whom we'll call Speedy, who alone had over a hundred thousand followers. Speedy participated on Twitch as a "Speedrunner." Speedrunners complete a whole video game as fast as possible and document their achievements with uninterrupted (and long) videos. Speedy called out the change as "garbage" and explained that Twitch had just become worthless for Speedrunners. Marcus knew that at least *five million* Twitch users were Speedrunners; losing them all would be catastrophic. Marcus alerted Twitch CEO Emmet Shear about the issue, and the new ("well-researched") limit was removed a week later.

Although the company addressed the mistake, the experience highlighted a clear disconnect between how users valued archived videos and what Twitch leadership (including Marcus) thought they valued. One irony is that much of the Twitch staff were then (and remain) active members in both the Twitch and gaming communities. Yet Twitch still got it wrong! Marcus said that the insight fundamentally changed how Twitch relates to the worldwide community.

Company leaders realized that they needed to listen more intentionally and carefully because different members have different priorities, and they constantly evolve as a community. Twitch began hosting over one hundred Twitch partners, all of whom are high-level members making their living on Twitch, to spend several days with leadership at the company's San Francisco headquarters. Even though Twitch is an online tech company connecting people through video, the staff listens to members' priorities over days and in person to understand them more deeply (personal communication with Marcus Graham, October 2016).

Effective member research does not necessarily need big investments of time or money. Sometimes speaking to as few as ten people can provide meaningful insight. And if you can't find ten people to talk to you, that's a meaningful insight too.

In Carrie's work, she often runs surveys among many customers and then invites respondents to speak further. Next, she will connect with select customers by phone for what she describes as a "discovery" call. This gives her a chance to learn about the customers' goals in both their work and personal lives. Because community works best when it supports progress toward a goal, she listens to where these customers want support, whether they yet recognize this or not.

GOALS FOR DISCOVERY CALLS

- *Assess whether there is a group with a shared identity (based on values) and purpose that seeks to connect in a community.* If there are such people and they already have a satisfying place to connect, it may be unnecessary and ineffective to create another. In fact, it can be harmful to fragment an already close community.

- If you believe that it's worth creating a community, then *determine the purpose* of such a new community. You need to learn how members will grow, be enriched, and get supported as they come together in a new way.

- Start building relationships with participants who will be candidates for "founding membership." (We will discuss founding members later in this chapter.)

Without interviews, you'll be left with assumptions. Whether you recognize it or not, this leads to making choices based on stereotypes. When investing in brand communities, we must remember that each person is a complex human being, and when we learn more about these individuals, they will inevitably surprise us. Community members relate very differently than traditional customers. They return to grow and contribute, not just transact.

Understanding the Stages of Community Maturity

The beginning stages of community building are usually rough and often filled with doubt. If you don't question your decisions daily, then you're probably doing it wrong. This is because none of us actually knows how a group will respond in a dynamic world each day. People are complex. Great community leaders are more facilitators than dictators. They know that they don't have all the answers, so healthy questioning is an important part of the experience.

Researchers have described community stages in many ways. All the named stages here are intended to help us understand what's going on and what to expect next. We encourage you to recognize these four distinct growth stages, which we've distilled from several sources: [1]

1. Inception
2. Establishment
3. Critical mass
4. Segmentation

Inception Stage

In the **inception stage**, the founding members constitute the community. The community starts because there is a need (for support, knowledge to share, create relationships, etc.). Founding members' discussion will provide clarity on why the gathering is needed and who should and will get invited. We will discuss choosing and working with founding members later in this chapter.

Establishment Stage

A good benchmark for identifying the shift from inception to the **establishment stage** is when the returning-participant rate reaches and then remains at about 50–60 percent.[2] This means that half or more of participants return for more connection. In an online community, you will see members begin discussions on their own. Members will generally self-organize for experiences. They will be unwilling to wait for leadership to execute ideas or events.

Norms—for example, common terms, behavior patterns, and discussion topics—will establish themselves. Rules for communication and participation etiquette will surface.

As total numbers grow, members will select roles within the community. Some members will lead discussions, some will provide support, and many will look for both support and knowledge. Some will step forward as leaders; others remain as followers. Some members volunteer information; others use the shared knowledge in their own lives.

The only way to get to the next stage is for leadership to recognize the ways that members want to contribute and then to extend trust and resources to encourage this best-case development.

In digital spaces, some participants may remain lurkers. Lurkers may read messages posted by others, but do not actively contribute to the community. Nevertheless, they are present and take value from their experience. Lurkers live in a gray area between visitors and members. They will show up and constitute an important part of online communities.

Critical Mass Stage

The **critical mass stage** is marked by additional members taking on leadership roles and upholding community guidelines on leadership's behalf. This is typically done by the core 1 percent of members. Obviously, members must be invited, allowed, and supported to take on these roles and the authority that comes with them.

At this stage, resources come to the community without leadership needing to bring them all inside or specifically asking for them. Some participants may, for example, offer a space at which to host an experience; members may ask permission (or not ask) to host their own member events. Leaders must recognize this as offering contribution instead of strictly as transactions.

Other brands may ask to partner for events or promotion because they want to connect with the community/audience to which you now have access.

At this stage, there will be a "need for a more explicit and formal organization with regulations, rewards for contributions, subgroups, and discussion . . . In this stage, . . . trust and lasting relationships emerge."[3]

Segmentation Stage

In the **segmentation stage**, a community branches off into subcommunities (figure 4.1). These subcommunities are a type of inner ring; not all members fit in all rings. (For a more complete discussion of inner rings, see *The Art of Community*.) For example, a main group of beauty enthusiasts might branch off into segments of skin-care enthusiasts, makeup enthusiasts who are moms, and people who only use environmentally friendly makeup. These segments, or inner rings, may develop their own subnorms and more nuanced focus that live under the umbrella community's values and purpose.

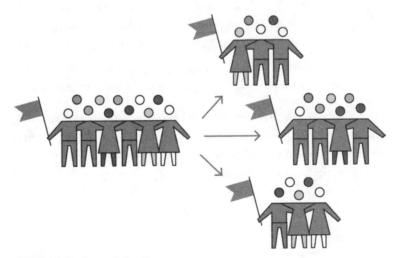

FIGURE 4.1. The Segmentation Stage

The four stages are only broad descriptions to help us understand what's at hand. Some stages may exist concurrently, typically in two contexts: (1) You have already built an active audience connected to your brand before you launch the brand community, or (2) your community is particularly newsworthy and goes "viral."

In both cases, you can easily have members who are already connected at a more mature stage when new participants rush in to join without norms, expectations, or familiarity with the organization.

Reaching Critical Mass

The critical mass stage is what all brands hope for—a group of people connected enough and large enough to somehow make a change together. In movements, this stage is often called the "tipping point."[4]

We look for these indicators of critical mass:

- *Resources come to the group* without leadership asking for them. This can include volunteer time, event planning, formation of subcommunities, and more. Asking for resources will remain important: It never goes away. In fact, the stronger the community, the bigger the asks will become.

- Participants *find the group* without direct invitations to explore membership. At some point, participants will get enough value from participating that they'll share the experience with others in camaraderie. It's great when people find you, but the real celebration comes when the community delivers enough value that others want to share it.

- *Organizational priorities will shift away from growth* toward serving a stable size for more satisfying engagement with current members.

At critical mass, leadership begins a balancing act between attending to growth and nurturing satisfying engagement with those already connected. Some communities don't need growth for their purpose, so they can focus only on engagement. Most brand community leaders want growth, so their balancing game will just remain part of what they do. Many leaders then wonder what leadership needs arise at critical mass. Here we provide a quick summary:

WHAT TO DO

- Separate responsibilities within the organization. Some people focus on growth, others on programming. Communication and coordination between leaders should remain, but no one can optimally serve those two priorities simultaneously.

- Carefully check back in on your purpose at regular intervals. Ensure that the community is still serving the purpose. If not, get back on track.

- Facilitate and support relationships between veterans and new members. It will become easy for new members to remain disconnected from veterans who already have friends and can forget to invite, include, and support newer members.

- Give more responsibility to the community to give feedback about what is (and isn't) working, and to manage the parts of the community that they are most passionate about.

AVOID

- Forgetting and ignoring those who got you to a more mature stage.

- Becoming a dictator as management needs grow with a larger community (remember Twitch almost losing Speedrunners).

- Moderating inconsistently. Members leave if they can't trust leadership to handle the space.

- Relating to your community as free labor. The fact that you've built an engaged group willing to do things on your brand's behalf does not mean they always will. They can and will leave you if you abuse their commitment.

Choosing Founding Members

The beginning is the most fragile and sometimes most frustrating and scary time. We all wonder whether our efforts will ever come to anything. **Founding members** are the early members who get the community from its beginnings to the critical mass stage.

The term *founding member* may not fit with every community's purpose, especially if you consider yourselves to be beginning organically. The term is used here only to help distinguish members who support the community from its inception and help build it into something more stable. You may prefer to call them inaugural leaders, early adopters, original participants, early fans, or anything else. No matter the term, they're crucial to success.

Many brands hire someone to organize and nurture a community who may not fit the profile of their prospective brand community members. Shira Levine was an experienced online community leader, but not (yet) a beauty fan when she led the Sephora Beauty Insiders community relaunch; by contrast, Danielle Maveal was a "maker" when she helped build the Etsy maker community. The founding members may not understand how to form a community around shared values and purpose, or they may not have the skills needed to do so. Hiring skilled help can be a great support.

The members invited in the beginning are important because authentic community grows around core values. The wrong founding members can bring toxic values into a nascent group. For example, a volunteer for women's political campaigns who is primarily there to find new romantic partners would make a bad founding member.

Traci Cappiello was a volunteer founding member of the Google Places community. These participants share public reviews within Google Maps. Traci first discovered the community when Google hosted events for reviewers. She joined because she wanted a way to share and "showcase" her native New Yorker knowledge. Traci is now a program manager for Google Local Guides, a group of "power reviewers" (personal communication with Traci Cappiello, September 2019).

She explained,

> I started writing reviews on Google Places for fun . . . and was invited to attend some of the first events ever where I met people just like me. Finding people like me who loved exploring in such a fast-paced city was key, and I met both locals and transplants who explored with me . . .
>
> Knowing I ultimately help millions in making better decisions with their time and money is the true reward . . . I knew I was one of the first members in NYC (and eventually the world), but didn't know that it would grow to be a 100 million+ global community of people passionate about sharing more than reviews.

Note that Traci helped found the community around Google Places because she wanted to share something and connect with others for exploring; she was not looking for a trade relationship with Google.

If founding members who lack camaraderie stay, both their words and behavior will show outsiders that your purported values are mere propaganda.

When starting a community, we *recommend starting with three qualified founding members*. Research and experience indicate that then growing to (as few as) ten will provide a strong foundation for the continuing journey to the critical mass stage. In the real world, founding members typically already know one another because they're connected by the core values bringing the fledgling community together.

FOUNDING MEMBER QUALIFICATIONS

1. *They live the values* of the brand and the brand community.

   We already know that what we do speaks far more loudly than anything we say. If it's an outdoor recreation community, then you need people who get out to recreate. If it's a motorcycle touring community, then you need people who ride motorcycles. Even more important, you want people who are already invested in growing in the way that the community will help participants grow.

   The founding members' choices, behaviors, and vision will set the tone for the community culture and priorities. Imagine a volunteer community in your hometown whose founding members never take the time to volunteer or support other volunteers: not likely to succeed.

2. *They already take action* in value alignment.

   The community helps *focus and support the values and life choices that the founding members have already expressed*. The new community participation doesn't serve as a "fixit" or "motivation" for them to take action in this area of their life. Anyone can see they're already in action. Imagine a Beatles fan club founding member who buys a Beatles album for the first time because they joined the community: That wouldn't make sense.

   The true commitment and accomplishments of the founding members should inspire prospective members because they want to grow as the founding members have grown and continue to grow.

3. *They have opted in.*

   This is straightforward and should sound obvious by now. "Voluntelling" people that they're founding members is unfortunately common. Such a misguided effort is a classic example of leadership unaware of how to create community. We recommend that you share this book with anyone who doesn't understand this!

4. *They clearly understand the community purpose.*

Communities grow around values and succeed with purpose. If members don't know or like the purpose, then they aren't helpful. In fact, they're a distraction.

5. *They are, or can be, in ready and responsive communication.*

People who won't respond or exhibit care can't build a core team. Too many leaders seek such people because they have a well-known "name" or because they think the participation will improve in time. New communities are stronger when they avoid such obstacles.

FITBIT RELIED ON JUST A FEW

Fitbit makes wearable electronic fitness trackers. Now a part of Google, its products measure fitness data, including an individual's calories burned, sleep patterns, and heart rate. The company now has over $1 billion in annual revenue and more than twenty-seven million users.[5]

Early in the company's history, there was an online forum where customers could connect with one another, but it was unstructured and moderated by a well-meaning software engineer who had no strategy for the space to support either members or the company.

Allison Leahy was then hired as Fitbit's community manager. She wanted to find a way to connect users and enable them to support the new company in developing useful fitness products and, of course, grow in size.

She created what Fitbit called the Community Council. First, she noted which members contributed the most in the then-current forum. She invited twenty of those already engaged members to form the new council, which would relaunch the users' community to make it both livelier and more useful. She didn't invite the most vocal members. She invited those who were kindest, shared good writing, and were most helpful to other members. The founding members for the new community would all volunteer to create the tone, model behavior, and provide content for future members. This process is called "seeding" an online community (personal communication with Allison Leahy, March 2019).

All the forum members who received invitations accepted. Several told Allison that they were honored to be asked, and some thought themselves unworthy. Most had no online community experience. Many were retirees who enjoyed supporting others remotely.

Before more members were permitted inside, those twenty founding members created real discussion threads on the new platform. Each one had demonstrated they were ready and willing to support other members pursuing health goals. Two weeks later, Allison "removed the gating" so that other Fitbit users could see the discussions and choose to join. Membership "exploded." Visitors discovered a resource genuinely ready to help them with fitness goals and connection. Most of the volunteer founding members spent twenty hours a week supporting members.

Today, the Fitbit community is a meeting place for customers to exchange solutions and advice for Fitbit products and to discuss health goals and lifestyle. The platform hosts over two million posts on more than five hundred thousand topics. Four of the founding members still volunteer as moderators of the community.

The takeaway is that Allison didn't need fifty thousand starting members, or five thousand, or even fifty to build an online community with global reach. Just twenty committed people with the right camaraderie was plenty.

There are two common problems when prospective founding members are invited to participate:

1. They don't know what is expected of them, so they can't or won't meet those expectations.

2. They don't know how to contribute.

When inviting and supporting founding members, you must make clear the *actions they'll be expected to complete*. That conversation will help both them and you understand *how they can contribute* to the community purpose.

Allison at Fitbit understood the importance of making clear what she expected from founding members. Before her community grew worldwide, she asked for *many* things from her founding members. In the beginning, however, she asked for at least four unambiguous contributions:

- Share honest opinions on the new online forum design, look, and feel.

- Flag content worth moving from the old forum to the new platform.

- Refer other candidates for founding member invitations.

- "Seed" (start) conversation threads on the private new platform.

Ideally, your clear and specific requests (almost certainly different from Allison's) will provide an exciting invitation for founding members to express the values they already exhibit and live.

If the "what" and "how" questions about contribution don't get addressed, then founding members will be confused about their role and value, which leads to disconnection. When the more junior members see this happen, they won't know how to derive value from their own participation because they see even elders grow disconnected and miss direction. Start the relationship right with a conversation clarifying how founding members are properly qualified and how they can (and should) contribute.

Remember that, in the real world, not all founding members will keep their commitments. This is both regrettable and typical.

It is also unfortunate that we have to remind mirage community leaders that people who don't want to contribute (because they have been "voluntold") aren't helpful. Coerced volunteers will cause distractions and create friction, impeding cooperation between leadership and truly motivated members.

If you can't find or attract founding members, then there may be missing trust with your brand that you must address before any real brand community can work.

Founding members may not commit to continued participation for a long period (years). This is fine. Lives and priorities change. Founding members get the community to critical mass. If they do that, then they have nobly served their role. Ideally, they had lots of fun too.

5

TEAM SELECTION

Your team size and structure will reflect the goals you aspire to support for your organization. The appropriate team size and roles for your brand community will be influenced by several variables.

- *Community size*

  The number of community leaders should be big enough to deliver value and keep the inside safe enough for both members and visitors. These tasks can include building and maintaining the technical platforms that connect your community. Three leaders for a two-thousand-person Harley-Davidson community isn't enough. Too many leaders, however, can easily become too much: Twenty leaders for a fifty-person authors' retreat will feel oppressive. (Charles notes, "I know because I've experienced it.")

- *Activities (frequency and type)*

  Activities should be frequent enough that visitors can easily find them when they learn about your community and grow excited to visit. This usually means that there should be regular events that members can plan for. One retreat a year *might* be enough for a business school alumni group, but it certainly won't be for political activists who are working in a dynamic social landscape with new technology and risking their safety for the work.

- *Community maturity*

  New communities need a higher leadership-to-participant ratio than do established communities, because original processes, traditions, and expectations are developing. This takes a lot of listening, experimentation, thought, and explanation. Mature communities beyond the critical mass stage can lean on already formed and contributing subcommunities (inner rings) and elders who share the management load.

There is no single best number for a team size. Obviously you need enough people, experience, and knowledge to accomplish your goals. HEC Montreal professor Caroline Aubé's research indicates that in general as teams grow bigger, the quality of members' experience decreases. In bigger teams, we find more interpersonal aggression and boastfulness.[1] Authors Jon Katzenbach and Douglas Smith write plainly in *The Wisdom of Teams*, "Ten people are much more likely than 50 to successfully work through their individual, functional, and hierarchical differences toward a common plan and hold themselves jointly accountable for the results."[2]

So, even though team productivity *may* be good in larger teams, individuals grow less happy with the experience. Katzenbach and Smith also state that groups bigger than twenty-five have difficulty working as an effective team.[3] In short, because we're concerned with the retention and quality of our teams, we're better off keeping individual teams only large enough to handle goals.

Appoint (at Least) One Person to Be Responsible for the Community and Self-Organized Activities

Accountability makes a difference, so ensure someone is accountable for community efforts. Ideally, make more than one person responsible. Together, they can start community among themselves as they experiment with connecting others. How many people, what they do, and how they support the community will differ with each brand.

Both Twitch and Airbnb work with two-sided marketplace business models. Some members provide inventory (web content and experiences), and others purchase. Each firm employs teams that work every day to care for and grow relevant communities both in size and deep connection. The work is so involved that they do several things all year round:

- Travel and host events on several continents
- Host members at world headquarters
- Make their own direct contact information available
- Monitor online discussions every day
- Measure both qualitative and quantitative research after each event
- Design and send gifts around the world

We know a person who served as the head of community for a Fortune 50 company with more than nine thousand retail stores across the US. We'll call him David. He was hired to help "connect" and improve the relationship between headquarters and the vast retail staff. The company wanted better collaboration among departments and less animosity among headquarters, distribution centers, and thousands of stores. David discovered that vast parts of the company weren't even talking to one another. Because many stores sold medication, poor communication with distribution and headquarters meant that customers didn't get critical service on time, and many simply walked over to competitors. After observing and listening to the concerns and frustrations, David proposed setting up an invitation-only online platform to provide the first space for discussion and collaboration among departments. One area was designated "bright ideas," where employees could share innovative ideas generated from their unique perspective. It solved many communication problems. This included giving headquarters direct access to "what the stores were saying" about timely and ongoing problems. David's efforts to connect critical parts of the company led to higher store employee engagement, more efficient employee work time, and innovated operations. David is especially proud that the increased direct communication enabled the company to recognize and handle several sensitive situations that could have grown into public relations disasters. David's work took years to grow truly effective, and internal research showed that the company culture did change.

Transitioning Volunteers to Paid Staff

Formally hiring current volunteers can be a good way to start building a paid team. Ideally, your volunteers have already built trust within the community so that when entrusted with formal and greater authority, they can get support from their existing informal authority.

Volunteers are typically people who have shown they already contribute in ways that reflect their internal motivation. That motivation can expand with new responsibilities, opportunities, and resources. Bringing them on as paid staff can be a good way to formally recognize their contribution.

If you choose to hire a volunteer as staff, protecting internal motivation in the community is important. It's critical to communicate to participants that the *hire is not payment* for earlier contribution. Such a relationship would be transactional and would erode internal motivation within the community. (See more on protecting internal motivation in part 3.) Rather, appropriate hires are to *recognize contribution and now support further contribution.*

So, yes, please hire volunteers who demonstrate that they're competent, helpful, and driven. And avoid hiring people simply because they're members. Membership alone never makes someone qualified to do a job well.

Community Management Expectations

We are often surprised how little leaders understand what effective brand leadership will look like and what will need the most attention when growing a community. This section will help you recognize what membership needs will look like from a leader's perspective.

Focusing on a Strong Core: The Pareto Principle

No matter how large or small your community, a small core will provide most of the work and value. Many community leaders don't understand this, and will complain that "not everyone" is very involved. That's just how it is, just about everywhere.

The **Pareto principle** (also known as the 80-20 rule) will show up in many areas in your community, not just in membership involvement. The principle predicts that *no less* than 80 percent of success (or results and value) will come from *no more* than 20 percent of resources. This applies to time, money spent, people, phone calls . . . nearly everything. Author Joseph M. Juran named the principle after a nineteenth-century Italian economist, Vilfredo Pareto.[4]

For example, whatever your favorite community is, our guess is that you experience at least 80 percent of what you love about it during no more than 20 percent of the time you spend in it.

The Pareto principle is also regressive. What do we mean? Think about a group you like that has about ten members. We are willing to bet that two of the members did the vast majority of the (helpful, important, or effective) work that made the group worthwhile. Now consider a larger group, with about one hundred members. Our guess is that approximately twenty (or fewer) core members did the bulk of the important work, and of those, four did at least as much work as the other sixteen in the core membership (because 20 percent of twenty is four). This means that 4 percent of all resources often can deliver 64 percent of results from a resource set. We can even drill down another level: 0.8 percent of resources can produce about half of all success.

Charles explained this principle to a firefighter who knew at least two hundred firefighters in her area community. He acknowledged that he knew almost nothing about fire rescue or the firefighters she knew, but he guessed that if she had to choose (on the basis of their proficiency) who would rescue her in an emergency, there would be eight firefighters (the top 4 percent) she would choose to respond as a team instead of all the other 192 combined, and he guessed that she already knew exactly who they were. She paused for a moment, obviously startled by the bold guess, and then said, "Absolutely!"

The Pareto principle doesn't apply to *every* set of resources, but it does apply to a startling number. This lesson is to help you understand that it's normal, predictable, and perfectly fine that members' participation will typically look radically unequal. Who those most active people are and how many participate at what level will shift over time. Just remember that contribution and effectiveness will remain very imbalanced. Notice how the participation imbalance looks graphically in figure 5.1.

We call the most involved 20 percent (or less) the *core group* or core membership, and the membership including the less involved 80 percent (or more) the *general membership*. There is nothing wrong or bad about general membership: (Virtually) every community has (and needs) these people. Besides making up the bulk of the community, the general membership can provide motivation, excitement, and the most data about overall community health and value. The core members are just more important and more effective in making a community work.

We call the top 4 percent (or fewer) *critical members*. When you understand the Pareto principle as applied to membership involvement, then you know to identify the top 4 to 20 percent and to focus attention on what they want and appreciate, and how they prefer to participate.

Your invitations, events, messages, members, visitors, funders, and time invested will almost all work within a Pareto distribution. This means that, for better or worse, the vast majority of all these components will prove fairly

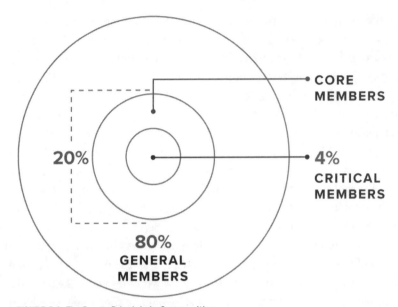

FIGURE 5.1. The Pareto Principle in Communities

ineffective. A small minority of each of them will deliver (overwhelmingly) the most results—4 to 20 percent is the effective portion. This is normal and can indicate that your efforts are working.

Recently an Oakland Adventure Club board member mentioned that the board wanted to bring on new members who will take on many responsibilities now handled by older members. She explained that there were, in all, about sixty club members. In conversation, she confirmed that about twelve members were overwhelmingly doing the work (at least 80 percent of it) to keep the club functioning and that three were real pillars for keeping the community working. The uneven responsibility here is both irritating and completely normal. There are many ways to newly involve more members, but "normal" is always going to look uneven.

When we learn about a community with, say, 5,000 members, we know that most (approximately 4,000 of them) will remain largely uninvolved. About 1,000 (core) maintain some significant engagement, and 200 (critical) really make things work. Two hundred committed people can accomplish a lot of important stuff. You may have already figured out that of the two hundred, forty of them are super-involved, and almost certainly there are eight serving critical and outsized roles for the community. It's probably true that if those eight leave, the community, as the members know it, will collapse. Yes, eight people out of five thousand can collapse a community as it is.

Who participates at each level will shift over time. What matters is understanding that even inside very large organizations, there's a surprisingly small group that wields great influence. It is terribly important that the most influential remain so because of their integrity and effectiveness and not because systems and tradition entrench the top core.

Online participation seems to work within an exaggerated Pareto distribution (still consistent with the Pareto principle). Early studies indicated that most online "communities" experienced a 90-9-1 contribution rate.[5] This means that, of visitors, 90 percent were passive consumers, 9 percent were active contributors, and 1 percent were so-called supercontributors. This was the case with early online communities, such as eBay's seller community (based on personal communication with Shira Levine, April 2019) and Wikipedia users.[6] It is impossible to eradicate all "participation inequality," so don't try! Your goal is to grow the "effective contribution" group either by gross numbers or as a percentage of the whole community (or both).

This is one reason why, when we hear brand leaders brag that they've built communities of millions, we roll our eyes a bit. We know that most of those numbers largely consist of names on a list (mirage community). The active participants are always a fraction.

Let's look at some real-world numbers.

We've already mentioned the online streaming platform Twitch a few times. By any standard, there are many members involved and committed to the global Twitch community. This includes engaging in gatherings around the world and in art projects, and connecting daily.

Twitch attracts more than 150 million unique viewers each month. Only 1.5 million members (1 percent) broadcast the content that all other members watch. A mere fifteen thousand (.01 percent) of those broadcasters attract the bulk of viewers, and 30 percent *of all traffic* is driven by only 150 individual broadcasters (.0001 percent) (from personal communication with Twitch's Marcus Graham, April 2019).

Marcus confirmed that if those 150 people were suddenly to stop participating simultaneously, "Twitch would be devastated. It is hard to comprehend how much that would hurt the organization." Consider that those 150 people represent only the tiniest percentage of Twitch participants. There is no question that if a particular .002 percent of members (about three thousand) stopped participating, Twitch would end as members know it. It doesn't matter that 150 million others participate at some level each month.

The global beauty retailer Sephora hosts an online community of twenty thousand of its most important customers. The company's research revealed that members spent twice as much as Sephora's average customers. When Shira Levine, then head of community, started her role, it was known within the company that a single community member, nicknamed Vera100 here, was responsible for creating fully 30 percent of all community content.

To be clear, we hope and expect that much of your membership will contribute and offer value to your communities. What matters is that you see that, even when tens of thousands or tens of millions are involved, a scant few really make the community what it is and shape how it serves members.

As a leader who understands unbalanced participation and effectiveness, you are responsible for protecting *the participants who make your community proceed toward its goal(s), reflect the core values, and keep the inside safe.* Given that leadership attention is limited and that only some ideas and priorities can get resources, there are two important jobs that respect the unbalanced participation.:

1. Pay special attention to the core and critical members' needs, concerns, and aspirations. They're special to the community, so treat them that way.

2. Find the effective core members and encourage, support, and resource them on a path that invites them into the critical member ring. This is also called identifying and investing in new leaders. This is how your community will grow. If members feel "held back" from contributing, they'll seek somewhere else they can flourish.

The inner-ring principle applies directly to your core and critical membership. Ensure that they get invited into an inner ring with appropriate privileges. It is one way to encourage and protect them.

There are always participants who just want to know what they can get for themselves—every day, meeting, event, hour, or minute. Although all participants should receive value (or why stick around?), focus your attention on those who are willing to contribute for others. Community requires mutual concern for others, and core members must demonstrate this for all.

The prioritization of a fairly small subset in a brand community, and honest but lesser engagement with most, reflects how personal friend communities are experienced and increasingly trend in general. Brown University public policy fellow and author Marc Dunkelman writes that Americans' interpersonal connections have changed and continue to change in ways that make close relationships more important. He describes community relationships as being divided into three rings (not to be confused with the inner-rings principle).[7]

1. The outer ring of a broad network of people we rarely meet or with whom we only share one experience (e.g., a concert, conference, or party)

2. The middle ring made up of people we know well enough that we can ask favors of them. We form lasting bonds with these folks over years. These connections are not as close as family and not as distant as mere acquaintances.

3. The inner-most ring of close friends and family.

Dunkelman argues that for a number of reasons (including the explosion of people connected by social media outer rings), the middle ring is shrinking. *Americans seek more relationships in the outer and inner rings and consequently the experiences that offer these relationships.* It is therefore important to allow visitors to experience some community events (outer ring) and then offer intimate experiences appropriate for members to build close relationships. These innermost ring members will make up your core. If communities offer largely "middle ring" connections, then they're offering something that is largely unwanted.

We want to be clear here: The high-performer distinction does not mean that high-performing members can or should participate outside the principles that make communities work. Although they may (and should) get special privileges, communities work when they serve members in growing into who they aspire to be, and where the inside is safe. If high performers don't contribute to this growth and safety or if they distract, erode, or ignore these fundamental principles, then whatever else is true, they're eroding the community.

You can get the greatest makeup artist in the world to come to Sephora events and carry on about makeup trends and eye shadow application, but if that person is an aggressive jerk making the inside unsafe, then the knowledge may be great, but they are harming community. Any community is by definition bigger than one person. If someone isn't accountable for supporting authentic community, then at some disruptive threshold that individual must leave.

Remember, most people can get lots of data from books and video. Members get value in community from relationships (connecting). Leadership must hold high performers accountable as members no matter the outsized value they bring.

Community Management Expectations

There are no self-managing communities. Someone has to do the work. Your community's leaders keep the inside safe, refocus activity toward a goal (as needed), restate the values, and share the important stories. Although there are different management styles, forms, and formality levels, there needs to be management.

Management is a unique branch of knowledge. This book works to support leaders in distinguishing and applying principles for making brand communities work for both members and organizations. How you set all this up for your particular participants, purpose, era, place, resources, and so on needs a specialized and nuanced conversation. We'll address some common community management questions. [8]

Do brand communities need full-time attention?

The answer to this question depends on the answer to a different question: How much do you want your brand community to succeed? Effective communities demand much more attention than every new community leader predicts. We can predict how much attention it will take for you about as well as we can predict how much attention your marriage and parenting need. Maybe you can grow a healthy marriage and be a good parent by devoting two hours every Sunday. We doubt it.

Twitch's Erin Wayne, for example, is reachable by dozens of Twitch city leaders around the world. They know they can reach out any time they need to contact Twitch, and they do.

If you've got a real brand and you want a real community that actually serves members, grows, *and* supports your organization, this endeavor will almost certainly need at least five times the amount of thought and time that you think it will.

Should we not even start because it will take a lot of time and work?

Sometimes the answer is yes. And this may be why you're reading this book. Most likely, there are people out there who you believe want to connect to do something new, important, fun, and/or simply satisfying. That sounds like a good reason to experiment with community building and see what grows and what needs get served.

When should we hire/appoint a full-time brand community manager?

Like marriages, every organization, context, and aspiration differs from all others. What it took to create a fan community for Lady Gaga cannot simply be duplicated to create a fan community for a different pop star in a different time. Only you can reflect on where you are, what you want, and what it will take to cross the distance.

The following are questions to consider when thinking of appointing a full-time community manager:

- How much time are you spending now?
- What influence do you aspire to create?
- What impact are you creating now?
- Will the value of a strong brand community warrant the investment?

As you answer these four questions, you should be able to get a sense of whether a full-time community manager is appropriate.

Network Effect

Leadership must always ensure that the community is enriching (serving) members and offering experiences consistent with shared core values. In the beginning, when your community has only a few members, this may be hard. A Miata drivers' community can offer relatively little Miata repair help if there are very few Miata owners participating. (In other words, more participants could offer more help.)

As you grow from the inception stage to critical mass, you're working toward a tipping point, when the community provides real value (e.g., easy car repair advice) to essential stakeholders.

In a brand community context, a working definition of the **network effect** is that the more people who use (or participate with) a resource, the more value it offers. User ratings sites like Yelp and resources like Google Maps are examples of resources that get better over time, thanks to the network effect. However, most Yelp reviewers and Google map editors aren't in community. Said differently, they're not growing mutual concern. This isn't bad;

it's just distinct from brand community building. Note that Nish Nadaraja at Yelp invested in building a brand community among Yelp's top "elite" reviewers because he recognized their importance for Yelp's success.

Communities can benefit from a network effect as well, but only when the growth is managed and limited. This is because a successful community shares core values, not just visitation or casual participation. If adding people leads to more participants without the shared core values, then the new participants erode community strength even when you have bigger participant numbers to brag about.

Remember, giving away free pizza in downtown Oakland will get you bigger participation numbers. It just won't make a better community. For the record, we're all for network effects. Just make sure you invest appropriately for both network effect and membership connection.

Two-Sided Marketplaces

A community can serve more than one distinct type of member (e.g., Harley owners and motorcycle repair professionals). **Two-sided markets** (also called two-sided networks) are economic platforms that bring together at least two distinct user groups that provide each other with network benefits. A platform that primarily offers value by supporting connection between (at least) two types of affiliated customers is called a multisided platform.[9] Examples include "credit cards (composed of cardholders and merchants); Health Maintenance Organizations (patients and doctors); operating systems (end-users and developers); video-game consoles (gamers and game developers)."[10]

Brands that serve two-sided markets can be life changing, even lifesaving. But they don't necessarily create community. Travel brand Airbnb, online broadcasting brand Twitch, and company review website Yelp all invest in community for their two-sided platform business models, but not all users and customers are involved in these companies' brand communities.

When working toward the critical mass stage in a two-sided network community, you must understand that you have at least two inner rings. (See *The Art of Community*, 87.) Each has different goals and needs (e.g., the differing goals for Harley riders and motorcycle mechanics). Although there is often overlap between the two rings, the participants' engagement will look very different, and you'll need to think about how you'll serve both.

In the beginning, this always looks like a "chicken-and-egg" challenge. What to create first to attract the other? *Always start with engagement on the "supply side" from the community creator perspective.* (In our example, start with the motorcycle repair experts.).

This is important because without the "supply," there is no opportunity for the customer/users to progress toward their goal (of getting that supply). Further, supply-side members often are excited to connect in friendship, celebrate, and learn from one another while they develop toward the goal of finding more customers/users. Twitch (broadcasters), Etsy (makers), and Yelp (local reviewers) have all discovered that this is exactly what happens among their supply-side members.

Offer the members on the supply side what will engage and bring them to connect, *and then* build growth on the "demand" side (Harley riders).

AIRBNB CONNECTS THE SUPPLY SIDE

Airbnb is an online accommodation and experience booking platform with well over two million hosts offering overnight accommodations or unique vacation experiences to customers around the world. The business model is, as we've described, a two-sided market. The hosts offer the supply (inventory) to all Airbnb customers. Said differently, without high-quality, committed, and successful hosts, Airbnb would have nothing to sell.

Most of the hosts aren't connected in community, but Airbnb understands that connecting them into authentic community taps into the internal motivation to help one another and grow into better hosts in an ever-changing marketplace. Airbnb employs two separate teams to build community among (1) accommodation hosts and (2) experience hosts. It sends staff around the world and hosts more than one hundred events each year building community among its supply-side members. Airbnb leaders recognize the business benefits of the network effect; they also know that authentic community on the company's supply side both grows and protects that network effect. (Information here is based on personal communication with Guy Michlin, May 2019.)

Starting a community with "one side" usually takes more time than leaders want or expect it to. Success can require years of effort. When you commit to two sides, you'll need even more patience. In many ways, you're creating two communities, one for each set of core values and purpose, even if the inner rings overlap.

6

GROWTH PRINCIPLES

Many leaders expect too much too fast. This unrealistic expectation is partly fueled by reports from mirage communities who claim extraordinary growth and effectiveness. Remember that forging a single real, durable relationship takes time. Hundreds of relationships take more time than a dozen.

We have heard reports of communities that came together in one week, one weekend, or as a result of one concert, festival, conference, or the like. The braggart always discounts the months (more often years) that some formal or informal leadership invested beforehand to connect with, build trust with, invite, and arrange an experience for a group that shares camaraderie and an openness for vulnerability.

From a participant's perspective, the relationship can form (or start forming) quite quickly. Durable communities always take more groundwork. There is no shortcut.

Growth Expectations

The dream of achieving worldwide reach through laissez-faire community growth is a fantasy. The reality is that you and your eventual team will need to commit lots of time for the following:

- *You will personally ask for lots of stuff.* To be effective, you will *personally* ask for far more stuff than you ever thought. Many aspiring community builders imagine that announcing a new community leads to resources being sent over as needed. We've never seen this happen anywhere. So get good at asking for stuff. Or more accurately, ask poorly until you get good at it. You'll ask for stuff like this:

    Time

    Access

    Consumables

    Space

    Advice

    Help in tracking participation and performance

- *You'll almost certainly have to reach out and promote to find appropriate members.* The myth says that a good community is so exciting in the beginning that viral enthusiasm will naturally grow it. This won't happen. The people who say they've seen it have left out a lot in the telling.

If people haven't heard of you, don't know what you're about, and/or don't understand the value available, they won't invest their time or anything else.

Even if you choose to keep your invitations and membership secret and so avoid traditional promotion, you'll still need to tell nonmembers who you are in compelling ways. You'll have to invest so that they can learn all they need to know. If you're not investing the appropriate time, work, or money, you'll see stagnation (at best).

- *You will make many direct invitations and receive few responses or participants.* Think about the communities in which you participate and to which you feel connected. How many of those did you discover via a social media post, a mass text message, or a marketing email? We'll guess that the number hovers near zero. This is true for everyone else as well. Don't expect others to connect to your community that way either. To get a better yield for your fledgling community, you must make many (many) direct invitations.

Most of these will never get a response. We know that. Keep offering, and some of your invitations will draw the right participants.

• *You will host many events and experiences that few people will attend.* There's a myth that if you can include the "right people" (influencers) in the beginning, the community will start strong on day one. This is never true. It may *appear* true because a community leader (elder) has brought along an existing community to fold into the new one, but the hard work still had to be done somewhere sometime.

The myth also may *appear* true when someone mistakes a mirage community for actual community and declares instant success. Declaring instant success is not the same thing as achieving real success or a real community. Communities take time to build because they are not groups or tribes that share value but no connection. They are far more than convenient gatherings. They're made up of people first finding each other and then caring for one another. When starting a community in the real world, if you're normal, you'll wonder *at least* a few times whether you're wasting your life, because it will look as though no one cares.

• *You do not have to lie about how big, fast, or diverse your community is growing.* When you hear about overnight communities or global expansion in a mere year, someone is measuring something other than community. We discussed false metrics in part 1.

Participants go to a community to connect with people in that community. Finding something other than a community there (like a mirage) makes it no fun. There is no good reason to lie about what you don't have yet while building the real thing.

• *You will always put mission (purpose) first, growth second.* Whenever we've seen growth prioritized as number one, it erodes the community value for those seeking connection and engagement with others who share their values. A community will deliver value because it serves members in a way that warrants their time and attention. Growth for growth's sake helps no one in the community.

To build a community, we build trusting relationships. This is why communities are so much richer for both members and organizations compared to lists, groups, or mirage communities. Real communities are durable and fun.

Creating these trusting relationships takes *much* more time than simply sharing information or offering a transaction. Yes, groups can be both fantastic and effective, but they are not the aspirational outcome of the leadership we're teaching in this book.

Because growing the fundamental relationships in real community takes time, you can never expect a quick investment to deliver terrific returns in the short term. Don't use marketing campaign measures to identify or justify an ROI for community investments (because these measures are used in, well, marketing). Marketing may sell stuff, but it won't deliver the same brand enhancement as an authentically connected community. Yelp's Nish Nadaraja noted that of course everyone wants to create a community quickly. He knew it would never work that way. His team respected the pace of relationships to build a real community that proved both effective and durable.

In our experience, *expect to invest at least eighteen months of work before the possibility of really powerful and clear outcomes show up for your organization.* The success you seek may take longer. That's still healthy.

With that said, in the first eighteen months, deep individual relationships can develop, friendships will form, good times will get recounted, and funny stories will be shared. We'll discuss helpful metrics in part 3. Like an apple tree without fruit yet, important growth will happen.

Growth Plan

Communities act and feel very different, and are managed differently, when there are three members versus when there are one million. You should anticipate that your community will change radically as you grow *even if the core values, purpose, and member types remain the same.*

A bigger group needs different management. The mistakes made by mismanaging will harm when the management doesn't recognize appropriate style for the group at hand. Many leaders don't level up communication and organization when the numbers grow. Others enforce policies as if thousands are involved when informal agreements over a phone call would suffice.

As a general rule, the more trust and mutual understanding that are in place, the less communication that is needed. Conversely, with less trust and mutual understanding, there needs to be more communication.

When five friends meet for a picnic, they don't have to explain why they're meeting, what they'll do, or that finger- and chopsticks-ready food is best. If they invite five hundred others, then more explanations, instructions, and RSVP confirmations will become necessary to avoid disasters in parking, food setup, and trash disposal.

Whether you're starting a new community or guiding your current one into growth, you as manager and leader are responsible for planning the growth. What the appropriate structure will look like and how you will change will vary as radically as communities vary. If you're hosting a picnic for a hundred cat-adopting families, then you'll need less communication and training than if you are hosting a twenty-person climb up Mount Kilimanjaro.

The areas you'll focus on for growth will differ depending on the community's maturity stage.

INCEPTION STAGE GROWTH

- The founder develops direct personal relationships with founding individuals.
- The founder invites involvement in a single bounded inner ring.
- The originating leader or leaders create the majority of content and events.

ESTABLISHMENT STAGE GROWTH

- Leaders encourage and support members to invite others to visit and join.
- Leaders encourage and support members to create content and events for the community. This includes giving them permission, tools, and invitations.
- Management establishes rules that members can enforce without involving the founding members. The rules protect the community tone, purpose, and safety.

CRITICAL MASS AND SEGMENTATION STAGE GROWTH

- Established leaders train new leaders to grow and manage.
- Experienced leadership trains leaders to train the next leaders.
- Established leaders create moderation, behavior standards, and escalation policy guides for consistency across segments.
- Established leaders create systems for platform growth and event planning.

Making Subgroups (Inner Rings)

Because challenges grow as we manage a growing community, *subcommunities* (calling these *subgroups* is OK) offer an easy and effective way to manage experiences for members without the distracting politics, communication confusions, and conflicts that inevitably arise in larger groups and teams.

Subgroups provide additional support for several community-enriching features, described in the next sections.

MORE PARTICIPATION

Subgroups support connection in part by simple time math. The amount of time any one person can reasonably speak and share in an hour goes down as the group expands. This is one reason we like to break up large groups into pods of five or fewer as soon as possible at an event. (Three is even better.) Five people can each equitably share with the group for twelve minutes in the course of an hour. It's hard to feel connected to others when sharing about yourself for just a minute or two. Time math is one reason that event leaders get disappointed and confused when they put many people in a room and see little connection develop. Often, participants simply don't get enough time to feel connected *even if* they participate fully. Time math is one reason that "campfire events," discussed in part 3, are so important.

CONVENIENT INTIMATE SPACE

Beyond the time math, smaller groups make it much easier to create an intimate (safe) space where members can share vulnerability. Creating such a space for fifty is not impossible, but is a far more delicate and demanding task than is making an intimate space for six. When we break up a group of fifty into ten pods of five, we create campfire experiences that can't happen with all fifty people participating.

INCREASED GATHERING FREQUENCY

Smaller subgroups also improve the frequency with which participants can gather. Even if venue options aren't a challenge, scheduling return times for more people is more challenging. Community strength comes from relationships growing over repeated meetings. If the meetings don't happen because they're difficult or expensive to host, then you lose potential deepening.

ACCOUNTABILITY

Smaller groups support accountability. With a small group, obviously, it's easier to notice when members don't or aren't able to fully participate in conversation, collaboration, or anything else. In some cases, you will want to call participants back to expected tasks; in others, you'll want to encourage them to participate where you notice they may not yet feel welcome or supported. A single call asking if a member is OK when others noticed they were missing can radically improve the feeling of connection.

MORE VISIBLE OPPORTUNITIES

Smaller groups help members notice and recognize opportunities where they can contribute and make a meaningful difference. For example, it is far easier to volunteer to make a meal for five friends than to commit to prepare a meal for fifty to one hundred. Also, when members extend themselves beyond their comfort zone, it's way easier to maybe fail for five friends than for a crowd of fifty.

UNIQUE CHARACTER

Each subgroup will develop its own character, which, in aggregate, will offer a broader range of ways for participants to find a place where they'll recognize that they fit in.

● ● ●

We've seen leaders ignore the importance of subgroups so many times it's painful. The most common mistake we see leaders make is starting an event by asking all the participants to introduce themselves, including some (random) information, one at a time. With any group of more than fifteen, this activity should be done in subgroups of no bigger than ten (we prefer eight). In a big group, no one remembers names, learns something relevant, or shares anything private. Given that participants entrust their time and attention to us, we can at least arrange for them to connect within a campfire experience (subgroup) intimate enough for the possibility of real connection.

Both Airbnb and Twitch invite local subgroups to experience shared events. Both brands do create large events (Airbnb Summits and TwitchCon), and members find their own subgroup and the brand staff relevant to their participation within the events.

Developing Leaders

Successful growth can only happen with new leadership maturing to lead a bigger community with more activity. A bigger and more segmented community offers more opportunity for leadership to contribute.

We think of leadership development as consisting of two parts:

1. Identifying future leadership
2. Training leaders to support the community

IDENTIFYING LEADERS

Picking the right people for any team is notoriously difficult. The biggest and most famous brands in the world struggle with this.

You're looking for leaders who want to *enrich the community* (not just themselves) and relate to the role as a responsibility, not a reward. Their actions reflect the group's values (whatever they are). Because visitors will only meet a few people, they will judge the community based on local leadership. So make sure your new leaders express the community values in word and (more important) action. Selfish and arrogant leaders will, unsurprisingly, characterize the community as arrogant and selfish. Picking people at random is, therefore, a bad idea.

Create some kind of application process. It does not have to be formal or complicated. Focus on finding people in whom the core values show up in their lives outside the community. Assess whether they can meet the expectations for leadership.

Interviews are a terrible tool for picking the right people. There are many reasons for this, of which two are key:

1. Interviews show us how people talk about themselves in a wholly artificial sit-down conversation. This is not what we want leaders to do in their role, and we won't be able to determine how they'll handle the real community leadership stuff.

2. Despite what might be our best intentions to welcome diversity, we overwhelmingly tend to pick people like us, in terms of class, accent, style, gender, smell, background, whatever. We think we make rational choices. We don't.[1]

The problem is that no growing organization succeeds when the entire leadership shares the same strengths (people person, technically adept, detail oriented, etc.). Such patterns mean there will be missing strengths. You've probably seen an organization where everyone could think big . . . and nobody could execute the necessary details. Or leadership that was technically adept . . . but couldn't inspire connection and commitment. To avoid these pitfalls, look beyond interviews.

The best indicator of an appropriate choice is evidence that the person already can do and does what is needed. This includes specific skills (hosting events, writing, teaching, etc.). You want to see that this individual already serves community members (formally or informally) to help members succeed in something. An experienced labor organizer we know notices first who among participants is a "hand raiser"—someone who volunteers to help others with the challenges, risks, and emotional fatigue of confronting a bad employer. She then invites the hand raisers into community organizing leadership.

Erin Wayne at Twitch oversees the team that supports more than forty Twitch groups around the world. She'll only consider working with new leaders in an area and make their group official after they've met three requirements:

1. They host two events with at least twenty participants.
2. They actively post about their group on social media.
3. They use a live online discussion platform to connect members.

Meeting the minimum requirements tells Erin that the new community leaders are highly motivated and willing to do the actual work to bring people together. She also says that these baseline requirements knock out at least 90 percent of the people who want to serve as Twitch group leaders (personal communication with Erin Wayne, June 2019).

When you recognize someone with the internal motivation to serve, the ability to do the specific job, and the willingness to take on the responsibility, then training makes success more likely. (Training can include sharing this book and *The Art of Community* for foundational understanding.)

TRAINING LEADERS

Obviously there are more roles requiring appropriate training than we can list here. The following are some foundational principles to support your training approach.

Create a list of skills your leaders will learn. People participate in community to grow in some way. This list will help leaders understand how they'll grow and clarify to you how you'll help them grow. For climbers, it may be important that they teach safety systems; for online gamers, how to moderate a chat forum; for Airbnb hosts, producing a fun event. If they don't like or don't care about the list in the beginning, you both want to know this. Change your expectations before the relationship isn't fun or rewarding for either of you.

Provide resources that help them learn the skills you've listed. It truly amazes us how many organizations skip this part. This might include access to media, books, or websites—better yet, access to others who have already mastered the skills. Offer new leaders introductions to people inside the organization and groups outside with more experience and a willingness to support. Further, introductions are usually never enough for real mentorship to develop. It's far better to also create an agreement between a mentor and trainee on how, how much, and how often they will connect so that growth can develop.

Connect leaders with other leaders and senior managers so that internal mentorship can grow, and wisdom and learned lessons get shared. This means actually introducing them. Explicitly tell each person on both sides of the introduction why you're connecting them and what you hope may come of a new relationship between them. Not all introductions will develop into something profound. But when this step is omitted, it shows that managers don't know how to develop their new leaders. They're leaving new talent in the cold. It's both lazy and bad management.

New leaders will need time to learn their role. This is especially true if they're setting precedent, making changes in a new time, or addressing a system that isn't working. Almost none of us get things right the first day out. Remember that you're picking people who want to learn and serve—this must remain in the forefront of your relationship every time you work with leaders.

Retaining Membership Expectations

To limit unnecessary or unhealthy turnover, managers must acknowledge and thank the participants on the journey. This is especially true for those who supported the work from inception to something significant. No one sticks around with people who skip the appreciation. We will discuss principles for acknowledgment in part 3. Here note that special events, tokens, and special access go a long way toward letting your core membership know that you appreciate their contributions.

With that said, membership turnover is normal. Life circumstances change. Babies get born, parents get sick, jobs move. Don't waste emotional energy fretting over changes in your community that reflect dynamic changes in the world.

In fact, it is very important that members can leave. If they can't leave, you will get stuck with people who don't want to be there. If members stick around because they're coerced or shamed, they become dead weight or, even worse, toxic. They'll take time from leaders, and they'll prove to new members that the enriching connections participants seek can't be found in the community. The exit door must always remain open. This can mean fewer participants and a more fun, effective, and resilient community.

Just as no one can predict how their family will grow and change, no one can predict—or control—how a community will change. People are inherently unpredictable. In other words, a time will come when the current brand leadership must give up significant control over what the community does and how members think of themselves. This may seem scary (and there will be scary moments, no doubt), but it's also what makes communities more exciting, interesting, and fun than, say, a strictly scheduled event series. A strict plan quells helpful creativity.

Consider IkeaHackers, who are enthusiasts of the giant furniture and household goods brand Ikea, but who operate outside Ikea's control. For eight years, IkeaHackers members convened on a website, sharing ideas and skills for customizing Ikea furniture. Gizmodo described the site as "a place to talk about [Ikea] love and share creative ideas . . . a burgeoning community of fans who are excited about Ikea and the hidden genius of its products."[2]

In response to the community, Ikea threatened to sue, citing trademark infringement. Although the legal merits of Ikea's objections were dubious (no one was confusing IkeaHackers for Ikea), the site was shut down—but only briefly. As you can imagine, the threats and apparent corporate bullying created a lot of anger, so much that Ikea executives eventually learned the lesson of "letting go" and permitted IkeaHackers.net to keep its URL, but only after many fans and journalists expressed bafflement as to why a global brand would threaten its own worldwide fans.

The painful experience apparently taught Ikea leadership about how communities can serve brands. Ikea designers now see the hacks as a learning resource. One design manager is quoted as saying, "We look at them and ask ourselves 'what are people trying to tell us about our own products.' . . . It's a really good way for us to learn.'"[3]

By contrast, Etsy structured its online member platform so that any member could (and did) set up their own subgroup and invite whomever they wanted to have join. Any conversation could take place inside the subgroups as long as members followed the general platform guidelines. Today the platform hosts more than six hundred thousand discussions for over seven million members.[4]

Efforts to keep total control as you grow will erode or destroy your success, so you must let go of what you can live with, as long as the new directions and groups remain true to the community's core values and purpose. It may feel uncomfortable, or downright scary, but this is what success looks like.

Communicating for Growth

When you want the community to grow, there are at least four types of communication to regularly share. Of course, "regularly" will vary depending on the community and its activity. If important events occur every week, then weekly messages may be good. If there's only one annual gathering, then weekly communication is overkill. Only you can determine what's right. No one wants to get inundated with communication, and no one wants to be kept in the dark either.

The following are the key categories for communication that support growth:

1. *Things getting done* related to the group values

   In the Harley community, meetings, group drives, leadership changes, and special events would all count. Reporting on a member's new garden layout would serve little or no purpose.

2. *How the community is changing and the future vision*

   This includes how the organization, its members, and things outside the community are changing. This helps participants understand where the community was (organizationally, emotionally, financially, pragmatically, etc.) and where leadership envisions going. Typically, this is shared as stories.

3. *Invitations to members* so that they can contribute right away

   Without invitations, communication remains "news updates." Few of us need or want more news updates. If the only response you receive from members is "good for you," then your communication doesn't inspire connection or involvement. In short, you're not inviting powerfully enough.

People who feel connected and share values want to contribute. Everywhere we go, we see leadership failing to invite members enough to access the willingness (and excitement) in those members to make a difference. If you're complaining that members aren't contributing enough and you aren't making regular invitations, then at least one element of the problem starts with your inadequate communication.

4. *Transparency*

To feel connected, members want to know what, how, and why things get decided. This is particularly critical in for-profit brand communities because members know businesses have a profit motive and that profit motives and community goals may conflict. Carrie has seen that nothing makes members angrier than when they suspect (rightly or wrongly) that a for-profit company is acting unethically or against brand community interests for profit-maximizing reasons.

It won't matter what considered intentions lie behind a choice or outcome. If you are not transparent in communicating what, how, and why decisions are made, division and anger will harm all the goodwill built to date.

Alternatively, when you intentionally offer transparency and actual vulnerability (regarding mistakes), the trust and support extended by a brand community is unmatched anywhere else in business.

REDDIT'S LESSON ABOUT TRANSPARENCY
Through a painful and expensive experience now called "ChooterGate" or "AMAgeddon," Reddit discovered how communities react to a lack of transparency. Victoria "Chooter" Taylor was briefly the point of contact between Reddit's volunteer moderators and brand leadership. While she served in that role, community members became upset about unannounced and unexplained platform and policy changes intended to address in-site harassment that had gone unaddressed for years. Victoria was considered "the website's primary employee tasked with keeping [the] community less susceptible to abuse" and "often seen as the only path for the website's volunteers to alert the company's executives of harassment or a lack of

transparency."[5] Members were shocked when Victoria was apparently fired with no explanation or further insight into how and why changes were being made. In response, within a day, more than one thousand groups within the site effectively shut down their parts of the site in solidarity and thus closed off Reddit's most trafficked areas with millions of subscribers.[6]

Volunteer moderators Brian Lynch and Courtnie Swearingen wrote in the *New York Times* that the "primary concern, and reason for taking the site down temporarily, is that Reddit's management made critical changes . . . without any apparent care for how those changes might affect their biggest resource: the community and the moderators that help."[7]

Within two weeks, the Reddit CEO stepped down, and community volunteers spoke out widely about their continued distrust of the company.[8] That month, *Wired* magazine summed up its article about the debacle with "Company management seems to have realized it needs to act more visibly to close the rift between the business and the unpaid community members who keep it afloat."[9]

TWITCH INVESTS IN TRANSPARENCY

Some years ago, Twitch users created a new game called Twitch Plays Pokémon, which any member could play using Twitch chat. The novel game exploded until well over 2.5 million people participated. It was an in-group phenomenon. When Twitch later updated its video archives system, the entire Twitch Plays Pokémon archive was accidentally lost. Marcus Graham, then head of community, knew that this would anger many thousands of members. He recognized that one option was to keep the mistake a secret for as long as possible until, if possible, Twitch could share some good news about the problem.

Marcus also knew and still knows that both sides of the Twitch marketplace (broadcasters and viewers) are connected to one another in far more than transactional ways. They trusted Twitch to support those relationships and the space in which they connect. Aside from Twitch fixing the lost archive, the Twitch community needed to hear right away, many times, and in several mediums that Twitch was attentive, had learned that it had made a mistake, and was investing engineer time to make the fix (personal communication with Marcus Graham, October 2016).

Marcus immediately went to the Twitch Plays Pokémon social media "hubs" (people with many followers) and reached out to at least 150,000 of the users to honestly share the mistake, the impact, and the plan to recover the archives. It took four engineers weeks to recover the media.

Although many customers were angry, Marcus could see in online forums that they trusted Twitch because leaders admitted their hurtful mistake, invested resources to correct it quickly, and even looked deeper to learn how to prevent such mistakes in the future. Customers gave Twitch another chance.

Part

3

DEEPER IDEAS

Ideas matter.
How we think about things,
about persons,
about states of affairs,
makes a difference.
—**Margaret Farley**

7

LEADERS' AND MANAGERS' ROLES

Now that you know how to recognize a brand community, how they often support organizational goals, and the principles for growing them, we can go deeper into ideas you'll need to understand in order to create communities that serve both members and organizations. No matter what your community growth stage or what outcome you seek, these topics will remain critical. Many leaders misunderstand each area, and the misunderstandings often create something toxic. The chapters of part 3 will discuss these five critical areas.

● ● ●

All healthy and mature communities have people who lead them with some kind of formal or informal authority. Because we're discussing brand communities, the authority will almost always operate formally. Authority typically rests with elders. In fact, members often grow into elders when they gain authority. The elders with authority constitute the diaconate. (*The Art of Community* discusses the roles of elders, the diaconate, and authority in more depth.) In this context, authority figures are often designated by the title *manager*.

In brand communities, managers must attend to five basic responsibilities:

- Serving as (or finding/hiring) gatekeepers
- Keeping the inside safe enough
- Welcoming members
- Delivering promised value
- Advocating for the community

Serving as Gatekeepers

For the community to work, it's critical that not everyone in the world be considered an appropriate member. (*The Art of Community* discusses this in depth in the chapter on the boundary principle.) For a strong and tight-knit community, you want only those people who embrace your specific values and purpose (i.e., those with whom you share camaraderie). As Priya Parker writes in *The Art of Gathering,* "You will have begun to gather with purpose when you learn to exclude with purpose." In fact, she argues, "over-inclusion is a symptom of deeper problems—above all, a confusion about why you are gathering and a lack of commitment to your purpose."[1]

Gatekeepers are responsible for helping the right people get inside and keeping the wrong people out. This is a terribly important responsibility. Many wrongheaded leaders don't do this job responsibly or, even worse, never acknowledge this role.

If you're building a Harley-Davidson riders' community and you let in Charles and his Miata-driving friends who want to discuss Japanese roadster design at every event, you're doing a bad job. This is why riding a Harley is key to joining a HOG chapter.

You can of course discuss Japanese roadster design at a Harley riders event. Transportation, safety, and mechanical design are often interconnected. But as a Harley owner, you'll do that with people who remain excited about how that relates to the Harley experience, lifestyle, and identity.

Self-selection is not the same as "everyone belongs." Leaders may be confused, thinking that avoiding discrimination means allowing everyone in all the time. This is a recipe for shallow experiences and unsafe gathering spaces. You must choose whom and why you let inside the boundary to ensure that the values and purpose are honored.

If you consider everyone an insider, then there are no outsiders. This is the same as no community, because no one can tell who's inside the community.

You may invite everyone to visit certain events and discover whether they share camaraderie. The gatekeepers only allow the right people into novice and membership inner rings. This can happen either informally or formally. You may need to systematize the journey from visitor to novice and then to full member. (Research the Commitment Curve for how to map that journey.[2]) Recognize that each level is exclusive to some degree.

Making the Inside Safe Enough

Because of its importance, we've already mentioned several times that to make sharing vulnerability possible, leaders (elders) must protect the community's inside as a container for respectful conversations and conflict that avoid abuse and disaster. Disaster often results in shunning, abandonment, and community breakdown. Conflict is inevitable, but abuse and harm are not. City University of New York professor Sarah Schulman clearly articulated the relationship between (inevitable) conflict and the harm that makes communities unworkable:

> [Harm] begins in its earlier stage as Conflict, before it escalates and explodes into tragedy. Disaster originates in an initial overreaction to Conflict and then escalates to the level of gross Abuse. It is at the Conflict stage that the hideous future is still not inevitable and can be resolved. Once the cruelty and perhaps violence erupts, it is too late. Or at least requires a level of repair outside of the range of what many of us will do without encouragement and support. Conflict, after all, is rooted in difference and people are and always will be different.[3]

We call it *fronting* or *avataring* when participants only show us the parts of themselves they are comfortable revealing to strangers. We front when we want to play it safe. There's nothing wrong with this: No one is going to share their deep vulnerabilities every time they get on a commuter train. But fronting impedes connection.

Participants go beyond fronting only when they feel safe enough to do so. The more that participants go beyond fronting (because they feel safe), the more connected they'll feel, and community strength grows.

There is no such thing as "completely safe" for everyone all the time. Counterproductive coddling threatens to squash any risk or uncomfortable growth experiences.[4] Difficult, confronting, and growth-inspiring conversations should and will happen.

The safety standards for a Berkeley prayer community and for an Oakland mixed martial arts community are, and should be, very different. No matter: To flourish, each must promote basic inclusion and respect that enables participants to learn and grow—to consider new perspectives and ideas so that they learn from differences they discover. This is "safe enough."[5]

Whether you call them guidelines, rules, standards, or something else, develop clear guidelines that prohibit

- Harassment

- Abuse

- Bullying

- Hate speech

- Name-calling

Carrie has drafted dozens of guidelines. Through her research and experience, she has identified the most common activities regulated within online communities:

- Copyright or intellectual property violations (most common of all)

- Illegal activity

- Any harassment or hateful conduct, including discrimination, hate speech, bullying, or targeted attacks

- Impersonating other users

- Spam and scams

- Sexual content or nudity

- Any violent conduct: extreme violence, graphic violence, threats, gore, obscenities

- Harming others or acting maliciously

- Unwanted sharing of private information (aka doxing)

We offer this list as a starting point. Your community will discover its own specific needs and challenges. Copying this list and declaring your guidelines done is not enough. Look for guidelines for brands you admire and use them to inform what's appropriate for you.

Invite feedback for your guidelines regularly, and really listen. Guidelines must remain dynamic as people, times, and contexts change. Enforce them consistently. Train and even remove leaders who don't role-model keeping others feeling safe.

At some point, your community's standards will be tested. When this happens, managers must

1. Address any harm done.

2. Acknowledge the impact.

3. (Re)assert the standards for the community.

Many leaders don't want to take the time, risk, or responsibility to do this job well. Most of us want great results without work, risk, and responsibility. This doesn't happen. When you ignore bad (emotional, physical, aggressive, abusive) behavior, whether you like it or not, you're endorsing it. That's how participants see it, and that's what we consider passive consent.

Safe (enough) is especially critical when bringing together participants sharing identities where some stigma, trauma, or shame has existed. For example, within Alcoholics Anonymous, sharing about weaknesses, failures, and struggles is critical for community bonding and mutual support. Without safety established to allow this, the gatherings remain a well-intentioned effort where participants politely front together.

Accessing vulnerability (at some level) and getting past fronting almost always follows the precedent of a leader or elder demonstrating vulnerability first. The precedent cannot be fake, convenient vulnerability, but the real deal. Participants must also feel confident that the leadership can handle the situation if anyone does violate guidelines or the conduct code for the space.

TWITCH STRUGGLES WITH SAFETY

In recent years, Twitch invested heavily in protecting the safe space on its platform by enforcing strict standards of zero tolerance for both hate speech and harassment (personal communication with Bobby Scarnewman, July 2019). This was an important investment because there was dangerous behavior by members that made the platform distinctly unsafe. This included "pranks" that called in fake crimes to coax police SWAT teams to raid unsuspecting broadcasters.[6]

There is understandable criticism that, with over one hundred million users, Twitch is not as transparent or consistent with policy enforcement or consequences as some would like.[7] Nevertheless, Twitch's Marcus Graham and Bobby Scarnewman both acknowledge a twenty-four-hour-per-day ongoing effort.

Because Twitch broadcasters produce hours of live media, virtually all that they say is extemporaneous. One prominent broadcaster who goes by Trihex used a slur intended as a joke to refer to a friend.[8] Twitch understood that the slur was neither intended to insult the friend nor taken as an insult. Twitch also knows that when content producers broadcast live for hours, they cannot carefully consider every no-harm-intended joke. Despite this, the broadcaster had violated the "no hate speech" guideline and was disallowed from broadcasting for weeks.

There are several good lessons to recognize in this Twitch example. First, the rule was established and made known to participants before the infraction, so the recognized violation was not a surprise for the member. Second, the intention of the hate speech didn't matter. Twitch doesn't want to parse intention and impact for every violation. If it did, then members would play games hiding and reframing hate speech. Third, there were attentive elders (moderators) to enforce the standards. Last, and just as important, the penalty did not eject a member from the community; he experienced a consequence that allowed him to return and even participate more maturely. In fact, the broadcaster hosted a fundraiser for a relevant nonprofit when he returned (personal communication with Bobby Scarnewman, July 2019).

If you ignore taking responsibility for keeping the inside safe, two things will happen.

1. Participants disgusted with the inside behavior will leave.

2. The remaining participants will dial back their participation because risking themselves to share vulnerably is no longer safe.

Both outcomes are terrible for building community.

REDDIT AND STACK OVERFLOW ADDRESS SAFETY

Reddit contains over one million subcommunities referred to as "subreddits." In addition to site-wide rules, each subreddit keeps its own specific rules that evolve as members and times change. Evan Hamilton, Reddit's community team manager, explained that each subreddit can have one or more moderators (sometimes dozens) who enforce the rules both swiftly and consistently. This includes banning rule breakers (personal communication with Evan Hamilton, April 2019).

Reddit provides training and tools to thousands of volunteer moderators and invests in their development through dedicated subreddits. Moderators can and often do meet one another both online and in the physical world. In fact, Reddit staff go on a "roadshow" to meet moderators around the world in person. When they meet, they create a shared experience in a shared space. This is all part of a commitment to ensure that inside users feel safe—so that they'll return. Without returning users, Reddit doesn't have a business. Today Reddit consistently ranks as one of the twenty highest-traffic websites in the world.[9]

By contrast, let's reflect on the experience of Stack Overflow, a brand that connects programmers from around the world seeking programming answers from its members. A Stack Overflow staffer we'll call Oliver joined the team when the site ranked as a top-fifty website worldwide. He remembers the pride among programmers in the community early on and the widespread commitment to help one another. He also remembers how programmers cared for one another on the site and worked to support each other in the then fairly small programming field.

As the worldwide demand for programmers exploded, the demand for help on Stack Overflow also exploded. Oliver noted the difference between old and new programmers. Economic, racial, gender, age, and geographic differences caused unnecessary friction among members that eventually showed up in aggressive and hurtful behavior on the site.

Nonetheless, the demand for peer-to-peer programming help was so acute that user numbers grew rapidly. Stack Overflow leaders largely ignored the toxic and hurtful language because they appreciated the growth. They overwhelmingly prioritized projects and features that generated revenue over activities that would also proportionately grow the community team or improve user relations. One Stack Overflow employee described the site as "the most toxic programming site in the world. Our users basically get bullied over there."[10] Oliver said executives invested limited time and money into community health and safety for at least five years because they didn't see a profit return for it.

> The predictable happened: Many of the best contributors to the community left,[11] and when they did, the site's value for other users plummeted. Moderators quit faster than they could be replaced. The company raised $40 million in investment and then two years later let go of 20 percent of the workforce.[12]

Welcoming Members

Welcomed, connected, seen, appreciated—these are all *feelings*. These feelings arise only when we know *someone has noticed us and expressed their appreciation for our participation*. This is why managers must ensure that all participants are welcomed. The type, length, and form of welcome will change depending on the community and context, but what doesn't change is that participants must be welcomed by someone, if not by several someones.

By *welcome*, we mean that participants must understand the following:

1. Someone notices they arrived.

2. They have access to someone to speak to, connect to, and receive guidance from if needed.

3. They experience a facilitated connection to other participants (such as an introduction).

4. They can (or do) receive guidance on how to navigate the experience at hand.

For example, at events,

- Are they allowed to speak or post at any time, or must they sit, watch, or listen?

- Can they come late?

- Do they join a cohort?

- Must they stay for the entire event?

- Is food up for grabs or saved for others?

- Will a planned program stop conversations within the hour, or is the whole event intended for conversations?

The welcome both manages expectations and facilitates growing the feelings of community as much or more than does fulfilling any technical need that attracted the participants.

This year, Charles pursued membership in what we've been calling the Oakland Adventure Club. Members may use the club's forty-bed lodge nestled in the Tahoe woods. They pride themselves on being a community that plays together and grows together as friends. They are, by definition, a brand community.

When Charles arrived for his first overnight visit as a prospective member, he expected to meet Janet, the member who was hosting him for his visit. He had just finished a four-hour snowy drive to the lodge and had taken off his shoes in the vestibule when Janet saw and approached him. The first thing she said was "Hi, I'm Janet . . .

- Don't put your shoes there; they go down the stairs.
- Don't put your bags there; they go in the locker room downstairs.
- You're not supposed to use this door because it lets the heat out.
- You need to sign in on the board which room you'll stay in.

The instructions and explanations went on for twenty minutes! Although everything she said was relevant for a prospective member who doesn't yet know the lodge policies or layout, what was missing was a welcome that let Charles know that he was seen and appreciated as another mountain sport enthusiast.

Janet isn't a bad person, but she had no training or guidelines on how to orient prospective members so that they would *feel* welcome. Imagine how visitors would feel if hosts started with a welcome that reached out with acknowledgment and appreciation first, and only then transitioned into rules provided by a supportive elder:

> Hi, Charles. Welcome! I'm Janet. I'm your host. I'm so excited you're considering the club. We're looking for new members, and you've driven up on a snowy night. I'm hopeful this will be fun and that I'll get to know more about you. I'll help you understand the club as I can. First, though, it's cold and you've had a long drive, so how about some tea before we handle the bags and a lodge tour?

It takes less than thirty seconds to offer the welcome suggested here. It can change a whole experience.

Delivering Promised Value

A manager's first job is to ensure that whatever is promised to participants will be found in the community. This can include information, training, friendship, or even just a good time.

If we expect to find a great Harley mechanic when we visit a Harley riders' community, then of course it helps if a leader ensures that there's a way to find one there. If I'm expecting a one-on-one conversation with the Harley-Davidson CEO, when I arrive, I may be surprised when I don't see an opportunity for this.

In addition to ensuring that the promise is fulfilled, leaders must ensure that participants are clear about what is in fact the minimum promise. There may be an invitation to meet the CEO at some point, but that would be a bonus in most riders' communities, not a promised offering to everyone, every time.

Leaders need to understand that ensuring there is value to find is *not* the same as inviting visitors into a group and then *hoping* they'll find value. Worse yet, we have seen visitors *blamed* when they didn't find the promised value.

Charles was invited to a writers' retreat billed as an opportunity to connect with more experienced thought leaders and to access their wisdom and support in growing as a thought leader. When he showed up, it became clear that drinking wine was a far more important activity than learning how to more effectively address social problems (as thought leaders). When asked for feedback, Charles and four other new authors shared their disappointment at the lack of attention or investment to help all of them grow more effectively. The new authors were told, "You should join the board to change this." This was surprising because the new authors were visiting for the first time, not seeking to take over an organization after three days.

One of the failures here is that the elders didn't understand that to keep the community relevant and attractive to visitors, they needed to support participant growth. In this authors' group (as with very many groups), the elders ignored this responsibility in favor of social reminiscing. Not surprisingly, every new author left.

When planning any content (blog post, references list, video, gathering), your first question should be, "What will participants get out of this experience that enriches them?"

Whenever we invite members into participation, we ask for some commitment from them, no matter how big or small. They're committing time, opportunity cost, association, and often money. As a leader, you have a responsibility to ensure that the experience is at least worth their commitment! Said differently, *opportunity must consistently provide more value than members' other options in that moment.*

If you don't know what the value offered is, or if you just hope that "they'll figure something out," then you're in real danger of violating this responsibility. Just inviting strangers to share nachos in a specific room at a specific time doesn't provide much value: We can all order nachos in our own rooms.

"Making and deepening friendships" might be the value you want to deliver in a particular space. Although this can involve sharing nachos, note that delivering on the "making and deepening friendships" part requires more investment than just ordering dinner. We suggest making introductions, providing a comfortable space, offering name tags, prompting a conversation about shared values and interests, and demonstrating patient listening.

Advocating for the Community

A successful brand community manager will advocate for members' needs and vision to the ultimate brand leadership.

Leaders who don't listen or don't want to listen to their brand community's needs and vision typically prefer an exploitative and extractive relationship with members. When members recognize this, the community's power to deliver value both to the brand and to its members will almost certainly erode—in a catastrophic and spectacular way. Remember that influencing the brand is one value that members seek when they get involved at all.

You can think of the community work as building a trust bank. You may build a high balance with years of service and demonstrated commitment. Refusing to listen to members will deplete the bank balance quickly. Constant listening, cocreating, and delivering on promises will increase the balance.

Airbnb has learned this lesson firsthand. Many Airbnb hosts were frustrated with the original method customers used to rate hosts. At an Airbnb-sponsored gathering, a company product manager sought direct feedback in person and discovered previously unheard frustration. One of the lessons he learned was that the then online feedback system didn't give users adequate tools to provide deep, nuanced, and contextualized feedback. Airbnb now regularly and formally invites product developers to join user events because the brand knows it can discover more hidden opportunities (personal communication, Danielle Maveal, August 2019).

Of course, not all voices in a brand community are either equal or helpful. It's OK to choose whom you listen to. You can filter using any criteria appropriate for your brand.

Airbnb serves well over two million hosts. Not every one of them sits down with developers. The brand invests a lot to invite the most successful hosts to share how the Airbnb platform can better serve them. The wisdom here is not that you must take time to listen to every member all the time, or design by committee. The lesson is that there must be a way that membership can contact brand management in a meaningful way to build and protect trust.

8

CREATING SHARED
EXPERIENCES AND SPACE

I n part 1, we spoke of the importance of shared experiences for any brand community. Although community shared experiences can include both planned and surprise events, here we will address planned events, as these are the kind that leaders organize. We'll refer to these as "events" for simplicity.

The principles discussed here apply to both "paramount gatherings" and local gatherings. A paramount gathering is a large event for the whole community, where members can meet one another, learn from elders, and participate in the community maturation (or evolution). The paramount gathering invites people to convene from wherever they live globally. Members share in rituals. (See *The Art of Community* chapter on the rituals principle.) The community's most senior elders and organizational leaders attend. Examples include CrossFit's CrossFit Games, Twitch's TwitchCon, and Salesforce's Dreamforce.

Event Specification

The more specific the values, the more specific the interest.

Imagine that we plan two chocolate-tasting events. The first will be a four-hour seminar on contemporary interpretations of Mayan chocolate tradition and introductions to the artisans reviving the practices. The second will be a ninety-minute tasting of Hershey's new seasonal chocolate flavors with all-you-can-eat s'mores. Although both are chocolate-tasting events, each will appeal to different participants, based on different interests founded in different values.

The first will likely draw participants interested in history, culinary tradition, and avant-garde foods. The second will draw people who like sweet things and maybe lots of them. One isn't better than the other. What matters is that, as participants gather at each event, they will see and (possibly) meet others who share their interests.

Many community builders unfortunately fail to consider how (or whether) their events reflect community values. Too many seem to believe that inviting strangers to a bar after a day of work for a happy hour will naturally lead to a community. We don't understand how inviting us to a noisy room to stand around drinking with strangers bonds us to anyone. If shared events work best when they reflect the community values, we have to ask, What values get reflected by generic happy hour bar events?

To be clear, it isn't bad to like or attend happy hours. They just don't usually serve community building as much as a more values-driven event.

Because communities bond over their shared values, the more an event could be or is attractive to all communities (i.e., any values), then the less valuable/effective/interesting it is likely to be for your specific community. The more specific the community values, the more specific the community events should be.

Carrie identifies as a woman entrepreneur and really likes meeting other women founding and growing their own firms. Through years of investing in growing her connections to this community, Carrie has discovered that she actually *doesn't* like attending generic female founder meetups across Seattle. They are simply not specific enough to her interests. She's discovered that she cares far more about meeting founders of any gender, creating sustainable "calm companies" with a social purpose prioritized over executive egos.

She avoids events that promise panel discussions on general business practices. She also avoids networking happy hours because they offer only superficial connection. She does seek out events connecting people and efforts for social good, because she's confident that her specific values will match the specific programming and the crowd.

Sephora practices this in its community as well. The company calls its managed customer community with over one million members the Beauty Insider community. Sephora leaders understand that, although all members within the brand community care about makeup and beauty products, there are many different interests within that boundary. In fact, the company has segmented members into forty groups (and counting). Leadership is savvy enough to make sure that no offline event ever tries to interest all members all the time. This makes the company's programming *way* more interesting for participants.

The "Sephora" beauty convention is a great example. *Glamour* magazine has called it "the beauty equivalent of going to Disneyland."[1] Tickets are limited and hard to get. Sephora's "insiders" have advance access to tickets. It is a giant event comprising many four-hour-long "master classes" on different beauty methods, including classes on hair, skin care, and makeup. Members come to learn from skilled masters in specific disciplines.

Other events invite members to meet celebrity beauty stars, and others invite fans in for special Sephora announcements. Each kind of event appeals to different members with different interests within the beauty enthusiasts community.

Later in this chapter, we will discuss intimate experiences and campfire spaces, and the importance of including fun. You'll learn how you can support connection during shared experiences.

Invitations

In practice, participants understand how an event will reflect community values because the host establishes the intention (explicitly or implicitly) in the invitation. The shared event experience starts with the invitation, no matter how formal or informal. In fact, the invitation's level of formality (whether a brief text, a personal phone call, or a parchment letter) may help guests understand how important, serious, exclusive, or momentous the event will be. In Priya Parker's guide to gathering with purpose, *The Art of Gathering*, she explains that the invitation is one way to share the "tone and mood" you intend before participants ever show up.[2]

One of our favorite examples of a team using invitations powerfully comes from the multibillion-dollar online home goods retailer Wayfair. The engineering team that handles the checkout features hosts a monthly Wednesday breakfast in the office, where team members hand make Belgian waffles. Each month, they invite another team with whom they work to join. A specially printed (and a bit cheeky) invitation to the "Wayffle" breakfast is always hand delivered to guests. Emily Levada is a Wayfair executive whose role is two levels more senior than the team, and she specifically shared how special she felt when someone sought her out to deliver the invitation personally. The card quality and the personal delivery help other teams understand how important and special the event feels for the hosts (personal communication with Emily Levada, October 2019).

A powerful invitation tells guests the real (community-oriented) intention of the event. For example, we could invite you to our Oakland event next Friday by messaging you like this: "We'll have drinks and pizza at our place next Friday. You should come." You've no doubt seen an invitation like this many times.

Think about whether the invitation feels more compelling and prepares you to connect with others if we invite you to the same evening with a phone call: "Reaching out to let you know that we'd like to see you again. Next Friday we're inviting neighbors over who we'd like to know better. This is to grow friends nearby as we build a life in Oakland. We'll have drinks and pizza. Will you join us?"

You may not like this event (you may not like Oakland), but you can see how the second invitation sets up the experience so that participants understand that it isn't only about a carb-loaded dinner.

We might attend an Oakland active citizen event in a beer garden, but only if the invitation says more than "Join us for a beer-garden evening." It'll say something to the effect of, "We want to build friendships among those taking time, doing the work, and even risking safety to make Oakland safer and cleaner. This will be a time to check in on our neighbors investing in Oakland." The event will sound even better if it's held in a room quiet enough for comfortable, meaningful conversation.

As we make an event more intention specific, it may appeal to fewer people. This is a good thing. For community building, it's far better to attract fewer people who accurately understand the intention and are excited by it (quality participants) than to draw many people who are indifferent, unaware, confused, or misguided by the intention (volume participants). Community building requires participants to connect. If you attract the wrong people, the right people then discover the wrong people exactly where they want to connect.

Whether informal or formal, effective invitations encourage people to participate more and enrich themselves and others. So, no matter how big and complicated a community may grow, community is really created one invitation at a time.

Intimate Experiences

The small grows to big—never the other way round.

Community leaders who talk to us about building community often envision building to a membership that will eventually fill an arena. Indeed, teams at Salesforce, Twitch, and CrossFit have all achieved this.

Although it's possible to grow to such a level, remember that people don't feel connected to your community because they joined a big crowd in an arena. They feel connected because of the *individual conversations, private moments, and vulnerability* that they experience with other participants.

We call these "small" experiences **intimate experiences** because they feel intimate even if they take place in a giant room, a field, or an arena. They almost always occur when we are physically close to others, in both planned and, very often, unplanned ways—for example, while waiting in a line, sitting in adjoining seat rows, or even eating a meal close by.

As leaders inviting people together and creating experiences, we need to allow and support with time, space, and permission the intimate experiences that connect participants.

Of course when participants share intimate experiences, they begin to form or deepen relationships. These participants won't just feel connected to the individuals within the intimate experiences; they will also feel closer to the greater community. Further, they will very likely feel more appreciative of and connected to the brand that made the intimate experiences and connections possible.

Campfire Principle

To encourage rich intimate experiences, leaders should use the **campfire principle**. This doesn't mean that you literally create campfires (though you can). The principle means that leaders create the kind of experience and space often found around campfires.

At campfires, we have *proximity, permission, and conditions* to connect meaningfully with others. Most important, *campfires are small enough that everyone can participate, if they choose, and feel seen.* Proximity and permission are fairly self-explanatory. By *conditions,* we mean factors that give people the context to share private conversations that can grow into vulnerable and memorable relationships. This can entail handling any variables that will distract or inhibit a possible vulnerable conversation—noise, interrupting messages, time limits, menacing oversight, anything.

Twitch's Bobby Scarnewman described campfires as giving participants "a chance to open up and say what's really on their mind and what they've been trained not to say in uncontrolled settings."

Even as a campfire group grows, participants remain connected around the fire, and the conversation on one side can differ from the one on the other (intimate experience). But we still experience the intimate campfire together. Campfire experiences are where community relationships actually begin, and they enrich whatever bigger event is going on around.

We can create **campfire events** at which participants can find an intimate experience. We can also offer **campfire space** where there is no planned event, but participants can use the available space for intimate conversations.

When we plan big events, we want to ensure that we've planned or (at least) allowed for campfire events and spaces within the big event. This will include ensuring that participants get invited to and can find the campfire experiences whether through self-selection or by invitation only.

Imagine that we have invited you to a weeklong brand community summit for five hundred leaders, to be held on Hawaii's Oahu North Shore. Now imagine that during that week, we invite you to join just six of us to watch a sunset sitting around a beach campfire, sipping jasmine iced tea. You can probably predict that the evening's conversation, sharing, and laughter will be much more meaningful to you, and will connect us more deeply, than all the time we spend among the hundreds of summit participants. Although intimate experiences may occur during the big five-hundred-person event, they'll happen far more often within campfire spaces. And although intimate experiences can and do form serendipitously, they're much more effective if you plan for them.

A planned campfire event within a big event (say, our summit) can be any event where participants will experience intimate enough space, time, freedom (permission), and conditions to share an intimate conversation, even if it's in a space set up within a big arena. At our summit, walks on the beach, meals at tables of eight people or fewer, musical jams, or discussions on niche topics can all count.

In principle, you can just offer a campfire space with seating and a fire ring (real or metaphorical!), or you can plan a campfire event (including singing and skits) with invitations.

The important point is that no one will gather around a campfire if there is no campfire space.

For example, our Oahu summit will be far better if we plan ahead and provide a dozen cozy spaces with seating, comfortable lighting, and ocean views for new friends to sit together. Standing around a parking lot is much less fun, but that's exactly where many events figuratively (and occasionally literally) leave participants to gather intimately.

To apply the campfire principle to an arena event (or any big main-stage event), you must arrange areas where participants can feel comfortable gathering and speaking in an intimate experience.

When we attend events, we can tell right away whether the producers understand this basic principle by the spaces they set up. If all the resources are set up for a main stage and the intimate gathering spaces are an afterthought (or simply missing), then we know the event is all show and that the leaders deprioritized bringing people together.

Campfire spaces can appear obvious, but sometimes are recognized only by trained eyes (now yours). Go back to the imaginary Carrie and Charles five-hundred-person brand community Hawaii summit. Now imagine that we invite all five hundred to an evening beach campfire. Are we going to plan for one giant campfire for five hundred people (plus crew) milling about? Or would it be better to set up several fires in different areas so that the spaces are more intimate? If we were really sophisticated, we'd set up several campfires and also (1) a walk down the beach in groups of no more than six, (2) a silent surf meditation gathering with reflection over tea after, and (3) a ukulele sing-along at the hotel. Each one serves as a campfire event with its own space. Planning several campfires means more intimacy at each.

There is reason and value in creating a main-stage event that can draw people together. The wise organizer also creates smaller campfires to encourage and add intimacy.

Consider that the travel to and from venues (walking groups, carpools, and shuttle rides) can also serve as campfires. In fact, we see this all the time, even while participants and planners frequently miss it.

Can you build a campfire online? Of course! But you'll see now that they're often missing. Online campfire spaces are missing if leaders have invested all their resources into a fancy landing page and newsfeed, while neglecting a forum to join specialized and intimate groups, engage in a conversation about specific needs, or explore niche topics. The online spaces are also inadequate when they're filled with distractions including irrelevant advertisements, links to other groups, and unrelated updates. The distractions tell members the space isn't protected.

Imagine a telecommunications brand inviting your IT administrator, Maria, to join a support community for your company's new business internet package. If Maria logs in and discovers an invitation to "Ask questions and get involved," without any qualifying questions, the host company is treating the space as an arena. Sure, a community supporting an internet package is less sexy than . . . almost anything we can imagine. But for some, such a support community can be a job saver. Those participants are seeking campfire experiences to get just the right help when they need it from just the right people who understand them and their pain.

So if instead, this brand invites participants to find a group for their specific needs and user types, provides a way for participants to introduce themselves to those with similar needs, and personally invites them to a group call for collaboration with others in their organization, it is using the campfire principle.

ETSY'S TREASURIES

Etsy's "treasuries" are a good example of the campfire principle employed online. Members were invited to curate these "pop-up" collections of Etsy items based on a theme of their choosing. The treasuries would then expire after three days. Themes included "made in Chicago," "breast cancer awareness," or items from a particular team. Attached to each treasury was a place where members could chat about the collection and theme. Some galleries inspired thousands of comments. Treasuries provided the possibility of a constantly new, relevant, and fairly intimate space for members to celebrate and acknowledge both things and ideas they cared about, away from a larger audience. (This information is from personal communication with Danielle Maveal, an Etsy founding team member, September 2019.)

TWITCH'S CAMPFIRES

Twitch also specifically uses the campfire principle online. Twitch's Erin Wayne said plainly "There is a campfire for everyone on Twitch." Each broadcaster's channel provides a campfire space. Twitch considers each broadcaster channel the broadcaster's own "corner of the internet." "They get to choose what their home looks like" (personal communication with Erin Wayne, October 2019).

When participants arrive at Twitch's home page, they're asked what kind of content they like to watch. Twitch provides hundreds of "tags" (e.g., *action, horror*, even *birthday*) so that members can filter options to find other members who (almost) exactly share their interests. They can also pick channels by the most popular at the moment or by brand-new "undiscovered" broadcasters. Twitch also provides recommendations to help steer users.

When inside a channel, members make the small online space special and recognizable in many ways, including special "emotes" (graphics that indicate an action such as laughing), chat rules, colors, celebration behaviors, inside jokes, meetup schedules, and more.

Fun

One of the most important components to include in events is fun. If a gathering isn't fun, then consider canceling it or redesigning it to include fun. Like us, you may think this obvious. Unfortunately, we've both attended events where it was clear that no effort was invested to make it fun (at all). Remember that for relationships to form, participants must return for more events. If the events aren't fun, who wants to return?

The good news is that there are many ways to make events fun, and most of them don't include tacking on silly elements to a boring day.

We're big fans of Stanford professor Stuart Brown's work understanding the importance and influence of play. He shares what he calls eight play personalities that can help us understand what features help different people relate to experiences as play.[3] The distinctions can help us recognize how our different events can relate to different kinds of people.

PLAY PERSONALITIES

Artists and creators. Fun involves making things that are beautiful, functional, or goofy. These people may also enjoy taking things apart, repairing, and restoring. This can include decorating.

Collectors. Fun includes the thrill of collecting the most, best, or most interesting objects and/or experiences. Although the experiences might look like exploring, collectors want evidence that they've "collected" a new experience.

Competitors. Fun involves competitive games with specific rules. Competitors play to win.

Directors. Fun involves planning and executing events. Directors are organizers. The planning can be as much fun as the outcome.

Explorers. Fun involves adventure and exploring. This provokes imagination and creativity. Such exploring can be expressed through physical, emotional, cultural, or aesthetic experiences. There must be a component of discovery.

Jokers. Fun involves nonsense and silliness. It often looks like foolishness.

Kinesthetes. Fun involves movement. This often takes the form of athletics, dancing, or yoga. Kinesthetes like to move their bodies through space. Remember that the movement, not competition, is the focus.

Storytellers. Fun involves creating and experiencing thoughts and experiences in a story. Many kinds of performers are storytellers.

The play personality distinctions can help us understand that not everyone will consider every fun event fun. We may notice that members group together within one play personality and focus on particular events accordingly. As leaders we can experiment with different kinds of fun events.

Etsy created an online marketplace for "makers." Obviously most of the company's events offer fun to artists and creators who connect to learn skills and make crafts together. This is plenty of fun for them.

If you want to learn more about fun, please read *Play: How It Shapes the Brain, Opens the Imagination, and Invigorates the Soul*, by Stuart Brown (with Christopher Vaughan).

Shared Space

All communities must have shared spaces to retain long-term strength. **Shared space** is a venue for meeting that *allows participants to ask for help and deliver support.* Whether they do or don't depends on several factors. We'll speak to those later. In this discussion, *space* can mean a physical location or a digital location where participants can meet.

Posting cool stuff in an online space is never enough. Watching someone speak or perform in a space is better than nothing, but groups with no aspirations to community can watch things "together" (think of concert audiences). The shared space serves community building when there are *avenues for participants to share who they are in some intimate (and vulnerable) way and understand that they can both ask for help and offer support to others.*

What counts as a shared space will differ depending on an event's scale, because obviously the shared space must serve the event size. For many intimate experiences, an intimate space is needed—such as a restaurant table for six Harley riders exploring the California coast. But if you're participating in a giant experience, then a much bigger space is required, such as several downtown Atlanta buildings for the Academy of Management conference.

Think of an event you attended recently, at which you considered yourself connected in community, perhaps a meal with family. What made you feel connected? Our guess is that you had (at least one) conversation with six or fewer other people (at a time). In that conversation, you recognized that you shared (at least some) values with the others. Almost certainly, explicitly or implicitly, someone offered support in that intimate conversation. This doesn't happen by accident. The space is the container that sets the conditions and tone for that vulnerability.

An intimate space is the kind of place that encourages or facilitates intimate experiences. Although the space and experience are related, they are separate elements. Leaders very often encourage and facilitate intimate experiences by offering comfortable and helpful intimate space.

Even when we participate in a giant event, our most important memories almost always consist of an intimate experience nested within the giant experience. You've probably attended at least one giant sports event—collegiate, professional, maybe even the Olympics. The memories that tie you to the other people who were there generally don't involve thousands of other spectators. They're mostly connected to the dozen or so people around you.

Imagine your excitement upon receiving an invitation to share dinner with your favorite music artist, Lady Gaga. Now imagine showing up and discovering that this means you will share dinner with her . . . by video and with thirty-five thousand other invitees who will watch the live stream in a Los Angeles stadium. Will you feel more connected to Lady Gaga or her fan community? You might be happy to have received a free ticket to an event she leads, but otherwise it would probably feel weird to "share dinner" with Lady Gaga miles away (which is one reason why artists don't do this). Part of the problem is that you aren't sharing space.

You may have fond memories of watching a winning game with friends, and remember how much the experience helped you feel connected. We believe you. *You shared space with them.* Had you watched the same win on your phone on a beach alone, we're confident that you wouldn't feel the same strengthened connections with others. Shared space matters when knitting community. It influences how community bonds grow.

If we don't consider, prepare for, and invite people to the right shared space, participants will not experience one of the key elements that bonds a community.

Digital space can count as shared space. To be effective, there must be some digital boundary that participants cross in order to enter into this space. Online community members may have to log in to a dedicated site or download a special app to interact with others. In this way, insiders can be confident that participants include only those with appropriate convening values.

Once inside, participants must be confident that there are hosts (elders) who protect the safety inside the space and ensure that the experience reflects the convening values.[4] The boundary crossing and host supervision make the digital space special and thus a community shared space.

Principles for a Good Physical Venue

In the best venues for community events (whether a chapter meeting or a national convention), you must control the "end-to-end" experience as much as possible. If strangers can stroll through your event, and others can make distracting noises or keep the lighting too bright (or too dim), they can erode the effectiveness of the space.

Many event producers choose terrible venues for connecting people. They may do so out of lack of resources, lack of research, or lack of empathy. But it pains us when we see a crowd of people who want to connect and the space inhibits what could otherwise be an intimate and powerful experience.

The next sections describe some principles to consider when choosing your venue.

ENSURE SAFETY

Participants can hear one another, remain calm, and share themselves, confident that they choose who hears, sees, or judges them.

When there is a history of aggression or reason for concern, you can share a code of conduct beforehand that, as necessary, establishes both appropriate behavior and how to report violations. Ensure that all organizers and volunteers are aware of this code and the reporting process.

CONTROL THE PRIORITIES

Selling drinks, meals, or tickets should never be the top priority for a community leader. This is a marketer's priority. Although the space may offer options (such as raffle tickets), you must control what priorities get protected. Ensure that no one else chooses when, how, or in what medium to get participants' attention. We often see competing people with divergent priorities using announcements, video screens, "experiences" (e.g., photo booths), and the like pulling participants away from intimacy and connection. Although media and activity diversity might help an event appear more interesting, the host must ensure that participants experience a space protected as a container for intimate connection. For example, five-foot-tall video advertisements looming over conversations always have an impact, whether you notice the influence or not.

ENSURE ACCESSIBILITY

You must ensure that the right people can find and get inside the venue. This often means considering questions like "Can a veteran in a wheelchair, a parent with children, members without cars get to and into your space?" Further, you must ensure that those in attendance are culturally welcome. Hosting a women filmmakers' symposium at the Hustler Casino is one obvious example of a poor choice.

Sometimes barriers exist that go unnoticed until the right questions get asked.

Charles visited the Oakland Adventure Club earlier this year. He noticed that the photos on the walls depicted dozens of only Caucasian people. How welcoming does a place that displays photos only of white people feel to an Asian American visitor?

HOG gatherings are often held in bars. This can be great for people who drink alcohol. But if every event is hosted in a bar, it will exclude people who don't drink alcohol or even avoid it.

You will have to consider how welcome your visitors feel in your spaces no matter what else you want them to feel.

MAKE IT COMFORTABLE

This sounds obvious, but it clearly isn't for many planners. Consider noise, lighting, appropriate furniture, temperature, luggage storage, even coat storage. Charles presented at a conference at which luggage and coats were strewn around the learning space because no one had provided an appropriate place for either. All of these kinds of variables can distract participants from the reason for their gathering.

Make sure there is sufficient seating and spaces for private conversations, recharging electronics, and quite places to retreat to. If you can't provide all the comforts you'd like within one venue, you can share suggested local businesses and public spaces where participants can go for a break—hopefully with new friends.

MAKE IT FUN

We all like to go to places that are fun! Places that are cheap and easy for *you* are not necessarily fun. Carrie recently attended a Seattle-based conference that offered optional midday dance classes so that participants could get out of their heads and feel refreshed, silly, and connected. Organizers scheduled no other programming during this time, so it did not force attendees to choose between fun and learning. The conference was held at Monkey Loft, a high-ceilinged warehouse furnished with bean bag chairs, hammocks, plants, and craft tables. There were some spaces for loud music and others for contemplative silence. Carrie loved the care the hosts exhibited in offering a fun space in the middle of a conference.

ARRANGE SEATING FOR A COMMUNITY EXPERIENCE (NOT OBSERVATION)

Furniture arrangement powerfully influences people's behavior, whether in favor of connection or of observation. We've attended far too many "community" events at which the chairs all faced a microphone at the front. We call this "auditorium" or "lecture" arrangement. This cues participants that they're expected to sit down, shut up, and watch. Which is precisely what they do.

For more connection, set up your furniture so that participants can easily see one another, turn to each other, and chat. Dividing a gathering into "pods" of six people is a simple way to start.

Remember, round tables themselves of course don't create community naturally; they only help make a setting. Leaders must turn attention toward the attendees' pods so connection can happen. Round tables used where participants all face a stage are mostly a waste and typically just plain uncomfortable.

CONSIDER ALL YOUR SENSES

By far, it's best to ask attendees ahead of time about their special needs and accommodations, such as wheelchair access, elevator needs, companion animal accommodations, and language interpreters (including for sign language). If you don't ask, you will almost inevitably exclude some who fear the space won't accommodate them comfortably. There's also a real chance you discover you can't accommodate the people who show up because you're unprepared.

SIGHT

- Put the light where you want attention. (Candles on dining tables are great for drawing attention to the center.)

- Dim those areas that would visually distract from where you want participants' attention.

- Notice what is ugly, dingy, or dilapidated. This clues participants that you don't care about the space (or them).

SMELL

- Notice what smells clean, fresh, sour, dirty, or rotten. Clean the space of dust and debris.

- Add flowers, open windows, and replace stinky furniture or carpets.

- Only use minimal (if any) potpourri, perfumes, and other strong manufactured odors. Many people are sensitive or even allergic to such artificial smells.

SOUND

- Notice where and when it's noisy. This distracts whether you think it does or not. Some attendees will be more sensitive to sound than others, and loud music or noises can overwhelm and even trigger fear or panic.

- If unexpected noise shows up, such as a maintenance or cleaning crew, manage it so that it pauses or finishes as quickly as possible. Pause your activities if you need to. Pretending the noise isn't distracting tells participants that the host is not protecting the space.

- Can participants hear what they need to at all times? If you expect interactive sharing to the whole room, prepare the appropriate microphones. We've seen producers want interactivity and then never set up the audio equipment to make this work. We've also seen music drown out activities, and too many speaking groups scheduled for one room. Each time, producers didn't consider the sound.

TOUCH

- Notice *whether* participants can sit, *where* they can sit, and *what* they can sit on.

- Notice tables, charging resources, and the space where participants will stand and walk. Ensure that all are comfortable enough for the time you'll invite them to stay and leave enough room for people with wheelchairs and other mobility devices to navigate.

- Consider all the surfaces that participants are likely to touch. Charles participated in an activity where an instructor invited participants to fall to the ground in a trust exercise. She didn't notice the skin-gashing rocks until Charles fell on them (really).

- Ensure that the space is warm enough and that people can regulate their temperature. Carrie knows of one community builder who, upon arriving at his venue discovered it was 50 degrees Fahrenheit. He sent crew to to buy dozens of blankets for attendees.

TASTE

- Food is almost always a good idea. Across many cultures, offering even a small amount of food means welcome. It reveals that the host cares about the participants. We agree with a restaurateur friend who believes that in many cultures, food is simply a proxy for community. When we bring food, we bring a piece of community.

- Notice where and how participants will get food when they're hungry, and how difficult that will be. If you want them to stay near, ensure that appropriate food is near. (This sounds obvious, but it isn't to many.)

- Note that if you arrange food because it's easy and cheap (junk food), participants with specific food needs may have to leave to get their own appropriate food. We have both done exactly this ourselves.

- Carrie notices that leaders in her circles provide the same snacks over and over. When she spends ten minutes arranging for something different, including gluten-free, vegan, kosher, and nonalcoholic options, "people's minds are blown" (sometimes that's all it takes).

Rejecting Conventional Wisdom

Most people don't study how to bring people together into meaningful and connecting experiences. They go with conventional wisdom. We're living in the loneliest era, so it's safe to assume that conventional thinking has failed us.

For example, bars are usually terrible places to build community. They are noisy by design, they expect us to buy drinks, and they fill the space with lots of stuff intended to distract us (screens, games, lights, signs, even pretty people). All of this pulls us away from protected intimate experiences.

Yet think about all the people you know who assume that a bar is a great place to build community. Consider that if your conventional wisdom isn't at least compatible with the time-tested wisdom in this book, then it's probably unhelpful, maybe harmful.

We mention this because chances are that someone you work with will reject the principles here, noting that events are "usually" planned another way (conventionally). Consider what wisdom they are drawing from and whether you want different results from those in the past. If you want different results, you'll have to set up and use your spaces differently.

Principles for a Digital Space

If your community started online or mostly connects online, creating physical space for participants to connect will greatly strengthen the community. We can't stress this enough. Consider Twitch, the online gaming platform with well over 150 million users per month. Although millions find and connect online, Twitch understands the importance of supporting dozens of small physical gatherings around the world; in addition, Twitch hosts two annual TwitchCons, to which tens of thousands pilgrimage. The company understands that no matter how big its community grows online, the physical gatherings strengthen the community.

Many brands invite customers worldwide to connect in digital space. Fitbit, Salesforce, and Sephora are all examples of brands that do this successfully involving tens of thousands of people. Designing a brand-appropriate digital space can be more challenging because we can't use all five of our senses. Due to these sensory limitations, digital spaces often do not create the depth of relationships that can be created in physical spaces. That's not to say there is no power or importance to online connection; we must just keep appropriate understanding and perspective.

Typically, digital community spaces work best in particular circumstances:

- As a supplement to an offline community

- As a space to discover others with shared identities, interests, and location

- Where participants' accessibility to one another is a problem

- When a stigmatized and/or vulnerable commonality brings people together—for example:

  Sexual challenges (disease or trauma)

  Survivors of trauma who wish to remain anonymous

  Marginalized identities and issues

  Mental health issues or neurodiversity

  Niche groups who feel geographically isolated (fan communities)

Six important principles for any community digital space apply to brand online spaces:

ENSURE THAT MEMBERS CROSS THROUGH A GATE

Participants must choose to participate and then take an action to cross from the outside into an inside space. In other words, they should not be able to find themselves inside your community space accidentally. For example, if they arrive in your community as a result of an online search, they should be aware that they arrive as an outsider. They must elect to become members. Such next steps may include downloading a specific app or entering a specific code.

WELCOME MEMBERS

Authentically acknowledge members as they arrive for who they want to be known as. Generic welcomes aren't enough. If you're welcoming software engineers to an open-source software event, then the welcome should clearly acknowledge arrivals as software engineers who care about open-source projects. The welcome should remind members of their shared identity as people who build software in a way that is open, accessible, equitable, and flexible.

ONBOARD MEMBERS FOR INFORMED PARTICIPATION

Visitors should be able to recognize and understand the values, culture, and (at least some of the) norms before they participate. For example, in forums that allow uneducated and immediate participation, the inevitable experience of repeat questions signals to participants that the space isn't well regulated and that the boundary is not protected. This is bad for authentic community.

Although barriers can limit participation (for instance, placing a requirement on the number of threads participants must comment on before they are allowed to post their own thread), appropriate barriers with accessible gates will protect meaningful engagement and connection on the inside.

ENSURE THAT LEADERS BOTH STEWARD PARTICIPATION IN THE SPACE AND MODEL IDEAL BEHAVIOR

This creates a context so that participants feel safe to go beyond fronting. Leaders should not only model the ideal behaviors of the community but also recognize others who do the same, both in larger and private spaces.

MAKE COMMUNITY GUIDELINES KNOWN, AND USE THEM

This establishes trust and safety. According to Reddit's Evan Hamilton, consistent and timely enforcement is the way that most successful groups create feelings of safety. Guidelines evolve over time with the community, and they mature in ongoing conversations.

Moderators must consistently and publicly moderate. This includes privately conversing both with harassment victims and with perpetrators.

There is no perfect way to write and enforce community guidelines. The good news is, you can search for community guidelines in use today. You'll find many examples to inspire your own.

ENSURE THAT THE LOOK AND FEEL CORRESPOND TO YOUR MEMBERSHIP

Look and feel here refer to the experience of such design elements as the colors, typefaces, and layout of a user interface. There is no one design option that will suit all communities. (Duh—there are no butterflies on the HOG website, but there are plenty on the Butterflies Community, a website for new moms struggling with their mental health.)

The wisdom on building successful digital community space is deep and nuanced. To understand enduring principles regarding the complexity of building such spaces, we highly recommend the book *Community Building on the Web: Secret Strategies for Successful Online Communities* by Amy Jo Kim.

There is no getting around it: to handle look-and-feel design, you will almost certainly need to work with an experienced designer. We recommend that you save yourself many headaches and months by bringing one on as early as possible.

To get to great look-and-feel designs, the best brands start with a prototype space and then invite a few members to judge and comment. You can respond to their preferences before a launch. Then, of course, continue to iterate over time. Both the community and times will change.

The following are just some areas you'll need to consider in your design:

- *Layout.* Ensure that it's easy to find ways to engage, including discovering events and new posts, and navigating to relevant subgroups. The layout should mimic mental models that members are already familiar with (e.g., the connections between a main group and subgroups). Consider how the layout presented will change, if at all, for first-time visitors, those who have transitioned to being a member, and then for leaders.

- *Buttons and calls to action.* Consider the most important thing you want members to do when they are in your digital space and ensure that there is an easy way for them to do it. Ensure that buttons that lead to actions are easy to find and recognize.

- *Imagery and iconography.* Consider how imagery will clearly communicate the purpose of the community. And consider how iconography, such as moderator badges, will signify special roles.

- *Member profiles.* Consider how profiles appear in the community and can be found. Also plan how much participants can customize them and update their own image or avatar.

- *Consistent application across channels.* The design should look consistent so that participants recognize and feel familiar with your look whether they're reading an email newsletter, attending an event, or replying to online posts.

- *Private spaces and subgroups.* Consider how members will break off into smaller groups to segment into specific areas. Consider whether anyone can join these spaces or whether members must be invited.

- *Search.* Ensure that it's easy to find past conversations and other members.

In the conversations addressing these seven areas, consider various perspectives related to experience, culture, physical abilities, age, member location, and any other relevant issues. Designing for accessibility is an enormous and vital topic for online communities. Many great resources exist to teach both experts and novices about accessible design. Carrie recommends *Accessibility for Everyone*, by Laura Kalbag, to support your efforts.

Conditions for Shared Spaces

A successful venue enables and supports participants' communication and connection. Two conditions must be in place for this to work.

- *Time for participants to talk to one another.* Participants must understand they're in a space with both time and permission to speak with one another. Scheduling events with every minute filled with attention directed toward a stage, videos, eating, administration activities, or skill learning doesn't give the participants opportunity for intimate experiences that build community. Something may get done, but it won't meaningfully deepen relationships.

- *Sound conditions that allow for real conversations.* If participants can't hear one another, they can't share a conversation. If you play music so loud that participants must shout to be heard, you're thwarting connection. We're surprised by how often event producers who say that they want to connect people choose venues (a loud bar) or events (loud concerts) where even we, community experts, can't connect with others.

In digital spaces intended for community connecting, the same rules apply. Participants must have access to a feature whereby they can share a private (intimate) conversation with a small subset away from the "noise" of the greater gathering. This allows for intimate experiences.

Features of Shared Spaces

For a community shared space to work, participants must understand explicitly or implicitly that the following four features are in effect:

1. *The space feels safe (enough) on the inside.* Participants must understand (usually by observing norms and examples) that the inside space is safe for them to express both (a) their pertinent values and (b) more vulnerable and intimate identity.

2. *A gatekeeper protects the boundary.* Participants must see (explicitly or implicitly) that one or more people are keeping outsiders out and that anyone who won't support the shared core values and purpose will be removed. An exclusive invitation or a nomination process can serve as a gate. The most important lesson here is that participants must understand that there is some kind of screening process and people protecting the boundary. (The boundary principle chapter in *The Art of Community* discusses how leadership uses boundaries in constructive ways.)

3. *Inside, members can identify one another as distinct individuals (i.e., there is clarity on who says what).* In communities, participants want to be seen and recognized, and to see and recognize other members. If this doesn't happen, it isn't a community.

This is one reason we are (fairly) adamant about name tags. If the inside is safe and participants really want to connect, then we should help participants forge connections and relationships that will carry on outside the community space. For whatever reason, there may be some cultural resistance to name tags. We find that when the leadership makes known the rules for the space and leads by example, the resistance dissipates. We tell participants, "The name tag isn't for you. It's for the people who want to talk to you."

In an online space, there may be good reason to hide identities for a time. In these cases, avatars (unmistakable visual representations of participants, including photos) remain important until true identities are revealed.[5] Total anonymity without reputation building and accountability *never* works in nurturing online communities. In fact, it exacerbates community-destroying behaviors such as bullying and harassment. Participants need some way to build up a reputation for contributing that is connected to their profile, even if the profile uses a pseudonym for exceptional reasons.

4. *There are prompts, facilitation, and/or permission from a host (leader-ship) for members to meet and express interest in other participants.* Typically, this means that elders model social connection and invite participants to connect as well. The modeling demonstrates the expectation that participants are meant to connect.

Most people in a crowd fear speaking to strangers without prompting. This is one reason the host's role is so important. Hosts can set expectations for a space that change the whole experience inside. Many event producers dismiss or misunderstand this.

When hosts explicitly invite all participants to connect with one another, often with a prompt, they are telling the participants that this is the expectation for the space. Even more important is the hosts' role modeling. If they only hang with their best friends, enjoy the open bar, and dance or sit solemnly listening to performed music, they influence the space more than most understand.

Simply telling people to "connect," "make friends," and "have a good time" never works. We recall a conversation with one community leader we'll call Thomas, who prefers to avoid name tags. He thinks they make any event a "networking" event. He then goes out of his way to introduce people who attend.

Consider the math: If there are two hundred attendees at a two-hour event, even one with no logistical distractions, how many minutes as a host can Thomas invest in connecting each guest? How does he know when he misses someone? Does he ditch guests who want to chat with him for, say, five whole minutes? What Thomas doesn't recognize is that his flitting between guests role-models for all that the space is intended for short, superficial conversations. Although he wants something more, that's all visitors see from him.

● ● ●

If you want to further explore creating meaningful shared experiences that move and connect people, we cannot recommend *The Art of Gathering*, by Priya Parker, highly enough. We hope her wisdom saves billions of people from pointless, boring, and disconnected events for years to come.

9

CONTENT STRATEGY

C *ontent for community building* means many things to many people. We've seen the term used to describe *anything* created to support a community. This includes the text on forms, large celebration events, and all the postings, announcements, and invitations for those events. It is hard to talk about appropriate content when the term refers to everything in every medium for everybody.

Here, the term *community content* describes resources and experiences that support three goals:

1. Organizing participants
2. Connecting participants emotionally
3. Educating participants in a manner consistent with community values and goals

Understanding how content can help and harm is deeply connected to understanding your members. If you aren't sure how well you understand your members, go back to part 2!

If your community materials don't serve the three goals we've listed, they don't count as community content here. It's content for something else, which isn't necessarily bad; it's just not community content. For example, community content differs from material that serves strictly marketing, customer support, and any other goals different from the three listed goals. We discuss how brand community serves those goals later.

Content Forms

There are two broad community content forms: media and shared experiences.

Media. This is any text, visual, or audio resource that supports emotional connection, organization, and/or education.

Shared experiences. These are events that emotionally connect, organize, and/or educate participants. Ideally, they do all three. It's best if these events are also fun. People generally dislike and avoid unpleasant events, and we (Carrie and Charles) specifically avoid unfun events ourselves.

When you offer content, it must be in *alignment with the community's purpose.* Otherwise it's distracting to your membership. Imagine inviting Harley riders to a DIY knitting workshop at Etsy's headquarters. You may think that this is so obvious it isn't worth mentioning. But we're regularly surprised by how many leaders offer content without considering whether or how it aligns with community purpose. Just because something is fun or interesting does not make it appropriate content for your community. And more content is not better. *More appropriate and community-aligned content is better.*

This principle allows you to cut distractions from your content offerings and show participants that you're gathering and serving them for the reasons they found you.

Now, you can host fun events because they're fun—for example, a Harley knitting and movie night. The wisdom to take away here is that you can't assume that any event is good for any community. If your Harley riders want to knit . . . buy the yarn. But! Do the research first, instead of sowing confusion about why an event is being hosted in your community.

In our experience, inappropriate, ill-fitting, or confusing events typically reflect desperation on the part of leaders. They don't know how events serve members, so they try "anything" or try to copy events that worked for others. That's a recipe for programming that confuses members.

The content must *serve participants' needs.* Remember, connecting (actual emotional connection) with others who share values counts as a need. If your event will help participants connect, then ensure you've structured it *so that they can connect,* instead of standing around wishing they could find deeper connection. And make the intention explicit in the invitation.

The biggest mistake we see is creating content that focuses so intently on a main-stage event that it leaves no room for members to participate, share, or connect. An example is an online live stream with an expert with no welcome from an elder or invited discussion before or after. Such events ensure that participants never reveal anything vulnerable or meaningful. Repeated events like this train members to perceive your "community" as a place for superficial transactional experiences.

Content Categories

Once you reach critical mass stage, your participants should create as much content as formal leadership creates, if not more. But leadership's participation sets the example for all members. *The content that you plan, encourage, and allow must serve particular purposes* so that participants get value when they experience it. The following sections offer an overview of content value areas.

Education

Educational content helps participants do something better and grow into who they want to be. The growth can take the form of skills or topic understanding (for example, motorcycle liability law). Even better, education helps participants grow internally into more mature and wise people, beyond their skills. (*The Art of Community* discusses how communities support growth externally and internally.)

For example, Etsy hosts craft and sales workshops where members learn both from one another and from experienced Etsy staff.

Stories

The stories your community shares reflect your lived values (not just made-up pretensions). Typically, important community stories refer to three topics:

- How we formed
- How we are changing
- How we affect the world beyond ourselves

Danielle Maveal, an Etsy founding team member, explained that Etsy headquarters posted stories about their communities on the official Etsy blog. The company would run monthly roundups about Etsy Team meetups, challenges, and triumphs. The stories together created a record of the changes and lessons learned among the leaders as they created a new platform for makers. Although Danielle admits that these posts were "low-performing content in terms of views," teams' seeing their names and initiatives on the Etsy blog "meant a lot to the Teams that worked so hard." In addition, this content modeled behavior and sparked ideas for other teams.

Group Identity, and Debate and Conflict

This content respectfully and civilly talks through conflicts and in doing so helps clarify the group's identity. Once the identity is clarified, some members may be inspired to leave. This can make the community stronger because those who decide to stay have a better understanding about their ongoing connection.

Welcoming Invitations

This regular content welcomes new members to participate. You may consider such posts to be frivolous, especially if they're frequent. We assure you they're not. If your community is growing steadily and members remain to contribute, you will reach a point where some members become "veterans" and others are the "new guard." Segmentation can be positive (even necessary), but segmentation should be intentional, not simply arise because there are few or no ways for older members to initiate, welcome, and get to know to new members. If the connections don't happen, an unnecessary and unhelpful schism (split) will become predictable (or inevitable). Such schisms of course inhibit experienced elders from supporting the maturation of younger members who seek guidance.

Instituting a formal welcome is critical for blending old and new groups. The activity gives veterans an easy way to contribute, and helps new members quickly feel seen, recognized, and acknowledged.

Even early in Etsy's growth, the company understood the importance of a strong welcome to all new participants, so it scheduled daily "Newbie chats" for all new members. Within these digital spaces, all those new to Etsy could connect with more senior members. The conversations established a relationship of welcome and support and modeled the communication tone within the community.

Celebration and Recognition

Content must *celebrate the people within the community*. Celebrating individual and group milestones, such as membership anniversaries, outside awards, achievements, and life changes, is critical. Each celebration reveals that members are recognized as whole people, not only for their transactional value to the community.

Etsy, for example, still encourages local members to create "craft parties" to "celebrate creativity" and connect members. The guidelines specifically encourage leaders to "make fun a priority."[1]

Collaboration

Organizing time and space to create things together is critical to binding a community. Part of leadership's role is to steward members' helping one another. If a resource is needed in your community, whether for an individual or for everyone, you can create an experience where members gather to create or revise that resource as needed.

Danielle explained that in her time at the company, Etsy scheduled regular in-person "skill shares" where teams gathered to cocreate workshops to share skills broadly among members. Often at Etsy parties, participants would build something together—for example, "Adopt Me" vests for animals looking for new homes and tiny hats for preemie babies. The list of generous gifts made together is a long one.[2]

Cultivation of Friendships

Content that cultivates friendships helps a community feel more connected. Without it, your "community" may (almost certainly) feel like a transactional place to "get stuff"—such as information, access, or special deals. If this tendency is unchecked, your community will devolve into a group.

This content makes members and the community *more memorable* for participants. This content is often the *most common material* found in an online community space, which surprises many leaders who don't understand its value. Although content for forming friendships alone is never enough, a healthy community can produce a lot of this and remain relevant and strong.

Friendship cultivation most often appears in two related ways.

DISCLOSURE (SHARING SELF)

Participants *share (disclose) things they want others to know about them.* In the best outcomes, this leads to vulnerable sharing. No one feels connected with people from whom they must hide all their beliefs, identities, and values. When the disclosure is offered, participants discover shared commonalities even if they are "off topic" from group goals. In part, the connections grow because we like people who we think are like us.

Vulnerability is something that has to be "earned" by a group. In other words, sharing too much vulnerability too soon will distance people rather than bind them. What the right amount is, is determined by culture and subculture. We can't help you more than that here. The most important lesson to take away is that disclosing vulnerable truths can be really powerful in connecting members, so take notice of vulnerable sharing and encourage it. Also, be aware that at some point you must consider what vulnerabilities are best saved for very intimate conversations outside of larger-ring conversations.

ASKING FOR HELP

Participants *ask for help* and (ideally) find it. Communities transcend groups because of the mutual concern. When members provide help because they care, the fundamental core of community is present. In fact, if your community consists of nothing more than a few people who care about one another, asking for and offering help, you have a community far better than have many leaders with giant mirage communities.

● ● ●

Sharing of self and asking for help aren't things you can bargain for, force, or trick people into doing. In an effective community, participants offer these things because they perceive the community to be a safe space where they can do this. Self-sharing and help-seeking arise because you've adequately prepared and offered the space. In by far the best examples, leadership models self-sharing and help-seeking first.

Coercion may provide a spectacle of friendship cultivation, but it actually makes the space less safe. Invitations to participate must remain invitations and no more.

10

MOTIVATION AND ENCOURAGING PARTICIPATION

The use of incentives, rewards, and acknowledgments to encourage participation is an area that unskilled leaders often get painfully wrong. Misunderstanding how members are motivated, and "rewarding" them inappropriately, can destroy goodwill and a community.

Good leaders encourage participation regularly and often. Although incentives and rewards may appear similar, they are not. Misunderstand the difference and you will exasperate your community's participants and appear emotionally tone-deaf.

The complexity of incentives, rewards, achievements, and acknowledgments can go very deep. The following simplified discussion will help you avoid destructive practices and notice enriching opportunities.

To help clarify distinctions, we'll reference Carrie's own real volunteer involvement. In Seattle, she volunteers to do data entry for a nonprofit that helps train women political candidates. By any standard, the actual work is both boring and tedious. Nevertheless, she has volunteered her weekends to do this work. In fact, she even invites friends, who also join.

Why does this work? Are those Seattle political organizers stunning manipulators? Do they know the exact management levers to get volunteers to commit to tedious work?

No. Carrie returns because those leaders help her be who she wants to be. More specifically, they're supporting her to act on her internal motivation to commit to a cause greater than herself. This is what great community leaders do. In this chapter, we will dive into what's going on.

Distinguishing between External and Internal Motivation

Each person has a diversity of things that motivate them. Inexperienced leaders often misunderstand how people are motivated toward community participation and contribution. As a result, they will "give away" goodies (such as branded swag or gift cards) thinking that this will create participation, contribution, and loyalty from the recipients. Note: It's not a "giveaway" if you expect work in return; it's a bait and switch, and that's toxic to any community.

For the purpose of supporting community leaders, we're sharing fairly simple and accessible distinctions. First, understand that there are two basic kinds of motivation, external and internal.

External Motivation

External motivation drives us to action in order to get a reward or avoid punishment. Typically the reward is offered and/or given by other people. *They decide whether, when, and how much is awarded or punished.*[1]

For example, participants are externally motivated when they post media online to get likes, host an event to impress others, or compete to win an award. They aspire to get something that others control.

Some forms of external motivation in community are fine! These may include access to particular events, credentials, or resources (e.g., a clubhouse, grants, or a network). But if members participate *only* for external rewards, then you'll have a transactional group (i.e., a mirage community) because the connected relationships will be missing. In such a case, "members" are largely competitors for limited rewards that they earn or win. Usually, externally motivated participants don't build supportive, caring, and patient relationships with the competitors they've got to beat.

Internal Motivation

Internal motivation comes from inside us and feels like a natural part of ourselves. When we are internally motivated, *no one else needs to provide anything more to inspire us to action.* The (internal) joy we feel after an activity (such as volunteering to do data entry for women candidates) can be enough. Carrie doesn't volunteer for the fun, attention, awards, or obviously money, and never will. She wants to see women politicians succeed and is willing to contribute as needed.

Internal motivation can be described in far more complicated ways than we have here. For the purpose of growing community leadership, we will focus on three key conditions to support internal motivation. We referenced them in part 1, noting that in healthy brand communities, members are internally motivated to commit.[2] Participants show up and return when these conditions are met. To be effective, all authentic community invitations need a context that supports *all* three conditions:[3]

1. *Choice:* the ability to say yes or no to membership and participation.

2. *Connection:* connecting to other people. We've discussed connection a lot in this book. Members want to be recognized by others and accepted for who they are, and they want to know that others care about their welfare.

3. *Progress:* advancement toward a purpose.

We want to experience progress toward a chosen *purpose.* This can include growing toward *mastery* of an art, skill, or field. This progress can be expressed as a form of being. For example, chefs do many varied tasks, and a chefs' community can help us cook better. We may scrub pots with chefs because they help us *become* better cooks. In this way, we progress toward a goal of *being* a better cook.

When Carrie volunteers, she first chooses whether, when, and how she supports the organization. Second, she connects with others who share her values and purpose. Third, she progresses toward her purpose in helping women candidates win elections. That makes the experience worthwhile even though the actual work is really boring.

In order to effectively support others with their internal motivations, we need to understand what internally motivates them such that they want an opportunity to take action to connect and progress. This almost always means investing the time and work to learn what's honestly internally motivating them. (See the section "Understanding Your Members" in chapter 4.) When we authentically support their internal motivation, we will be shocked to see what people will step up to do.

In the real world, there's an unfortunate tendency among leaders to *recognize their own motivation as internal* and *wrongfully assume that everyone else is externally motivated* (i.e., that other people just want more cool stuff).

There are all kinds of internal rewards we seek in community. You may even identify some we don't know about. Very often participants seek one or more of these benefits:

- Wellness (well-being)

- Creativity/innovation (creating something both personal and new)

- Generosity (being a support to others)

- Aliveness/vitality (fully experiencing life)

- Fortitude (persistence in the face of challenge)

- Purpose (meaningfulness)

- Fulfillment (sense of accomplishment)

- Belonging (deepening relationships with others who share their identities, beliefs, or values)

All these are benefits often associated with internal motivation and are less likely to be supported by external motivation. This is one reason why simply making friends is a legitimate reason to join a community. Strong friends help us feel belonging, aliveness, and fortitude. Friends also are people with whom we can express our generosity. This can be a reason why you'll get mad if a friend doesn't call you when she needs a ride to a hospital. She withheld an opportunity for you to *be* a generous friend.

Ignoring one or all of the three conditions explains why so many communities experience failure. It doesn't matter how fantastic an invitation *could* be or how much participants really want to help. A single contextual element can make any opportunity distasteful. Coercion is just one example.

Community Internal Motivation

We want the right people to consider membership with at least some internal motivation. This is to say, we hope that they join without a cold calculation of a strict quid pro quo relationship with other people. Such calculations result in a transactional group relationship.

When Carrie originally volunteered to do data entry, she didn't do so because she was looking for a really boring activity done under fluorescent lighting to fill her Saturdays. She *chose* to do something to *be* a support to women candidates winning offices (purpose) and to *contribute* (progress toward the purpose) and *connect* with a community that shared her values. (To learn more about community identity and membership, see chapter 1 of *The Art of Community*.)

At the time, she would have considered any request or invitation that would help her *become* a contributor and community member. In this example, she was asked to do data entry on a weekend. She tried it once and returned for more because all the conditions for feeling internally motivated fulfillment were in place.

Imagine that we invite you to go on a weekend apple-picking outing with us. It will be an opportunity to get outdoors on a sunny day, make some friends, and of course enjoy some apples. We obviously won't pay you or trade for your participation, so you'll only join because you're internally motivated to do so.

Notice that no matter how much you'd like to apple-pick with us, an otherwise fun opportunity is transformed into something else as soon as we dismiss or ignore any one of the three conditions that support your internal motivation.

MISSING FREEDOM (COERCION)

- If you don't pick at least forty pounds of apples, we'll ban you from all social events among our friends.
- Everyone who refuses the invitation will be labeled as "not a team player" in our work group.

MISSING CONNECTION (ISOLATION)

- All day, you're assigned to work in an orchard corner alone so that you "won't have to compete for apples" or "get distracted" by other pickers.
- We insist that there be no talking in the field because some people are introverts and may not say that they prefer the silence.

MISSING PROGRESS (STAGNATION)

- You're neither told what to bring nor provided sacks, buckets, or ladders. Without appropriate equipment, you can neither collect nor carry to the car more than ten apples at a time.

- You're allowed five minutes to pick your apples and then told to guard the car alone while others pick in the field.

Leaders' ignoring any one (or all) of these three conditions explains why so many experiences fail to build community.

The most powerful way to support internally motivated volunteer participants is to *separate their contribution (such as work) from external rewards.* If we make rewards into things to be earned, then we create a transactional relationship that competes with outside market-rate returns (e.g., payment for data entry or anything else).

This does *not* mean that you cannot give valuable rewards to high-contribution and high-performing members. You can, and we support that wholeheartedly. But when you do, you must make clear that you're not giving meaningful material rewards because they're *earned.* You give the reward in recognition of the members' commitment, and/or to honor who they are and their importance to the community and purpose.

To give you more effective options, it's important to understand the distinctions between tokens and acknowledgment, as we will discuss later in this chapter.

Combined External and Internal Motivation

Often we are driven by both external and internal motivations. Many teachers, doctors, house builders, artists, chefs, and firefighters love to contribute because they know they're making a difference in others' lives (contributing). Virtually all of them need, and rightly demand, payment in exchange for their work. If they didn't, they couldn't and shouldn't continue. There is nothing wrong with this! Either or both kinds of motivations can be effective. What matters here is distinguishing between them so that we can deliver appropriate support in member relationships. If we don't, relationships (and participation) erode quickly.

When members participate for both internal and external motives, leaders must honor and deliver *all* rewards needed. We've seen many leaders criticize contributors because they need or demand external rewards for participation when leaders think all contribution should come with *no* external rewards. This is silly and very often extremely toxic. When leaders insist on ignoring the need to fulfill *all* appropriate motivations, they appear abusive and tone-deaf.

We know of a Christian summer camp that recruited twenty-something staff to run operations. The camp offered either no pay or very little. Each workday lasted more than twelve hours. When staff expressed a problem with the situation, they were told that "if they really were serving because of their faith and they really believed in the work, then they wouldn't want more money." This is both ridiculous and a good example of leaders ignoring the often connected relationship between internal and external motivation. Ignoring either one erodes the relationship and builds deep resentment.

Likewise, if leadership only fulfills external motivations ("The pay/reward/ exchange is enough"), then there should be no surprise why stakeholders feel unappreciated, disgruntled, and angry.

Our job as effective community leaders includes discovering the means and member relationships that serve both our community's needs and the contributors' needs. This includes *honoring all internal and external motivations.*

Rewards: Separating External and Internal Motivation

Let's clarify some important distinctions before we discuss how to avoid creating problems with incentives and rewards.

Incentives

An incentive is intended to incite action. An incentive *appeals to external motivation* for someone to take action. Typically, incentives work in a commodified transactional relationship. If we ask you to pick us up from the airport and you'll only consider it if we buy you dinner (to make it worth your while), then the offer is an (external) incentive. It's commodified when we then compare the dinner cost to hiring a car.

Tokens

A token is an item given to someone. It represents a relationship, a shared value, or both. A token specifically honors a recipient's internal motivation.

Tokens are never transactional even though the token item may be materially valuable, such as jewelry. A token's value lives in its representation of something nonmaterial. *It works in a relationship.*

Because tokens work in the realm of meaning (representation) and refer to a relationship, the person who gives the token makes a big difference. In fact, who gives the token can make all the difference. When we say "give," we don't refer to who physically hands over a token; it's OK to send a token in the mail, for example. Tokens work because of who gives them, so it's important that someone knowingly offers the token to represent a relationship.

Tokens are often given after a participant contributes in action. However, as noted, the token's material value is not the motivation for someone to contribute.

It's hard to overstate how powerfully tokens can serve a community. Many people—you may be one of them—keep special tokens the rest of their lives. Some examples of tokens include military medals, wearable pins, challenge coins, and any item passed from an elder to a growing novice to honor the novice's development.

If we ask you to pick us up from the airport and you want to do that to support us as your friends, we may offer you dinner. That dinner is not then an incentive. It is a token of our friendship. We provide it to honor our friendship and your internal motivation to help friends.

Acknowledgment (No Judgment)

In **acknowledgment**, someone specifically articulates the contribution a participant makes (or made), without judgment. Typically, this includes words that specify how the individual is making a difference. For example, "Carrie volunteered four hours of data entry this Sunday" acknowledges Carrie's contribution. There's no judgment of whether she did a good job or not. In fact, even if she did a terrible job, the acknowledgment remains honest and accurate.

The important aspect of acknowledgment is that it enables us to show others that we notice their contribution (or effort) without putting ourselves in a judgmental relationship. For one thing, there are people by whom many of us don't want to be judged; for another, there are times we just don't want to be judged.

For example, we (Carrie and Charles) are book writers, and neither of us wants to meet others at weddings where the conversation includes, "You're a writer! That's amazing! I could never write a book. You must have so much discipline!"

That's not a terrible thing to say to an author; it's just a judging (albeit positive) announcement from someone (a nonauthor) from whom we don't seek judgment. Consider that we don't mind getting judged on other occasions, such as when volunteering for a political campaign over months. Hearing we did a good job will be important.

By contrast, on her first day volunteering, when Carrie is frustrated by the database program, she doesn't necessarily want someone judging how well she's using it . . . because she's not good at it yet. A simple acknowledgment can be far more effective:

> Carrie, I notice you're putting in the time to learn the program. That's the only way to do it, and using the database is an important job here.

If someone tells us we're doing a "great job" or "good work" and we know we aren't (yet), then that person is just demonstrating insincerity, which erodes both trust and credibility.

Because acknowledgment excludes judgment, we can acknowledge someone who isn't doing a good job or isn't very helpful yet. We can acknowledge someone's time, commitment, intentions, and effort, regardless of the quality of the work. In fact, acknowledging someone's time, effort, and improvement can create the right context to share helpful criticism for improvement. So, even when Carrie is still lousy with the database, we can acknowledge her:

> Carrie, I see you came in on a Saturday to help. It's a reflection of your commitment to this work, and we'll only succeed with help like this from many volunteers.

For some people, using acknowledgment enables them to escape what we call the "death spiral of thanks and compliments." You know people who describe everyone they know or work with as "amazing," "the best," or "incredible." The hyperbolic words grow empty and annoying because everyone isn't actually amazing at everything.

At one of Charles's workshops, he worked with the head of a high school military academy. By every standard, the academy is a strong brand community. Every morning, the head of school inspected the cadets' uniforms and quarters to ensure that all was in order. He felt silly "thanking" each cadet for doing exactly what they're tasked to do every day. He then recognized that all they needed from him was an acknowledgment. "Cadet, your uniform is exactly right. Your quarters are clean and tidy." He may sometimes add "good job," which is a judgment. That can be great too. But he doesn't have to do it.

There is a gray area between acknowledgment and judgment: Whenever we draw attention to something (say, with acknowledgment), we judge it worthy of attention; also, when we acknowledge someone's contribution, we are implicitly judging it helpful and appreciated. Fair enough. There's an overlap between acknowledgment and other forms of encouragement.

When we're speaking to or about someone who doesn't want to be judged (because they're struggling or feeling vulnerable), avoiding judgment can make a very big difference. When we're connecting with others and want to avoid creating a judgmental relationship with them, then using the acknowledgment distinction gives us a way to do this.

We acknowledge you for taking the time to sit with this book in hopes of growing better at bringing people together. We don't know whether you made a good choice or whether you'll get better. We acknowledge that reading these words is part of your commitment to be a better community builder.

Recognition, Gratitude, and Appreciation (with Judgment)

Recognition, gratitude, and **appreciation** are three distinct and nuanced ideas. We're bundling them in this discussion because many leaders use the terms interchangeably. The important commonality is that all three include both acknowledgment and a value judgment. Obviously you can judge something without gratitude or appreciation. Community leaders usually recognize members because there is both evaluation and appreciation for someone's commitment and contribution.

In a healthy community, a lot of gratitude is shared, so we're assuming that this kind of judgment will come up a lot (as it should). An example is, "Carrie volunteered four hours this Saturday, and she did a great job" or "Carrie is a really helpful volunteer. She volunteered another four hours this weekend." The difference between this and acknowledgment may appear subtle.

Status is one way to recognize or acknowledge a member's contribution. In fact, we know that Twitch broadcasters have cried when offered a higher status because it acknowledged their contribution to the community.

Keep in mind that providing higher status simply for longevity ("seniority status") can be toxic for a community, because it doesn't recognize contribution, only longevity. Someone can be a pain in the butt for years and have longevity. Providing higher status because of contribution enriches community.

The important benefit to distinguishing these terms is that we then have a better lens for seeing what is the right kind of communication, at the right time, to offer in our communities. It gives us more tools to relate to and connect with members.

In community, we want to be seen for who we are and the contributions we make. When someone simply acknowledges both of these things, that is often moving, heartening, and enough.

To help you understand the distinction among acknowledgment, recognition, tokens, and incentives, imagine Charles getting advice from Carrie on improving his marriage relationship. Carrie tells Charles that many partners like getting flowers, so Charles decides to give his wife, Soch, flowers more often.

The examples in the next sections can help clarify how any one gift (flowers in this case) can very differently influence a relationship, depending on how the gift is presented.

Assume that Charles's wife remains with him because they each care about the other's well-being and like their connection. No surprise, the marriage is overwhelmingly internally motivated. This is to say it's not a transactional marriage for external rewards. Given that they have a son, the home holds a family community. It's obviously not a brand community, but otherwise all the principles apply.

Charles's plan is to welcome his wife home on Friday with a dozen roses. He hopes the gift will help her feel even more appreciated and connected in the relationship.

ACKNOWLEDGMENT TOKEN GIFT ROSES (HELPFUL)

Recognizing Soch's internal motivation to support the marriage and family, Charles can present the roses this way:

> Soch, I notice how much time and work you put into the house and our family even with a full-time job and work tasks late into the night. I notice that every day you check in with me and our son. These roses are for you to acknowledge your commitment and effort.

In this presentation, Charles *acknowledged* Soch's commitment and efforts. The roses are a gift given generously, and they *serve as a token* of his appreciation for her and her commitment.

Notice that there is no judgmental language. It's possible that she is in fact doing a poor job of handling both work and family needs. The words and gift remain honest.

Judgment isn't necessarily harmful. Still honoring the relationship, Charles could also express *gratitude* and appreciation:

> Soch, I notice how much work you put into the house and our family even with a full-time job. I'm appreciative of the time you take to care for us. I think you do a great job, and it makes a difference, making my life happy. These flowers are for you.

Here, Charles is *recognizing* her for her contribution. The flowers still remain a generous gift and a token of appreciation in the relationship.

TRANSACTIONAL ROSES (DESTRUCTIVE)

Charles could mistakenly believe that, while he's in the marriage because he values the connection, she's in the marriage for external rewards (stuff from him and from other people). In this case, Charles might present the flowers this way:

> Soch, welcome home. You made dinner four nights this week, mopped the floor, and bathed our son. For every chore you did well, I bought one rose until I reached twelve. Congratulations—you get a dozen roses from your husband this week for doing at least twelve chores well in the house!

We hope you got a sense of how much this will *not* help the marriage. Maybe you (appropriately) winced. We see this kind of mistake in bad community leadership far too often. The problem here is that Charles presented the flowers as earned in a transactional relationship. This dishonors Soch's internal motivation. If there was generosity involved, it's spoiled by transaction. She "earned" flowers through her actions. They're the same flowers from the same partner on the same day, and they now don't help her feel much appreciated as a partner—if at all.

EXTERNALLY MOTIVATING INCENTIVIZING ROSES (DISASTROUS)

If Charles were really wrongheaded and thought flowers would *incentivize* Soch as a reward, he would say something like this:

> Soch, I'd like to give you something nice because we're married and you care for our family. If you do chores in the house, including bathing our son, cleaning the floor, and making dinner, at the end of the week I'll give you one rose for each chore you do, up to a maximum of twelve. If you do a good job, I'll give you a big bouquet because you've been a good wife.

We hope this sounded ridiculous to you. We cringe reading it. In this case, Charles offered the roses as a potentially earned reward (bleh!). This isn't very romantic and, knowing Soch, it will certainly harm Charles's marriage. She doesn't want to be judged, counted, and rewarded for tasks in her marriage! She wants to be in relationship. She wants to be appreciated for who she is in the relationship and any gift to come out of generosity, unearned. She wants a partner who cares about her no matter what happens in her week.

● ● ●

Notice that the flowers work as a helpful relationship gift only when they're given to Charles's wife because he's expressing appreciation for who she is. She gets the flowers for *being* his wife, *being* connected, *being* committed, *being* important to him. Said differently, *the flowers only work while they remain a token (representation) and there's generosity (unearned giving) in the giving.*

Some people get confused as to how "just words" can make the same gift work fantastically or disastrously. They rightly point out, "They're the same roses!" "Just words" can make or break your efforts because the words tell recipients whether the gift lives within a transactional connection or a relational connection.

No matter how valuable the gift, if recipients want something that represents their precious connection to you, your presenting it transactionally will never fulfill their want. As an example, Charles can fly in one hundred plumeria leis because his wife "earned" them doing one hundred chores, but she'll never appreciate them as much as one orchid given with these words:

> Soch, I noticed this has been a hard week. You've had two days of work travel. There's been a screaming sick kid in the house. You couldn't go to the gym because of surprises, and I didn't make dinners because of late meetings. This single potted orchid is for you. It's for the dining room table so you'll see it every morning and be reminded both when you leave and when you return that whatever happens, you've got a husband who cares about you and appreciates your commitment to our family every day.

The distinction between earned and unearned tokens applies to all gifts shared within internally motivated relationships. It also applies when we want to reward people because they deserve it. The gift must remain a token, and recipients will know this because our words present it as such.

"Earned" Tokens

You may know of tokens that are "earned" for achieving some activity. We know that HOG members can "earn" a token pin for joining a particular group ride. Many summer camp kids "earn" beads or badges for completing an activity (archery, pottery, etc.). The examples are countless.

After all our insistence on tokens being relational gifts and not rewards, why do such "earned" tokens work? The reason they work is that the item received (patch, pin, bead, sash) has little or no material value in the world. For clarity, the bead or pin tokens cannot be sold either within or outside the community for any substantial money or trade value. In fact, the *only* consequential value of the "earned" token is as a symbol. So even if we say it's "earned," the recipient is only "earning" a symbol.

Imagine if the HOG riders and summer campers "earned" a $10,000 gift card instead of the pins and beads. The whole community's relationship to the rewards would change.

For example, Airbnb staff send specially made key chains in the shape of the Airbnb logo (known as a Belo) to important hosts. The only way to get a real one is as a gift from Airbnb staff who want you to have it. Often the Belos are given with a handwritten note expressing appreciation. In this way, they serve clearly as a token of appreciation.

Our favorite earned token example was shared by a friend who worked for a famous investment firm. Each staff person was given a small Lego set that represented a given investment project. Over years, staff collected Lego sets on their desks that others in the know could interpret as representing the history of deals worked on. All the staff felt pride in their own Lego collection that represented their cumulative contribution to the firm.

The Folly of Maximizing Cheap Tokens

When wrongheaded leaders see or learn that inexpensive token gifts can work to strengthen member relationships and commitment, some engage in the folly of *seeking maximum token efficiency* and scalability.

Earlier, we used the example of Charles giving roses to his wife, Soch. Presumably he was smart enough to present them as a genuine gift from a loving husband who wants her to feel appreciated for who she is.

Imagine Charles returning to Carrie and telling her, "She loved them!" and then saying, "I wonder whether instead of a dozen flowers each week, ten would do the same? How about every other week? How much less will the flowers work if I give them 20 percent less often? What's the most efficient return on flowers in my marriage? What if we consider adding her birthday gift budget to the flower budget?"

The important lesson here is that if a husband goes all the way through exploring the most efficient flower-gifting in his marriage, his spouse will rightly wonder why he's so stingy and will question the importance of the relationship. *This is because the effort undermines generosity in the relationship.*

We see this folly often play out even when multibillion-dollar brands consider what, when, and to whom token gifts should be sent.

Erin Wayne, Twitch's head of community marketing, oversees more than forty Twitch city groups around the world. They're called "groups," but they function as brand communities. Each group operates with local volunteer leadership and hosts several events a year for its members. One way Twitch supports the local communities is by providing Twitch-logoed items or "swag." Every year, Erin's team suggests kinds of swag and asks what kinds each group wants. Depending on costs, Twitch can provide a few expensive items (such as high-end hoodie sweatshirts) or many inexpensive items (hats). The local leaders choose.

The Honolulu group recently asked for Twitch-branded beach balls. They loved them so much Erin said they "flipped out" (i.e., got very excited) when they received them. Because of vendor relationships and volume, the balls cost Twitch only about $1 each. Each ball inspired more excitement among members than a $40-per-person drinks tab at other events. Erin understands the importance of the token in the ongoing relationships and never tries to maximize ROI on any given beach ball.

However, for those leaders who don't understand how tokens work, they'll wonder . . .

What exactly is the ROI for each $1 beach ball?

If balls work so much better than event drinks, isn't it best to eliminate drinks and send out more balls?

What's the cheapest ball we can send out to every group next year?

These questions reveal someone who doesn't recognize tokens or understand how they work. The balls only work because the gift (accurately) tells the Honolulu members that Twitch recognizes them, cares about them, listens to them, and wants them to (1) join freely, (2) build community among themselves, and (3) enjoy themselves (purpose). The token balls exist within a living relationship among the members, local leadership, Twitch staff, and Erin. As Erin put it, "You only get back what you put in. Swag is only one tool used in real invested relationships" (personal communication with Erin Wayne, June 2019).

More than sending out swag, Erin knows the name of *every* local leader around the world. Each one can and does contact her directly when they need help . . . and then her team helps.

Erin pointed out that the balls were a hit in part because they came out of a conversation where the Hawaiian leaders asked for something. Twitch responded to the request. The members recognized that Twitch pays attention to them.

To understand whether Erin's team is helping support and achieve organizational goals, a better question is, "What is the ROI of the *staff's commitment* to the relationship?"

Using External Incentives and Rewards the Wrong Way

We obviously can't know your participants well enough to tell you *how* to reward them. What we can help you understand is what kinds of rewards may work best.

Let's go back to our earlier example of Carrie volunteering her time to do data entry. As we've mentioned, the truth is, political data entry is tedious. Totally, absolutely tedious, mind-numbing, and exhausting. There are thousands of other ways that Carrie could volunteer close to home that would be more fun. And yet . . . she does the data entry.

What's going on here?

Carrie's not returning for external rewards. Imagine that Emily, the volunteer organizer, offers Carrie a reward of ten campaign points for every voter data page she enters. These points can be exchanged for hats, T-shirts, pins, or other campaign paraphernalia. If Carrie were externally motivated (seeking things given to her by others), this *might* appear to be an effective strategy, because Emily wants as much data entry from volunteers (including Carrie) as possible.

REWARDS WHEN THERE IS EXTERNAL MOTIVATION

Let's explore using external rewards. Unfortunately, even if Carrie were externally motivated, these rewards will work poorly at best.

1. The strategy will *only work short-term.* Emily is never going to offer Carrie enough rewards to keep her doing a tedious task on her free Saturdays. If Emily were to eventually offer Carrie enough rewards to keep her going, *Emily would end up paying Carrie.* Carrie would become a part-time hire.

2. If Carrie is doing this tedious work for external rewards, she will look for something to do that's less tedious to get those same points. Emily will have to offer increasingly more points for data entry and thus create a rewards death spiral.

REWARDS WHEN THERE IS INTERNAL MOTIVATION

The situation is worse for Emily if she has misread Carrie's internal motivation and offers external rewards. Because Carrie is internally motivated, she's doing the work to be who she wants to *be.* She wants to be effective supporting women candidates serving communities, and she wants to be connected with others with similar values and purpose. There is no point, T-shirt, or hat that Emily can give Carrie to help Carrie *be* an effective support.

When Emily offers external rewards (points), she undervalues and dishonors Carrie's internal motivation and, ironically, erodes Carrie's powerful internal motivation. Research shows that what will almost certainly occur is that Carrie will assign value to her tedious hours by looking at what the points are worth (a lot less than Carrie's labor and weekend). That will tell Carrie that her volunteer work isn't very valuable to the organization. So she'll stop and look for something else to do. More than likely, she'll look to volunteer where the leaders value her work and invite her to be effective and connected.[4]

Acknowledgment and Appreciation

Internally motivated people welcome acknowledgment and appreciation (A&A). *These are not rewards.* A&A honors the commitment already inside someone. It is never earned in a quid pro quo (transactional) relationship.

In Carrie's volunteer experience, Emily can acknowledge Carrie in many ways. A simple option is for Emily to speak to Carrie alone and say,

> Carrie, I notice you're spending many Saturdays in this office entering voter data. All of us consider this a painful and tedious job. This is important work for the candidates we're supporting because we need to know who to contact. Your time makes a difference getting our women elected.

Emily can also hold a short office meeting to acknowledge the day's work among all volunteers. She could include words about Carrie's contribution, along these lines:

> Carrie spent her Saturday entering voter data. She completed eighteen pages today. It's brutally tedious and painful work. Our database is more complete because of her time.

Emily can also express appreciation for Carrie. Here, *appreciation is a kind of acknowledgment in which we include a judgment.* Many times it may seem silly that we're distinguishing between the two. As explained earlier, there are times when others don't want to be judged and when we prefer to avoid serving as a judge. Recognizing that we can acknowledge someone powerfully without judgment serves as an important distinction.

To appreciate Carrie, Emily can say what we've already cited and add a judgment:

> Carrie's a strong volunteer who's willing to do hard parts of this work. [Or]
> I admire Carrie for her commitment.

Tokens

As we've discussed, items used as tokens can be effective or countereffective, depending on how they are presented. For example, gift cards are terrible tokens if they are "earned," but they can work well as "a token of appreciation." In online spaces, badges work as tokens when they're used strictly to acknowledge. This means they have no trade value but have symbolic value within the community.

You can make tokens symbols of just about anything, including commitment, accomplishment, or impact. Because they work in the realm of meaning, they are easy to make and share. But, as with all things, if we make too many, they lose their specialness.

Emily can acknowledge Carrie and add,

> Carrie, I'd like you to have this logoed sweatshirt to acknowledge your commitment. You've done tedious work that makes a difference, and I'd like you to have this because you obviously care about our mission and you support all of us working on this.

Because Emily infuses the gift with meaning, it doesn't live in a transactional relationship between the organization and Carrie.

In his work, Charles has given $20 ice cream shop gift cards to staff who've done an important job. The cards aren't worth much by themselves, but he makes sure the recipients know that the cards are given so that staff can celebrate their success with someone with whom they'd like to share ice cream. The card serves as a token acknowledging their success, and it facilitates a ritual (an ice cream outing) celebrating the same. For this to work, the card must pay for ice cream for at least two, and *Charles must make explicit that the gift is about celebration*, never about a transaction.

Rituals

Rituals are activities that have meaning. Appropriate rituals can be a great way to offer A&A. In mature communities, rituals acknowledge changes and milestones. Part of a community's value comes from offering connection to people who recognize one another for who they are. Community rituals allow members to see that their community recognizes both their changes and their accomplishments.

The topic of rituals is so grand and rich that volumes have been written discussing it. In this context, it is not wrong to think of *tokens as items* that acknowledge a relationship and *rituals as actions* that do the same. And yes, combining rituals and tokens is a fantastic idea.

Strengthening with Gamification

Gamification refers to using game mechanics to manage a group, usually by introducing competition among members.[5] Progress is noted within the competition through such tools as points, leaderboards, trophies, and badges.[6]

Gamification is designed to help motivate groups to do things—that is, get actions done. Picking up trash, crowdsourcing resources, answering questions, and returning to participate (in loyalty programs) are examples of many actions that can be gamified.

In community building, Gamification is effective only within very specific conditions. Gamification introduced impulsively or recklessly into an authentic community can deeply erode members' internal motivation.

It *can* help in getting tasks done. But we must remain very clear about whether our intentions are to yield short-term gains or to build long-term supportive relationships. A poorly organized game introduces uncertainty about participants' real motivation and even their contributing value. For example:

"Is Carrie doing data entry because she cares about women candidates or because she wants to win the game?"

"We wonder whether Carrie is really committed, because her data-entry volume is often in the bottom-half ranking among Saturday volunteers."

"Is Charles picking up street trash because he cares about a cleaner Oakland or because he wants the rewards?"

"We don't know whether Charles really wants to help, because he's never even close to winning the day's trash-bag count."

There is also the danger that game players will focus on the criteria counted and neglect the core community purpose(s). Charles picks up Oakland street trash several days a week. He knows that if a reward is offered for filling the most trash bags per week, he could win the game by seeking out the most bulky boxes, furniture parts, and discarded clothing. But what he really wants is a cleaner Oakland. So he's happy to pick up candy and cigar wrappers even though hundreds of these strewn down a block won't fill a single trash bag.

When participants (wrongly or rightly) believe they're losing status for losing the game(s), they're likely to ditch the whole experience. Charles would rather go pick up trash on his own block than get sneered at for not filling bags with bulky boxes.

GAMIFICATION AT ETSY AND CODINGAME

In Etsy's early development, the company posted a sales leaderboard on their forum that was updated many times a day. Because Danielle Maveal, a founding member, was a seller too, at the time she wanted her name posted on that winner's board. She now reflects that the board did motivate her to sell more. It also demoralized her. The ranking, and her failure to rank well, made her "forget the joy of selling" (personal communication with Danielle Maveal, September 2019).

Etsy eventually removed the leaderboard because leadership learned that the boards motivated the wrong kinds of contribution. The brand wanted to change the economy by promoting handmade creations, not mass-produced junk that sold well at low prices.

Codingame is a platform that hosts games that help members practice intermediate and advanced coding skills. Two years ago, its gamification was structured with two specific features: (1) There was a public leaderboard posting the all-time global points leaders; (2) points were earned for both solo and cooperative games.

According to Codingame's community manager Thibaud Jobert, leadership learned that players spent a lot of time on solo games to earn points quickly and avoid pacing themselves with other participants. Although there was nothing wrong with independent activity, it led to some negative outcomes. For example, in order to rack up points, many members copy-and-pasted others' code into their work. This didn't help players' own code learning, but it got them recognized on the leaderboard. Codingame rightly noticed that it wanted to encourage collaboration and experiential learning, but its gamification encouraged the opposite (Thibaud Jobert, personal communication, April 2019).

Codingame also recognized that the public leaderboard is an important feature of the community because it celebrates community members publicly as high achievers. So the company changed the leaderboard scoring to award more points for multiplayer games over solo coding. The change raised the profile of multiplayer gamers and thus encouraged member collaboration. Solo players still earn points for their participation but aren't publicly acknowledged on the leaderboard.

Bad games lead participants to expect transactional value for social contribution or connection. Just as offering rewards can erode participation, leading to transactional relationships, game winnings can do the same.

To ensure that our games support relationships within the community and do more than "get something done," we must attend to some key criteria. To help clarify these, we'll imagine a game to support Oakland street-cleaning volunteers.

MINIMUM GOOD GAME CRITERIA

- *The game encourages and rewards cooperation among participants.*

  It's OK for participants to help one another lift, carry, and load refuse together without penalty.

- *The rewards serve only to acknowledge participant success rather than provide real material value.*

The award has very little market value relative to the work accomplished in the game.

A pizza dinner for five is good. A week's trip for five to Hawaii is not.

- *Losing the game does not meaningfully harm participants' status.*

When Charles picks up garbage all day but fills only two bags with fast-food napkins and candy wrappers, everyone knows this can mean that he is just as committed and helpful as someone who filled more bags.

When Charles's seventy-four-year-old mother fills only one trash bag, slowly, all understand that her commitment is just as respectable.

- *The game is non-zero-sum. Everyone can grow by playing.* This typically means that participants "win" by growing closer to who they want to be, furthering toward a purpose, and/or just doing what they seek (i.e., bikers get to bike; paddlers get to paddle). This allows genuine appreciation for all players, including the last finishers within the community.

Everyone who participates helps make Oakland cleaner and spends time with neighbors who want to make a difference.

- *Sitting out is OK and not a status-losing choice.* Note that this criterion protects the freedom crucial in any internally motivated activity.

If Charles takes his dog to the vet or visits a sick friend instead of playing the game, he loses no respect.

- *It's never a problem that other members are winning.*

If Charles hands in one bag of candy-wrapper trash, that's not a problem.

There is no reason for Charles to sabotage other players.

- *Everyone wants winners to win.* Said differently, no one meaningfully loses status or resources because there's a winner.

When Charles sees the trash pickup tally by the top teams, he's excited to see how much trash got off the street and respects the work to haul it in. He loses no privilege, respect, or resources because there are new winners.

Please note that the last criterion doesn't mean that "everyone wins." Or that there is no top winner. The criteria ensure that winners win and losers win differently. This is how a community remains a community and avoids devolving into a backbiting, backstabbing, information-hoarding gang of frenemies.

GAMIFICATION AT CROSSFIT

CrossFit is a worldwide fitness brand with over ten thousand gyms (known as "boxes") offering high-intensity workouts incorporating diverse skills and movements. Workouts often include running, Olympic-style weight lifting, and gymnastics.[7] Many CrossFit boxes provide a great example of communities using gamification under healthy conditions. It's virtually impossible for any CrossFitter to dominate in all skills. Most workouts include several movements and are gamified so that athletes compete for the shortest time to complete all assigned repetitions or for completing the most counted repetitions (e.g., climbing up a rope) in an allowed time. At the end of each workout, participants post their score. Presumably one or more CrossFitters have completed the workout the fastest, lifted the most, and/or finished the most repetitions. At the end of each hour and day, it is easy to see who is top ranked for the workout.

In healthy gyms, the gamification works to bind the (CrossFit brand) community because the minimum game conditions are in place.

- Athletes can call out encouragement to one another, advise, and even physically lift up other athletes to support fitness improvement. (For example, a former US Marine once ran out to Charles on the course to run beside him and speed up Charles's pace when Charles wondered if he'd collapse. The physical outreach made Charles feel welcome and supported within the community despite his physical struggle.)

- "Winning" only means doing well that day, given an athlete's age, experience, and health. Athletes know that any given day's performance reflects earlier sleep, recovery, and nutrition influences. They also know that age, injury, and outside responsibilities (e.g., sick kids) mean that athletes arrive with differing potentials at the start.

- "Losing" the score ranking any day does not mean that an athlete isn't doing their best for that workout or is failing in their effort to meet fitness goals. In fact, respect is shared with athletes new to and struggling with the sport. Among members, it's widely known that it's easier for a practiced athlete to knock out twenty chin-ups than for a new athlete to do ten.

- Everyone who "plays" wins by exercising among friends and finding their limit for the day no matter their score or rank. This is as true for the first finisher as the last.

- Taking a "recovery day" (no strenuous activity) is always an option. All understand that athletes must respect their body limits and back off if that's what their healing needs.

- When an athlete breaks their own personal record (e.g., amount of weight lifted or shortest mile run time), all can celebrate the new gained strength. No one's performance erodes anyone else's success. There is no fundamental game reason to hope an athlete does poorly.

As a longtime CrossFitter, Charles has exercised alongside world-champion athletes and septuagenarian grandmothers. It is a magical thing to experience a place where world champions can and do genuinely call out encouragement to athletes struggling with the exercise of the day. It is inspiring to see new athletes visit and return because they feel welcome despite obesity, surgical recovery, and/or inexperience. This is possible because everyone who shows up understands that they win just by showing up. When just showing up, each athlete moves toward their purpose of building better fitness. In fact, the CrossFit culture uses a phrase often shared with new athletes: "The last person on the course beat everyone who stayed in bed."

Although the points show who ranks for any given day, they never matter in judging who athletes are being or how they're growing.

11

MEASUREMENT AND METRICS

We think of community measurements assessing three areas. Each area informs about a specific and important part of a brand community's success. Each area impacts on the success of the other areas. Or, simply put, failure in any one area will harm the others.

1. **Community activities:** experiences offered to members. These include programs, events, blog posts, trainings, celebrations, rituals, and so on.

2. **Community health:** Members' satisfaction that they feel supported, included and accepted.

3. **Organization outcomes:** Behavior, skill, or resource that supports organizational goals.[1]

This chapter will provide principles for how and what to measure. There is too much diversity among brands and communities to share exactly what you should measure at any time. You'll get to explore what's right to measure for your priorities.

Measuring Community Activities

Relationships just take time to develop. So, in early stages you can *measure the actions* to bring a community together instead of results. This can mean tracking actions that provide members value and a space that encourages connection. For example, it may be best to track how many invitations are made and how many events are offered. Leaders often need to offer many events to learn what appeals to members most or even at all.

Early-stage communities often don't yet create meaningful outcomes because they're too young. Moreover, even when your community does produce lots of outcomes, it's possible to lose community strength if insufficient attention is paid to the working relationships within the membership. In both cases, measuring community health separate from outcomes helps leadership work on ensuring durability so any good outcomes grow and persist.

We've mentioned several times that although there are many things we can measure quantitatively (motorcycles sold, event participants, contributing members, volunteer hours), all these measures can be manipulated by a community manager. For example, when you give away free pizza, more Oaklanders will show up. The stronger attendance doesn't mean you've got a stronger community. Although this is true, it's hard to build a strong community without events, places, invitations, and communication to bring people together. So measure what experiences are offered and the actions involved to offer them.

Measuring Community Health

There can be lots of activity (dancing, dumpling eating, or drumming) and not much community health. We can dance and eat around people we don't feel connected to, known by, or welcomed by. So collecting data that indicate members are connecting is also important. There is no single magical way to do this. A collection of proxy measurements can help us understand community health trends.

Three to five community health metrics are usually all leaders can track to inform them when and where problems need attention. Here are some metrics that in aggregate can help you see whether this is happening:

- *Gross size:* membership, visitors, attendees, readers.

- *Conversion rate:* how many people convert from visitors to members.

- *Churn:* how many members drop out.

- *Meaningful engagement:* Experiences that indicate participants develop or show mutual concern. What you measure will vary a lot depending on what your community does together. Look for how participants *contribute.* (Clicks don't mean much for community.)

To most accurately understand community health, qualitative research is by far the most important. Qualitative research investigates participants' reports on their own experience (feelings, motivations, perceptions) even though there's no standard for comparing their responses. Qualitative research often includes open-ended survey questions, focus-group conversations, in-depth interviews, direct observation, and the like.

Quantitative research (surveys with rating scales, for example) may help you recognize trends and surprises. For example, we can notice that more participants report feeling more connected after an event than reported at earlier events. Although we don't know what any one participant means by "feeling more connected," we can look for the trend as we create events.

Marcus Graham at Twitch knows that one of the brand's important competitive advantages is that the top two hundred broadcasters rightly *feel* connected with Twitch leadership and *feel* supported connecting with members. Twitch doesn't need ten thousand more broadcasters looking for free pizza; it wants the top two hundred broadcasters to feel so connected that they never consider leaving. Marcus knows that, at the end of the day, those relationships deliver both customers and growth. So Twitch asks important members how connected they feel.

We've seen many after-event surveys that ask about participants' satisfaction, enjoyment, or effectiveness. There's nothing wrong with great responses on these questions. However, if you're seeking to make participants feel connected, welcome, safe, enriched, seen, and/or appreciated, then they may not know what "effective" means for you. Participants' feeling "satisfied" by the experience may also mean very little if they feel neither connected nor appreciated.

Consider having members rate the following five statements on a Likert scale (from "Absolutely agree" to "Do not agree") and then track general responses over time so that you can learn how connections evolve among members.

- I believe others here care about me.
- I care about the others in this group.
- I think people here know who I really am.
- I believe that in a tough time, people here will help me.
- There are enough opportunities to connect and get to know others here.

Frankly, we've learned that most events are so unsatisfying and poorly thought out that participants are delighted when an event simply avoids being a boring, confusing, noisy, and/or aimless time. This is when your observation is important. You can notice whether, when, and why participants laugh, cry, hug, high-five, smile, cheer, dance, break out into long private conversations, trade contact information, share meals, and anything else that indicates that relationships are forming or deepening.

Twitch's Marcus Graham has access to participation tracking for over one hundred million users and still believes that measuring participation is always the hardest part. We agree with Marcus, who says that you can often see the importance and power of a community when things go bad (personal communication with Marcus Graham, April 2019). In bad times, we can see who supports one another, and how, when support is needed. But none of us want to create disasters as a way to see our community strength. Still, we need a way to see how things progress before bad times occur.

Measure Relationships

When it comes to community building (not necessarily promotion), we must understand that, in relationships (among friends, with your parents, with neighbors), successful growth is very often hard to measure. We agree with David Brooks's assertion that *"care is primarily qualitative. A community is healthy when relationships are felt deeply, when there are histories of trust, a shared sense of mutual belonging, norms of mutual commitment . . . and real affection from one another's heart and soul to another"*(emphasis ours).[2]

In chapter 1, we discussed the difficulty measuring qualitative experiences like mother's love quantitatively. We're revisiting the example for those who share this chapter as an excerpt and because the limits of qualitative measurements are important to this discussion. To understand how mutual concern (authentic community relationships) remains qualitative, and quantitatively elusive, consider again mother's love. We hope that you have experienced mother's love. With few exceptions, mothers care very deeply about the welfare of their children. Despite the fact that most of us believe that mother's love is critically important for many rewarding, satisfying, and enduring experiences in our families, it will be either hard or impossible for most of us to prove quantitatively that mother's love has grown or eroded in the past five years.

Measuring shared meals, phone calls, holiday visits, or any other activities may help you understand the relationship better. Looking at trends may inform your understanding of the relationship trend, but of course these measures will never accurately assess mother's love in your family (or ours), or even come close to it.

In relationship, the value or impact of each action, investment, or choice is hard to assess externally. The importance lives in individuals' experience. If you make the mistake of depending on external metrics to judge internal experience, then you're at real risk of being distracted by **surrogation**. Surrogation is the tendency for people "to confuse what's being measured for the metric being used."[3]

Wells Fargo provided a clear example of surrogation when it measured building long-lasting customer relationships by means of "cross-selling" metrics. Cross-selling for Wells Fargo meant that employees would sell more products to current customers. The result of using this metric, however, was that employees increased the number of new accounts by opening 3.5 million new customer accounts without customers' consent. Employees scored high on the metric, but they missed any truly helpful business goal. The company continues to pay for the mistake in at least a billion dollars in litigation costs and lost brand integrity.[4]

Community strategies can fall prey to surrogation, too. For example, your strategy may be to build deeper relationships between customers and the business, but if the only metric you use to measure progress is the number of messages sent from your employees to customers, your team may begin to send pointless messages to improve their numbers. This is especially true if their performance evaluation or even compensation is tied to these scores.

We all want to know when we're succeeding, and measurements that document progress are valuable to share with stakeholders. The difficulty comes when people who don't understand how communities work and succeed choose unhelpful metrics and then judge the success on those metrics using meaningless or misleading data.

At the end of the day, we don't think it is very important to measure mutual concern quantitatively. You know members care for one another when you see it show up as action. This can include volunteering, donating, attending events, or personally checking in on one another. This is often something that outsiders cannot see or feel.

Regularly Survey Self-Reported Measures of Belonging

We can and should collect subjective (qualitative) measurements of belonging. Learn whether your efforts are working or need a change by surveying whether and how much your members feel connected. No one makes all the right decisions from the beginning. Discover what will work by getting the feedback.

As an example, when discussing Airbnb's community investment, Guy Michlin, head of Airbnb host success and community, explained that the company both wants to know whether the events are helping build community and wants to make the research as burden free for participants as possible. Airbnb knows it's critically important that its hosts around the world remain connected to the company, because they provide all the experiences and accommodations for customers. So Airbnb creates dozens of events around the world that facilitate hosts' connecting with one another and sharing best practices and learned lessons. And after much research, Guy's team has settled on asking hosts two qualitative questions that tell them enough to guide the company's work (personal communication with Guy Michlin, July 2019):

1. How connected do you feel to other hosts?

2. How supported do you feel by Airbnb?

Measuring Outcomes for a Brand

The first step to measuring outcomes for your brand is to determine the outcomes you want. What you measure will of course be informed by the goals you want the community to support. In part 1, we listed seven organizational goals that communities can support. All members can't deliver on all organizational goals every day. You'll have to choose priorities.

Measuring community brand support success can become a very sophisticated and resource-intensive project. We'll just introduce some fundamental terms and tools. You can use them to help choose what and how you will measure for your goals.

When getting started, pick *one* of the goal areas and as few metrics within that area as possible that will still inform you that value is being delivered. You can always change your focus later when experience reveals new wisdom. Tracking and responding to too many metrics distracts and pulls attention from the actual work of building a community to critical mass stage.

You can imagine a community manager at Acme customer service brand focusing on improving the outcomes for all of the following areas to reinforce customer support alone:

- Reduce time lag to customer questions
- Increase in customer satisfaction scores
- Improvement in individual ratings of response quality
- Number of provided answers
- Reduction in new incoming questions
- Reduction in other support resources used
- Lowered staff time spent in customer support
- Increased product use

All of these are important, but monitoring every item on this list would make anyone dizzy and frustrated. Just measuring these outcomes could (and should) require an experienced full-time staff, and interpreting the data would be an additional challenge. Most people don't have the time or resources to monitor so much while building a community. Without that staff support, the list would be more distraction than tool.

Find a proxy for the impact you seek (data entered, volunteer days, people aware of your work). Measure things that your community can deliver *and control*. If, for example, you measure data entered by volunteers, the numbers can mislead if the community has no control over gathering the source data.

The following are common helpful metrics to review among community members:

- **Customer retention.** This may be the most important metric to watch because keeping a customer is five to twenty-five times cheaper than gaining a new one. This metric measures who returns to repeatedly purchase/experience your brand.[5]

- **Number of new customers.** The number of new customers in any given time period.

- **Customer satisfaction rating (CSAT).** This is a measure of how satisfied customers are with your brand experience. Typically, this is rated on a Likert scale from "Very dissatisfied" to "Very satisfied."

- **Net promoter score (NPS).** This is a proxy measurement for future growth that compares the number of brand promoters to the number of detractors.

- **Customer lifetime value (CLTV).** This is the prediction of the net profit of an entire relationship with any customer.

- **Change in sales revenue.** This is the increase or decrease of revenue in any given time period.

- **Cost savings.** This measures costs decreased because of strategy changes. For brand community leaders in customer service and talent retention, this may be the only metric they care about when considering community investment costs. This metric is often unimportant for marketing goals.

We've heard too many times that many brand executives will make community investment decisions only using measures that indicate what investments directly serve organizational goals (outcomes). There is no problem with measuring to ensure an investment is succeeding. The problem comes when focus on one area leads to decline in the other areas that shape outcomes.

Several internationally influential practitioners in world-famous, well-resourced companies shared that measuring the importance of and ROI for brand community efforts remains the most difficult part of their community building. Large companies hire PhD researchers to handle this. Most organizations lack the resources to hire advanced research teams or the capacity to track sufficient member activity.

Advocating for Community

The biggest challenge shared among the brand community executives we interviewed was advocating for brand community investment within their organizations. Such advocacy is difficult when success depends on members' *internal* experiences, yet organizational leaders demand quantified *external* metrics. Even among the leadership of global brand communities that clearly serve brand goals (including Etsy, Twitch, Yelp, Patagonia, and Airbnb), executives believe there still remain unmeasured benefits and value to their organizations.

Obviously, growing member numbers is good for audience growth. What else can help advocacy?

Compare Members and Nonmembers

One strategy is to compare the behavior and outcomes of members (variable) and nonmembers (control). Unfortunately, this strategy has an inherent problem in that the observed variable (members) has an inherent bias toward activity. For example, Sephora learned that its community members spend many times more than nonmembers, but we don't know whether big spenders are just more attracted to the brand community. It's possible that they *may* outspend the same without membership engagement.

Of course, this seems unlikely because an enthusiastic customer, engaged and well informed on exciting opportunities, seems more likely to buy more. This makes intuitive sense, but we simply don't know.

To account for this, you can use a "synthetic control." This means you find people who aren't participating in your community and also have profiles similar to those of your members. You may have to compare specific members and nonmembers (e.g., compare a Seattle-based author member and a Seattle-based author nonmember). Then you can track any outcome differences you like (e.g., purchases, volunteering, advocacy).

By any standard, this is very hard to do, and to get any good data will almost certainly require the full-time attention of at least one highly skilled person (likely with a graduate degree in research). We only know of well-resourced organizations that do this.

You can find more discussion on goal-specific measurement in appendix A: Brand Goal Practices.

Consider the Counterfuture

Many brands succeed just fine without brand community investment. We support this if the community will just become a distraction. Some organizations, in contrast, understand that a strong brand community is core to their competitiveness or survival (e.g., Etsy, Yelp, Salesforce, and Twitch).

You can think through and articulate the predictable scenario—the counterfuture—if your brand *doesn't* invest in community. Start by answering questions like these:

How will we attract the best talent? (by bidding war?)

How will we gain access to innovative input?

How will we distinguish ourselves from competitors?

How will we educate the market on sophisticated innovations?

How will customers learn to use our product without our help every day?

INTERNAL ADVOCACY EXAMPLES
YELP

Yelp's Nish Nadaraja noticed that other review websites incentivized reviewers with rewards, including gift certificates. He knew that this strategy could generate many, but not deep, reviews. He also noticed that these competitor websites could generate many more reviews than Yelp, but then the contributions decreased sharply. Further, on all the other sites, the honesty of the reviews was always in doubt. Reviewers only participated while they were (externally) rewarded. Nish knew that incentives could be used, but that they only delivered a quick action or reaction, not durable relationships.

Yelp committed to the Yelp Elite reviewers community as "a long-term play." Nish knew that Yelp's competitive advantage would be the quality of honest reviews. Readers needed to recognize that they were learning from genuine enthusiasts who were honestly celebrating opportunities in their area.

The community building would help Yelp (1) attract and (2) retain high-level reviewers involved in the company goals over a long term. It also (3) presented a barrier for any competition who also wanted those reviewers.

According to Nish, in the beginning it was hard to watch competitors rack up more reviews while he trusted that honest community investment would deliver better results in the long run. Of course, history has proven him right. He said that Yelp eventually became a place where visitors knew they would find fanatics sharing their favorite finds.

Although gross review numbers were important, in the beginning Nish didn't have good review volume to show other executives. He tracked indicators that the Elite members were forming relationships. At every event, he explicitly encouraged members to share contact information and connect outside Yelp events. Then his team could notice on the online platform how many people connected through the platform after an event and how many events they created for themselves.

Nish said that, without the supportive reviewer community, Yelp might have followed the well-documented trend of other review sites. And, he added, Yelp might no longer exist.

SALESFORCE

Earlier we discussed Salesforce's experience in its early days when the company was unable to adequately understand how its customers wanted the products developed. Part of its now proven solution was to form a users' community called IdeaExchange. The community helped managers distill what was most important for their customers. We learned through interviews that one of the keys to success is that cofounder Parker Harris mandated that managers share how the community "gets a say" on each new product release. This ensured that Salesforce's products remained relevant for its customers. The counterfuture was for Salesforce to largely guess what customers wanted and then backtrack (a lot) when it guessed wrong. Instead, the company dominated its industry for years.

ETSY

Etsy wanted a strong community to transform passive marketplace users into allies, advocates, advisers, and influencers. In aggregate, the community brought like-minded members into the work of supporting "makers." Danielle Maveal noted that the community made the original small start-up team feel bigger and facilitated bigger impact through its members' commitment (personal communication with Danielle Maveal, September 2019).

Further, when Etsy started, many crafters were not selling their work online. For Etsy to succeed, the brand needed to build trust with makers who provided the inventory in Etsy's two-sided business model (sellers and buyers).

When makers did connect as makers supporting one another, many helped market Etsy in meaningful ways, including creating craft shows, hosting onboarding workshops for new Etsy sellers, and solving member problems before Etsy customer service could respond.

Danielle added that when working with brands other than Etsy, she now creates an event series with the goal of increasing both positive sentiment about the brand and "connection and support among members." She then watches participant progress and performance metrics:

Does their activity on the website or forums increase?

Do they read more on the blog (reflecting more interest in the brand)?

Do they start their own volunteer community group?

When advocating for investment in a brand community, she shares the feedback, ideas, and excited communication among users. She then explains how the relationships affect the bottom line by reducing support costs, launching new programs and tools, and even inspiring internal employees. She can share with senior executives how community membership increases loyalty, reduces customer churn, increases positive brand opinion, and increases user value. She's seen that participating community members are more brand loyal than nonparticipants.

Highlighting member communication, she can show that members in a strong community feel happy and that the community's happy participants both "put up with more bumps in the road" and help those around them.

LAST WORD

Well, respect to you for following this work to the end. Most of what we've shared in this book wasn't invented by us. We're only the messengers and translators for insights gathered by elders over generations. Please do them all proud by taking their wisdom into the world.

The only communities all of us want to commit to and invest in include some generosity. In any worthwhile community, we believe that others will be generous with us when we need it and, even better, when we don't need it. In turn, most of us want to generously contribute to others in some way.

This is to say that if you're reading this book to bring people together, your community will only work because there is some generosity built into all the structure, vision, planning, and rules. Further, none of your planning works unless you invite others into generosity. Invitations are so critical, yet so many people skip them and then miss their importance.

We're pessimistic about loneliness and disconnection diminishing in our era. We're optimistic about the people who learn to bring others together and take action in their own way.

If you're stuck or afraid, remember that community always starts with an invitation. Community and belonging are created one invitation at a time. Humbly invite someone you want to know into an intimate conversation where you have the space, conditions, and permission to talk about things important to you.

It may go poorly or well. No matter—every minute you'll be building your muscles to connect people. And for that, we'll be *very* proud of you.

Bringing new people together never goes as well as we want it to. It usually takes (much) longer than we expect. Sometimes people don't seem to care. So we're sharing some wisdom from our heroes that reminds us that failure is OK and that the work remains important.

> All of us are in the same boat,
> all living in a world we never dreamt of,
> all sometimes losing our way,
> as we try to keep the world going
> until we have reared a generation
> who know better how to live in it.
> —Margaret Mead[1]

> You may have to face the fact that your work
> will be apparently worthless
> and achieve no result at all,
> if not perhaps results opposite to what you expect . . .
> Gradually you struggle less and less for an idea,
> and more and more for specific people.
> The range tends to narrow down,
> but it gets much more real.
> In the end, it is the reality of personal relationships that saves everything.
> —Fr. Thomas Merton[2]

We work with our teams to create materials, workshops, and experiences that embolden leaders to connect people important to them. We only know it's working when you tell us. You can contact us and get free worksheets at our websites: CarrieMelissa.com and CharlesVogl.com.

Appendix A

BRAND GOAL PRACTICES

Here you will find a deeper discussion of principles that can help a community serve particular brand goals.

Innovation Community Practices

If you want your brand community to support innovation powerfully, you must heed these principles.

Make Exclusive Invitations

The innovation community is an inner ring. Not everyone in the world or even in a given fan community gets invited or has an equal voice in the innovation conversation. Helpful ideas can come from unexpected people, but too many voices all treated equally will overwhelm designers, leaders, and strategists. In addition, not everyone is equally knowledgeable or experienced in the challenges at hand. When it comes to product development, outdoor apparel company Patagonia should be listening to mountain climbers, not necessarily leadership book writers (even if we like and buy their fleeces).

When focusing a community to support innovation, selecting even fewer than twenty members into an inner ring to provide the most prominent voices can work great. This manageable number reduces the noise and distraction that comes with too many voices collaborating on a new project. These inner-ring voices may bring ideas from obscure corners when helpful. You may consider inviting only your most loyal, dedicated, and creative members.

Some brands have millions of people already connected to them. Where there are many voices that could be relevant to the early development of the platform, there should be clear criteria for who's invited to codevelop. In the early stages, trying to create something that "is just right for everybody" typically leads to at best mediocre results (lowest common denominator) and at worst to paralysis. Choose whom the platform should best serve in the beginning and give yourself permission to develop it later with user feedback in time.

Offer Direct Contact with Elders

No one likes to share thoughtful feedback and then wonder whether it was heard, considered, or effective at all. This is especially true for the most insightful, knowledgeable, creative, and valuable members. Moreover, if innovation means understanding something in a new way or addressing challenges differently, participants will need to easily discuss nuance and questions with leadership.

Leaders must create a feedback channel with direct contact with community elders (authority). If you want your community to influence innovation because members have insight and perspective that helps, *they must have direct access to the people who can use the help for real-world results.* This may mean getting them in a room with product managers, vice presidents of community or chief executives, so that they see that their input goes where it makes a difference. Anything less and you risk looking, rightly or wrongly, as though your brand just doesn't value their participation.

Make a Public or In-Community Acknowledgment

Whether they are paid or are volunteers, members participate because they care. Their internal motivation drives the relationship. Honor this by creating a way to acknowledge their work as a special contribution. There is an almost infinite number of ways to do this. Gifts, tokens, public recognition, special events, special access, shared meals, and retreats all count. Make sure you use at least one.

It is common to create a symbol or special title, or to provide a special token to represent their contribution and inner-ring membership. Yelp has its Yelp Elite, Twitch names Partners, and Harley-Davidson issues special patches for riders' "colors" (emblems that typically get placed on leather riding vests and jackets).

Advocacy within the Organization

Organizational senior leadership could be overwhelmed with a long list of requests and changes coming from people they don't know, even if those very people are closest to the brand's needs and problems. We've learned that when a suggestion gets to brand decision-makers without context, the importance or priority rank of that suggestion can get lost in the communication. This means that brand community members must take in the innovation feedback from members and effectively (1) interpret it, (2) evaluate its relevance, and then (3) advocate for the innovation to those who have the authority to make change. If all else goes well but this last step fails, then most of the innovation support your brand community can offer will evaporate. No one likes to help think through changes if changes don't get made.

Here we'll share that in its early days, Salesforce offered a way for members to suggest and vote on requested features. This informed a priority list for managers. Further, executives ensured that a meaningful portion of all product releases were sourced from member requests. Speaking with members, noting the suggestions that garnered high votes, and reading comments among members informed executives even in the earliest stages of product development. Jennifer Sacks, a Salesforce executive, told us that the market-dominating products could never have been created without their user community's contribution.

As Salesforce grew into a worldwide firm, the original suggestion and voting system became overwhelmed. Managers could not respond to or synthesize so much communication. In response, the company launched a world tour so that staff could listen to members directly before redesigning the IdeaExchange. After visiting twenty-two cities, twelve countries, and four continents, Jennifer Sacks brought back ideas and feedback gleaned from hundreds of conversations with members. She advocated for the most important needs directly to product managers. As a result, member contribution made the newest product rollout radically different than what managers predicted before asking the community. To date, Salesforce has sourced more than three thousand implemented features from IdeaExchange. The company continues as a world industry leader (personal communication with Jennifer Sacks, September, 2019).

Talent Recruitment and Retention Recruitment Practices

You can refer to *The Art of Community* for a deep dive into principles that support the feeling of belonging in community. Here we highlight four critical practices to keep people connected.

Exhibit and Present Explicit Core Values

We all want to believe that our work is important and makes a difference. We know that people in community want to be connected and to progress in becoming who they want to be. So you need to ensure that there are opportunities for members to make a difference according to values that inspire them together. This includes offering training, opportunities for action, and enriching discussion connected to inspiring real (not pretend) values.

The Patagonia outdoor clothing company is among our favorite examples of a company that has invested in making the brand values explicit and then offering its staff opportunities to make a difference accordingly. The company's mission statement is "We're in business to save our home planet."

Patagonia makes its environmental protection values present in many ways. For example, the company uses its retail stores regularly as venues for environmental protection nonprofits and individuals to hold events such as film screenings, speaker events, and trainings. In addition, the company took headquarters employees outside to smell and touch cotton fields and dirt so all could understand the importance of shifting production to organic cotton. And each store has a grants budget to support nonprofits of its choosing.

Vincent Stanley, Patagonia's director of philosophy, said that the staff feel ownership of their work and the responsibility to make products safer and less environmentally destructive. When asked about recruiting talent, he laughed. Attracting talent has never been a problem, in part because people come and stay to share the company's real values. He said, "Applications are astronomical" (personal communication with Vincent Stanley, June 2019).

Celebrate

Celebration is a way to acknowledge how we change, grow, and succeed. If others see us as people (and not just as our service), they notice (and acknowledge) how we change and matter.

If you're not scheduling significant time and resources to celebrating, (1) people will notice, and (2) you'll get results that are entirely consistent with your inattention.

You may not need to call your best friend on every holiday and their birthday, but if you're calling them on none of those occasions, they'll notice. The neglect will also radically change your relationship with them.

The most important celebrations within communities are campfire events, discussed earlier in this book. There's nothing wrong with big spectacle events. They may even provide fantastic memories to share for years. But campfire events should be far more numerous. The members acknowledged must see that the people who know and care about them notice how they're changing and growing.

Tell and Invite Stories

The stories principle is so important that Charles wrote a whole book (*Storytelling for Leadership*) about how leaders can and should tell stories that matter. For the stories principle to work, leadership must create opportunities for members to both share and learn stories about experiences that formed or shaped them. These don't have to revolve around professional development or the most profound experiences. Members in community want to be accepted for their whole selves. We all have stories about how we formed our familial, career, philanthropic, spiritual, athletic, academic, and civic selves. If members don't have a venue, the time, and permission to share stories, then they likely aren't sharing them, and the potential to share identification and belonging is wasted.

Stories can be shared and learned in person or online. Which is better? Both.

Extend Opportunities to Grow (How Members Want to Grow)

No one remains committed to a community if it doesn't help them grow into who they want to be. If you want your critical people to stick around, you must ensure that they have a way to grow.

The inner rings in a mature community reflect a member's growth. In other words, you can't join an inner ring for mountain-crossing cyclists until you've grown strong enough to join cyclists crossing a mountain range.

Leadership must ensure that there are inner rings for members to aspire to join, and elders willing and available to support the journey. If you don't provide both, members will look for someone (or something) that can.

Customer Retention Practices

To ensure meaningful engagement, apply the following three principles in your community.

Hold Regular and Accessible Real-World Gatherings

Regular gatherings provide an opportunity for groups to grow intimate connections and feel supported close to home.

There is no substitute for bringing people together to meet one another and experience a space with shared values and purpose. This is so important that even Twitch, with more than 150 million online users each month, still gathers members in over forty cities each year for in-person meetings. Airbnb, with more than two million hosts, creates over one hundred gathering events each year around the world. It hosts large summits (paramount events) on three continents each year.

Invite Participation in Two Ways

1. Ensure that there is a venue where participants are *invited to share about themselves* in a safe place. There they must experience being accepted for who they are and for their shared values.

2. Ensure that there is a venue where *participants can contribute to (support) others* within the community if they choose. Members often look for a way to "give back" or "make a difference." If you don't give them that opportunity, they'll experience pain. Some (or many) will seek a better way to contribute—outside your community.

Provide Opportunities to Grow

Ensure that there is both opportunity and invitation for members to grow in some way they want. This can include teaching technical skills or, even better, supporting internal maturation. Often this can mean offering access to elders who can create experiences and share hard-won wisdom. Brand communities are extremely varied. Any way that your participants want to grow and you support them counts. In time, they'll be happy to tell you what makes a difference so that you can offer more of it.

This principle also means that we must be intentional in telling members that there are opportunities to grow more. A common way is to offer advanced classes, workshops, trips, or meetups that allow members to connect with more advanced practitioners once they have achieved a required level.

For example, Airbnb's "experiences community leaders" get special access to executives, research, and trainings that help them be better hosts and community leaders in life. Trainings are offered live online on topics including creating events and rituals, research techniques, and video production.

Marketing Practices for Community

To protect and grow a community, two strategies effectively promote success.

Offer Privileges to Community Members (Actual Members)

Actual members who have passed through a visitor stage and been approved by gatekeepers receive reserved privileges connected to the community purpose and values. These privileges can take almost any form. Special access is nearly always popular. This may include access to decision-makers within the brand, to inner rings inside the community, and to special help when they need it.

Fun examples we know of include HOG leaders visiting with Harley engineers and family of the founders at Harley Officers' Training. Similarly, Yelp Elite members are invited to many secret events at hot new venues.

These privileges are never, never transactional. They're offered as a privilege of membership, in recognition of contribution to the community, or as acknowledgment of shared values. The privileges honor members for who they are as people and members, not strictly for what they've done or how much they've bought.

Name Brand Ambassadors

Brand ambassadors constitute an inner ring within both the organization and the community. (See *The Art of Community* chapter on inner rings for the role of inner rings in communities.) There can be several types of inner rings—for example, for high-performing (elite), new, or specialized members. Other participants are told that the ambassadors are special (because they are).

One way to communicate ambassadors' special status is by bestowing a title. You don't have to call these members *ambassadors*, as Lululemon does. You can use any term that indicates specialness, such as *partner* (Twitch), *council member* (Fitbit), or *MVP* (Salesforce). Regardless of their title, the actual ambassador community members demonstrate with action the core values of their respective greater brand communities.

As part of their privileges, brand ambassadors typically receive *access to others like them and, importantly, to leaders within the organization whom they admire.* This means that when someone meets a brand ambassador, they're also meeting a member who can presumably influence brand leadership. This is part of what makes privileged membership special.

The best brand ambassadors can and do directly communicate with one another. They do so because they're part of both the greater community and an inner ring within it. Leadership can facilitate this connection through introductions and by creating shared intimate experiences.

One of the privileges of ambassadorship is *invitations to restricted shared experiences.* The events help ambassadors connect to support one another and help them feel that they're special to the brand and the community. Patagonia brings ambassadors to its California coast headquarters to connect with senior brand leadership and recreate together over fun meals.

As with any welcome into a special group, providing tokens makes a big difference. Ambassadors should get at least one kind of token that is available only to their inner ring.

SALESFORCE

Salesforce uses an ambassador principle with its MVPs, an inner ring of the volunteer Trailblazer Community that helps customers use Salesforce products. Approximately 250 MVP titles are awarded each year out of over one million Trailblazers. The designation is a profound honor. Each member is reevaluated each year. Erica Kuhl, former Salesforce VP of community, shared that the MVPs support thousands of other Salesforce customers each year. The designation is "about people truly caring for one another" (personal communication with Erica Kuhl, August 2019).

To support these ambassadors, Salesforce has organized an MVP Care Team. Salesforce offers all MVPs special access and experiences, including these:

- Induction ceremony
- Exclusive party for connecting members

- Front-row seats to Salesforce events
- Support for life events (e.g., tragedies, health challenges)
- Celebrations for happy life events (e.g., new babies and weddings)

Measure Marketing with Community

There are a number of metrics often used to measure whether a community is in fact serving brand marketing (promotion). Note that marketing efforts without community bonds can often deliver good promotion. An example is rewarding customers for referrals (which promotes, but doesn't support relationships). This means that marketing metrics don't necessarily tell us whether the internal community is strong. We recommend that you consider the metrics we discuss here.

Track Referrals from Brand Ambassadors (When Possible)

Not all new customers referred from brand ambassadors will get credited to the ambassadors. This may be because the ambassadors are representing the brand community everywhere they go. Explore how you can learn when sales or growth can be credited to specific ambassadors. Some organizations do this by creating special referral links for ambassadors to share. Some track customer growth and product use after ambassador-hosted events. As long as the ambassadors attract attention, serve members, and represent the brand's values, they play an important role in making an authentic community effective.

Said differently, as long as ambassadors are offering your kind of water to thirsty rhinos, they're doing their work.

Measure Content Created by Members

As we've said, not all content strengthens a community. Measure only the content that you know serves members' needs and growth and that supports participants' connecting. (Solving problems counts; vacation photos usually don't.) Meaningful and helpful member-created content is your watering-hole water. Anyone who makes your watering hole more attractive is helping your brand reach the people important for success.

Measure Traffic to Member-Created Content

If we want to know whether our watering hole is attractive and delivering life-giving water, then we want to see who and how many are coming for the water. When you've got many members contributing, you may have different flavors of water (in a good way). You can measure the traffic to the water offered.

BuzzFeed is an online news and entertainment outlet that has been ranked in the top three hundred web traffic sites.[1] Among the drivers for visitors are the entertaining quizzes, which invite players to answer fun questions about themselves. The company organized a social media group called BuzzFeed Contributors, a community of volunteer writers, many of them still in school. BuzzFeed learned that a single teen contributor in the community was the second-highest driver of traffic for BuzzFeed worldwide. By that contributor's count, she created 692 quizzes in one year alone.[2]

BuzzFeed made many regrettable business and staffing choices that eventually led to the layoff of hundreds of employees and significant visitor loss. We also think it's disgraceful for a for-profit brand to rely on volunteer labor for all (or nearly all) offered content. That said, the success of the BuzzFeed Contributor community in bringing in traffic highlights how dramatically a supported community can provide resources that draw others. Leaders can measure the draw of community-produced content to note one way that the community serves brand goals.

Measure Membership Purchasing

Last, we can measure whether, when, and how much members purchase. For many organizations, this can validate the investment to build a community. For example, earlier we mentioned that Sephora's research revealed that its online community members spent twice as much as the average Sephora customer. Sephora online community "superfans" spend ten times more than the average.

Remember that marketing is only one area in which communities can support an organization and that the selling can never usurp the service to members. Otherwise the effort will collapse.

Practices for a Support Community

There are several principles that particularly help support-focused brand communities succeed.

Build a Strong Online Platform that Facilitates In-Person Gathering

By facilitating an online venue for engagement and connection, you enable members to participate and grow anywhere and anytime. We see this in the robust online platforms set up by global tech companies such as Salesforce, Apple, and Dropbox. Customers can go to online brand platforms to find each other and offer volunteer help around the world.

That said, the rule that in-person meetings enrich a community still applies. If you believe that your brand-support community is valuable, then investing in physical meetups can strengthen *everything* created online. As we've mentioned, Harley-Davidson sells vehicles, Yelp hosts online reviews, and both sponsor in-person events in many time zones. Spotify, among the biggest music-streaming brands with more than one hundred million subscribers, flies its top community "Rockstars" to Sweden once a year to connect with one another and with the company CEO.[3]

Provide a Forum for Help Requests and Responses

You must create a forum where those seeking help can get help! Passing out a contact list is *never* enough. (Unfortunately, we see this all the time.) As always, at least one elder keeps the forum space safe for all activities and participants.

Acknowledge and Appreciate Contributors

There must be regular and meaningful acknowledgment and appreciation from elders in a way that both protects and honors contributing participants' internal motivation. Anything that commodifies the relationship is toxic.

Connect Community Contribution with Official Brand Staff

The support experience must be integrated so that the brand's staff can monitor how well the community serves members' needs. The staff must respond when support goes poorly, and *acknowledge when it goes well.* A build-it-and-forget-it model never works over the long term.

Weekly or (at least) monthly "share-back" meetings are necessary. Each side—both brand leadership and community leadership—can share how evolution and purpose progress.

Provide a Venue for Sharing More Widely (Off Topic)

Offer opportunities (with both space and time) where participants can share about experiences, identities, concerns, and interests outside the strict brand experience. Without this, you will create a mirage community.

Focus on as Few Metrics as Possible

An intense focus on what matters to your community—for example, average time to first response and average time to receiving help or a solution—helps leadership get relevant feedback on program success. We like the way Adrian Speyer, who leads community at online community software provider Vanilla Forums, put it: "If your community is focused on supporting your customers, you want to focus on metrics relevant to support. Don't measure how many puppy photos get shared. Choose a core metric that reflects actual community impact for your organization. A good example is measuring how quickly community members get the right answers they need. Everything else is a distraction" (personal communication with Adrian Speyer, April 2019).

Keep It Current and Relevant

Past community conversations become antiquated and unhelpful quickly, as products, uses, and users change. Leadership teams must keep support documentation relevant and current. The resources can and should be offered as a reference for customers so that members can avoid having to answer repeat questions.

Although it's the fantasy of nearly every CEO to inspire millions of customers to handle customer service, please know that this community goal just isn't a good fit for many brands. If you fail to make this work, it could be that you're asking a turtle to run a marathon for which you're unwilling to train either the turtle or yourself. (In other words, customers can't do it just because you don't want to invest appropriately.)

We know of two different finance companies we'll refer to collectively as Moneybirds. They tried to set up an online community so that customers would help one another with investment, administrative, and legal advice related to money. No surprise to many of us, their customers didn't want to sit at home and coach others about money confusion, frustration, and ignorance. As Shira Levine, who has grown many brand communities, put it simply, "Financial services are difficult. People don't want to help other novices figure out their money problems for free" (personal communication with Shira Levine, April 2019).

Practices for Supporting Movement Communities

Segmenting refers to finding different ways that participants can contribute and then providing inner-ring experiences so that they can connect and collaborate within their specialized segment. In other words, programmers want to connect with programmers, and event producers with event producers.

Segmentation is not a tool for manipulation. It allows participants with specific shared skills and values to connect more intimately and to together explore the ways that help them grow. This is particularly important in advocacy movements because the work may (almost certainly) go on for years. To develop the competency of volunteers and partners in their contributing skills, and to ensure that they feel connected over an extended time, it is imperative that they get connected with a segment that is relevant to their growth and intimate enough for developing friendships.

It is also both important and necessary that *segmented members are invited and included in more-general events.* Inner rings live inside a community boundary, not separate from it.

Participants can get segmented into more than one segment. Charles, for example, can easily get segmented into both writer and event-producing inner rings. Carrie will fit in both entrepreneur and organizational strategist segments.

The segments aren't used to separate people for the sake of separation. They're used to support participants in finding others in the movement with whom they share even greater similarities and to enable the development of more intimate experiences with a smaller group.

Segmentation must also remain dynamic. This means that once a member is in a segment (say, a wine-drinkers segment), they can change to another segment (say, iced-tea drinkers). Just as people's changing lives may make them want to find a new community (or leave an old one), so their lives may lead them to want to move from one segment to another.

There is no magic formula for segmenting. You'll have to explore what will work best for your members. In a political campaigning community, for example, there are several kinds of segments to consider.

- *Location.* Participants are physically near one another.
- *Issue.* Members collaborate on a focused issue.
- *Identity.* Members who identify in a particular way (as immigrants, lawyers, survivors, etc.) are together.
- *Overall leadership.* This is a group of those who will train others.

Grow Segment Leaders

All growing communities need elders, and each segment will need some sort of leadership (formal or informal). Jeremy Heimans, cofounder of Purpose, and his coauthor Henry Timms, CEO of the 92nd Street Y, recommend inviting new leaders to ascend in cohorts.[4] This means that as new leaders begin their training, they grow together with peers as opposed to learning alongside others at very different levels. This approach enables them to experience training at an appropriate level for them at the right time. Senior trainees forced to unnecessarily revisit fundamentals can become bored (and might grow disruptive). Forcing new people to go through material that is over their head only overwhelms them.

When appropriate, you can eventually invite mature leaders to train future leaders. This creates a self-sustaining organization that supports leadership development *after* having invested in foundational training.

Once you have sufficient numbers of trained leaders, *then* segment your member-filled inner rings in whatever way works best so that each is led by a leader, subleaders, and moderators.

Create a Platform with Necessary Opportunities

A platform to connect participants works best if it can accommodate several needs. If it misses *any* of the needs we've listed here, then the platform is at risk of failure because participants will seek a solution outside the community spaces. In other words, the following opportunities must be available on the platform.

- *Create endless segments and subgroups.* Segments help members find intimate experiences and develop deeper connections not possible if every experience is in a big crowd or filled with new introductions.
- *Elect leaders.* There must be a way for members to step forward and take on more responsibility. This is their way of contributing. Most

movements need leadership to come forward at least for moderation, event planning, content creating, and outreach.

- *Organize events.* Without events, there's little fun and few invitations to gather. Make sure there are many fun events!

- *Offer public recognition of leadership (e.g., badges).* This alerts new members whom to seek out for guidance and training. Without leadership designations, finding a way to participate remains confusing and time intensive. Members will wonder who's in charge of creating, leading, and managing teams.

- *Track member and volunteer retention.* If you don't know who is remaining, then you don't know whom you can count on and whom you're losing. In every movement we've looked at, getting membership to show up when needed is critical for success. Learn who your real members are. Just a list of email addresses never counts.

Appendix B

WORKSHEETS

You will find worksheets here that can be used to start a conversation with your leadership to clarify how you will suitably apply brand community principles to grow the right community for you.

Obviously there is too much diversity among organizations and goals for any static tool to serve all. You can start by reflecting on foundational ideas to ensure that you are building toward something that's suitable for your vision.

Worksheet 1: Selecting Founding Members

You start a community with a foundation of only a few members.

If you already have dedicated founding members in your community but haven't recognized them with such a title, then it's never too late to express appreciation for their commitment.

The following sets of questions can start a conversation about how to recognize ideal founding members. You can then choose whom to invite because they closely match what you seek. (Note that the unskilled choose members first and then the criteria.)

BEHAVIORS

- If you already have a platform or group, what are the relevant activities of the founding members?

- If you don't yet have a platform, what do your ideal founding members already do (in their free time or otherwise) related to the purpose of your organization?

- Have they shown willingness to participate in conversations about founding a community?

PERSONALITY

- What are the ideal personalities you seek?

  Some groups only seek hard-core competitors. Some seek patient contemplatives. Of course you can include many kinds of personalities. Just consider what kinds of personalities you envision will fit best.

AVAILABILITY

- What is the ideal availability for these founding members? (Daily, weekly, monthly or less?)
- When do they need to gather to participate in activities?

  Availability is influenced by a lot of factors (e.g., caregiving, studies, and work commitments). Consider what level of availability will be required to meet member needs.

INTERESTS

- What are the ideal interests of your founding members?

PURPOSE

- Do they understand the community purpose?
- Do they want to commit to supporting the purpose?
- How are they willing to support the purpose?

INVITATION AND COMMITMENT

- How will you invite them to join the founding members group?
- What are the steps for joining?

  You can consider an application, an initiation meeting, volunteer activity, or anything else.

- What do you expect these members to do as you start or reboot a community? (Note: It must be in line with both their needs and yours.)
- How will you inform them of what is expected of them?

Consider these actions to convene your first founding members:

- Name up to ten people (max) who fit the description you seek. Then consider additional people who fit much of the description and may serve as backup members.

_____

_____

_____

_____

_____

Ensure that you follow at least these steps in connecting with prospective founding members:

1. You contact prospective candidates to discuss a possible invitation for founding membership.

2. You and the prospective candidates engage in an individual orienting call or meeting to clarify expectations.

3. Invitees confirm commitment (opt in).

4. You send a formal invitation to each candidate, and it is accepted.

Worksheet 2: Selecting and Training Leaders

To reach critical mass, you must identify and train community leaders. Look for leaders who want to serve the community (not only themselves). You'll recognize these leaders because their actions reflect the community core values and purpose.

As communities grow and mature, new leadership must develop for community scale and enduring relevance.

The questions here can start a conversation to identify members appropriate for a training plan.

SELECTION

- How many leaders do you need for your current size? (In any early community, you'll need at least one leader for every ten members.)

- What actions should these members have already taken in your community to show their commitment?

INVITATION

- How will you choose leaders (invitations, nominations, or other selections)?

- What criteria must they meet to qualify?

- Will you need an application to participate?

- Who will reach out to candidates?

- What training will leaders need in order to gain appropriate skills?

- When and how will you connect them with other leaders?

- What elder will connect with them to support the training?

- How will you let them know if/when they cannot continue as leaders for any reason?

- How will you acknowledge leaders now and in the future?

- How will you offer transparent communication with these leaders?

Worksheet 3: Campfire Experiences

The following conditions are essential to a successful campfire experience:

- *Proximity (close space) for speaking to one another.* Participants must share a conversation-supporting space (a restaurant table, a beach circle, an online chat platform). All must be close enough to see, hear, and make eye contact with one another.

- *Permission to contribute and participate.* Participants must perceive explicit or implicit permission to talk with one another. Watching a presentation is the opposite of being given permission to talk.

- *Conditions.* There must be time when participants can freely speak in conversation. Distractions must be handled. This includes noise, interrupting messages, and menacing oversight.

With this understanding of the critical conditions, you can look at your planned campfire experiences to confirm that all the conditions are in place.

If you get stuck, run a Design Sprint activity called Crazy 8s. Give each participant a pen and instruct all to fold a piece of paper into eight squares. Then read the description of campfire experiences to them (see Campfire Principle in chapter 8).

Ask all to draw eight possible answers to this question:

What campfire experiences would you like for the community?

Put on a timer for four minutes and go crazy. (Each square should take about forty seconds to draw, and stick figures are fine!) Then return to discuss the ideas you like best.

Worksheet 4: Identify a Brand Community's Purpose

This worksheet can start a conversation to help answer core questions that influence what a brand community will look like:

Why are we building community?

How will the community enrich members?

What organizational support does it provide?

First, clarify larify the ways that community can support the organization:

- *Innovation:* creating *new* value for stakeholders

- *Customer and stakeholder retention:* keeping customers and stakeholders involved with the organization and providing value to the brand

- *Marketing:* informing the market of offered value

- *Customer service:* helping customers/users with service or products

- *Talent recruitment and retention:* attracting and retaining the people the organization needs for success

- *Advancing movements:* creating a fundamental shift in the culture or business.

- *Community forum:* making the brand a destination for a specific community

Start a conversation with your team where you address these questions:

1. How do stakeholders want to grow the organization?

2. What will a successful community help them do or be?

3. What resources can they offer a community to support growth and connection?

Once you have gathered responses to these questions, rank the answers on their importance in impacting your organization. The hidden purpose of your community may surface in the discussion.

Worksheet 5: Encouraging Engagement

Encouraging participation in the community is never as simple as giving swag, badges, and points. In fact, as we've discussed in this book, incentivizing with external rewards diminishes participants' internal motivation.

Although of course you need to acknowledge, reward, and recognize member contributions every day, you also should plan formal ways to do so. The following table reviews some of the terms we've been using in this book.

Review of Terms

TERM	MEANING	EXAMPLE	RECOMMENDATION
Incentive	An external reward offered in exchange for participation	Offer members a sticker for every post added to a platform.	Use incentives sparingly. When you remove the incentive, you will likely lose the participation they encourage.
Token	An item given that represents a relationship and/or a shared value	A member completes volunteer hours and the founder sends them a handwritten card and sticker honoring their commitment.	Ensure the token is often given by a community elder and reserved for those who have supported in action.
Acknowledgment	A specific articulation of the contribution a participant makes (or has made), without judgment	A new member writes their first article for a newsletter, and you say, "I notice you put in time to share this story. This is an important part of growing our community, and I see your commitment."	Use acknowledgment liberally, especially for new leaders and members, to help them feel seen.
Recognition, gratitude, and appreciation (with judgment)	Forms of sharing acknowledgment with a value judgment attached	A longtime member contributes their hundredth post to the group, and you add them to a special access group that includes a badge attached to their username.	You can recognize with higher status, privileges, responsibilities, and verbal affirmations.

Three conditions must be in place to support internal motivation:

1. Choice
2. Connection to others
3. Progression toward purpose

Answer the following questions with your team to ensure that you will encourage engagement in ways that help members feel seen and inspire them to remain connected.

ACKNOWLEDGMENT

- How will we express acknowledgment (written, video, call, email, etc.)?
- Who will express acknowledgment?

GRATITUDE/RECOGNITION

- What participation should definitely elicit gratitude and recognition?
- How will we express formal gratitude or recognition (written, video, call, email, etc.)?

TOKENS

- What participation should be recognized with a token?
- What tokens would we like to offer?
- Who will give a particular token?
- What do our tokens represent?

NOTES

Preface

1. B. Joseph Pine II and James H. Gilmore, "Welcome to the Experience Economy," *Harvard Business Review,* July-August 1998.

Introduction

1. The working definition in this book is informed by and articulated differently from that introduced by Muniz and O'Guinn in 2001. Albert M. Muniz and Thomas C. O'Guinn, "Brand Community," *Journal of Consumer Research* 27, no. 4 (March 2001): 412–32, https://doi.org/10.1086/319618.
2. "Cigna U.S. Loneliness Index," Cigna.com, May 2018, www.cigna.com/assets /docs/newsroom/loneliness-survey-2018-full-report.pdf.
3. "Cigna U.S. Loneliness Index."
4. Jayne O'Donnell, "Teens Aren't Socializing in the Real World. And That's Making Them Super Lonely," *USA Today,* March 20, 2019, www.usatoday.com /story/news/health/2019/03/20/teen-loneliness-social-media-cell-phones -suicide-isolation-gaming-cigna/3208845002/.
5. Ariel Stravynski and Richard Boyer, "Loneliness in Relation to Suicide Ideation and Parasuicide: A Population-Wide Study," *Suicide and Life Threatening Behavior* 31, no. 1 (2001): 32–40.
6. "QuickStats: Suicide Rates for Teens Aged 15–19 Years, by Sex—United States, 1975–2015," Centers for Disease Control and Prevention, www.cdc.gov/mmwr /volumes/66/wr/mm6630a6.htm.
7. "Suicide Replaces Homicide as Second-Leading Cause of Death among U.S. Teenagers," Population Reference Bureau, June 9, 2016, www.prb.org/suicide -replaces-homicide-second-leading-cause-death-among-us-teens/.

8. Jacqueline Lee, "Palo Alto: Cameras to Do Suicide Watch along Train Tracks," *Mercury News*, July 7, 2017, www.mercurynews.com/2017/07/05/palo-alto -cameras-to-do-suicide-watch-along-train-tracks/.

9. Vivek Murthy, "Work and the Loneliness Epidemic," *Harvard Business Review*, September 2017, hbr.org/cover-story/2017/09/work-and-the-loneliness -epidemic.

10. Scott Berinato, "What Do We Know about Loneliness and Work?" *Harvard Business Review*, September 2017, 10–12. (Reprint BG1705).

11. Emma Seppälä and Marissa King, "Burnout at Work Isn't Just about Exhaustion. It's Also about Loneliness," *Harvard Business Review*, June 2017, https:// hbr.org/2017/06/burnout-at-work-isnt-just-about-exhaustion-its-also-about -loneliness.

12. "Remote Work: A Guide to Conquering Remote Work Loneliness from Remote Workers around the World," Buffer, accessible at https://open.buffer.com /remote-work-loneliness/.

13. Quora, "Loneliness Might Be a Bigger Health Risk Than Smoking or Obesity," *Forbes*, https://www.forbes.com/sites/quora/2017/01/18/loneliness-might-be-a -bigger-health-risk-than-smoking-or-obesity/.

14. "The 'Loneliness Epidemic,'" Health Resources & Services Administration, January 2019, https://www.hrsa.gov/enews/past-issues/2019/january-17/loneliness -epidemic.

15. Ryan J. Dwyer, Kostadin Kushlev, and Elizabeth Dunn, "Smartphone Use Undermines Enjoyment of Face-to-Face Social Interactions," *Journal of Experimental Social Psychology* 78 (2018): 233–39, doi:10.1016/j .jesp.2017.10.007.

16. Kostadin Kushlev, Jason D. Proulx, and Elizabeth W. Dunn, "Digitally Connected, Socially Disconnected: The Effects of Relying on Technology Rather Than Other People," *Computers in Human Behavior* 76 (2017): 68–74, doi:10.1016/j.chb.2017.07.001.

17. Rani Molla, "The Rise of Fear-Based Social Media Like Nextdoor, Citizen, and Now Amazon's Neighbors," *Vox*, May 7, 2019, www.vox.com/recode/2019/5/7 /18528014/fear-social-media-nextdoor-citizen-amazon-ring-neighbors.

18. Laura Entis, "Can You Buy a Cure for Loneliness?" *Vox*, May 6, 2019, www.vox .com/the-highlight/2019/4/29/18511580/loneliness-co-living-coworking-friend -app-tribe-wework.

19. See https://www.twitch.tv/videos/328778515?t=00h26m42s.

20. United Religions Initiative Charter 2017, https://www.uri.org/sites/default/files /media/document/2017/URI-Charter-English.pdf.

21. Sister Sabina Rifat, "United Religions Initiative Report: Peace Group of Journalist Muzaffarabad, Aj&K, Distribution of EID Package to the Needy

under the Auspices of 'Peace Group of Journalist Mirpur Region,'" May, 26, 2019, https://www.facebook.com/236653296384526/posts/peace-group-of -journalistmuzaffarabad-ajkdistribution-of-eid-package-to-the-need /2130608856988951/.

22. Rich Teerlink and Lee Ozley, *More Than a Motorcycle: The Leadership Journey at Harley-Davidson* (Boston: Harvard Business School Press, 2000).

23. Mike Seate, "Harley-Davidson: The Evolution during the 1980s," *Baggers*, February 23, 2009, https://www.baggersmag.com/harley-davidson-evolution -during-1980s.

24. Seate, "Harley-Davidson."

25. Bob Lowery, "Harley Owners Group 30th Anniversary Celebration: Riding with a Passion," December 6, 2013, thunderpress.net/top-stories/harley-owners -group-30th-anniversary-celebration/2013/11/27.htm.

26. "H.O.G.® History: The Beginning," *Hog Blog*, September 26, 2019, blog.hog.com /insider-articles/h-o-g-history-the-beginning.

27. Margie Siegal, *Harley-Davidson: A History of the World's Most Famous Motorcycle* (New York: Shire Library USA, 2014).

28. "H.O.G.® History."

29. Gregory S. Carpenter, Gary F. Gebhardt, and John F. Sherry Jr., *Resurgence: The Four Stages of Market-Focused Reinvention* (New York: Palgrave Macmillan, 2014), 229–30.

30. Rich Teerlink, "Harley's Leadership U-Turn," *Harvard Business Review*, March 2000, hbr.org/2000/07/harleys-leadership-u-turn.

Chapter 1

1. Eb Adeyeri, "Ice Bucket Challenge: What Are the Lessons for Marketers?" *Guardian*, August 27, 2014, https://www.theguardian.com/media-network /media-network-blog/2014/aug/27/ice-bucket-challenge-lessons-marketing.

2. Göran Ahrne and Nils Brunsson, "Organization outside Organizations: The Significance of Partial Organization," *Organization* 18, no. 1 (2010): 83–104. https://doi.org/10.1177/1350508410376256.

3. Eric Werker and Faisal Z. Ahmed, "What Do Nongovernmental Organizations Do?" *Journal of Economic Perspectives* 22, no. 2 (Spring 2008): 73–92.

4. Giovan Francesco Lanzerra, "Ephemeral Organizations in Extreme Environments: Emergence, Strategy, Extinction," *Journal of Management Studies* 20 (1983): 71–95.

5. "Community works when it is 'controlled' by purpose. Community without purpose is chaos. Purpose without community is simply passion." Tim Kastelle, Nilofer Merchant, and Martie-Louise Verreynne, "What Creates Advantage in

the 'Social Era'?" *Innovations* 10, no. 3/4, https://www.mitpressjournals.org/doi /pdf/10.1162/inov_a_00241.

6. "An Introduction to Yelp Metrics as of March 31, 2019," Yelp, www.yelp.com /factsheet.

7. "About Us," Sephora, www.sephora.com/beauty/about-us.

8. Daniel Pink, "What Motivates Us?" *Harvard Business Review*, February 2010, https://hbr.org/2010/02/what-motivates-us.

9. Annual Report Pursuant to Section 13 or 15(d) of the Securities Exchange Act of 1934. For the fiscal year ended December 31, 2018, www.sec.gov/Archives /edgar/data/1370637/000137063719000028/etsy1231201810k.htm.

10. "The definition of vulnerability is uncertainty, risk, and emotional exposure." Brené Brown, *Daring Greatly: How the Courage to Be Vulnerable Transforms the Way We Live, Love, Parent, and Lead* (London: Penguin, 2012), 35.

11. Brown, *Daring Greatly*, 45.

12. Bonnie M. Hagerty, J. Lynch-Sauer, Kathleen L. Patusky, M. Bouwsema, and Philip A. Collier, "Sense of Belonging: A Vital Mental Health Concept," *Archives of Psychiatric Nursing* 6 (1992): 172–77.

13. "From Instant Pot to Instagram: Critical Lessons in Startup Community Building," *First Round Review*, https://firstround.com/review/from-instant-pot -to-instagram-critical-lessons-in-startup-community-building/.

14. "Yelp Metrics."

15. "#WellActually, Americans Say Customer Service Is Better Than Ever," American Express, December 15, 2017, about.americanexpress.com/press-release /wellactually-americans-say-customer-service-better-ever.

Chapter 2

1. Tim Kastelle, Nilofer Merchant, and Martie-Louise Verreynne, "What Creates Advantage in the 'Social Era'?" *Innovations* 10, no. 3/4, https://www .mitpressjournals.org/doi/pdf/10.1162/inov_a_00241.

2. Yasmine Gray, "5 Reasons Why Rihanna's Fenty Beauty Was Named One of TIME's Best Inventions of 2017," *Billboard*, November 30, 2017, www.billboard .com/articles/news/lifestyle/8046279/rihanna-fenty-beauty-time-best -inventions-2017.

3. Charles Arthur, "Digg Loses a Third of Its Visitors in a Month: Is It Deadd [*sic*]?" *Technology Blog, Guardian*, June 3, 2010, www.theguardian.com /technology/blog/2010/jun/03/digg-dead-falling-visitors.

4. Jolie O'Dell, "Digg's Decline by the Numbers: Plummeting Traffic, Waning Power [STATS]," *Mashable*, September 24, 2010, mashable.com/2010/09/24 /digg-traffic-stats/.

5. Eddie Wrenn, "Digg Is Sold for $500,000 - after Turning Down an Offer from Google for $200 Million Just Four Years Ago," *Daily Mail Online,* July 13, 2012, www.dailymail.co.uk/sciencetech/article-2173029/Digg-sold-500-000--turning-offer-Google-200million-just-years-ago.html.

6. Fortune 500, "Salesforce.com," Fortune.com, https://fortune.com/fortune500/salesforce-com/.

7. Daniela Sirtori-Cortina, "From Climber to Billionaire: How Yvon Chouinard Built Patagonia into a Powerhouse His Own Way," *Forbes,* https://www.forbes.com/sites/danielasirtori/2017/03/20/from-climber-to-billionaire-how-yvon-chouinard-built-patagonia-into-a-powerhouse-his-own-way/.

8. Jim Harter, "Dismal Employee Engagement Is a Sign of Global Mismanagement," *Workplace* (blog), *Gallup,* November 18, 2019, https://www.gallup.com/workplace/231668/dismal-employee-engagement-sign-global-mismanagement.aspx.

9. Emma Seppälä and Marissa King, "Burnout at Work Isn't Just about Exhaustion. It's Also about Loneliness," *Harvard Business Review,* June 2016, https://hbr.org/2017/06/burnout-at-work-isnt-just-about-exhaustion-its-also-about-loneliness.

10. Seppälä and King, "Burnout."

11. David Burkus, "Work Friends Make Us More Productive (Except When They Stress Us Out)," *Harvard Business Review,* May 2017, https://hbr.org/2017/05/work-friends-make-us-more-productive-except-when-they-stress-us-out.

12. Christine M. Riordan, "We All Need Friends at Work," *Harvard Business Review,* July 2013, https://hbr.org/2013/07/we-all-need-friends-at-work.

13. Seppälä and King, "Burnout."

14. Amy E. Randel, Benjamin M. Galvin, Lynn M. Shore, Karen Holcombe Ehrhart, Beth G. Chung, Michelle A. Dean, and Uma Kedharnath, "Inclusive Leadership: Realizing Positive Outcomes through Belongingness and Being Valued for Uniqueness," *Human Resource Management Review* 28, no. 2 (2018): 190–203, doi:10.1016/j.hrmr.2017.07.002; Sandra Restrepo, director, *Brené Brown: The Call to Courage,* Netflix, 2019.

15. Tom Ryan, "Lululemon Customers Want Spiritual Enrichment—and to Look Good," *Forbes,* May 15, 2019, https://www.forbes.com/sites/retailwire/2019/05/15/lululemon-customers-want-spiritual-enrichment-and-to-look-good/#6b690923b55e.

16. John Burns, "Pros and Cons of the Electric Motorcycle" (blog post), Motorcycles.com, May 25, 2018, https://www.motorcycle.com/features/pros-cons-electric-motorcycle.html.

17. Carrie Melissa Jones, "7 Lessons from Asana's Community Launch," *CMS Wire,* March 18, 2019, www.cmswire.com/customer-experience/7-lessons-from-asanas-community-launch/.

18. Felix Richter, "Infographic: The Explosive Growth of Reddit's Community," Statista Infographics, May 23, 2019, www.statista.com/chart/11882/number-of -subreddits-on-reddit/.

Chapter 3

1. Elizabeth Perle McKenna and Hahrie Han, *Groundbreakers: How Obama's 2.2 Million Volunteers Transformed Campaigning in America* (New York: Oxford University Press, 2015), 23.
2. Neil Stern, "Glossier: From Beauty Blog to Billion-Dollar Brand," *Forbes*, March 19, 2019, https://www.forbes.com/sites/neilstern/2019/03/19/glossier -from-beauty-blog-to-billion-dollar-brand-valuation/.

Chapter 4

1. Alicia Iriberri and Gondy Leroy, "A Life-Cycle Perspective on Online Community Success," *ACM Computing Surveys* 41, no. 2, art. no. 11 (February 2009); Jenny Preece, *Online Communities: Designing Usability, Supporting Sociability* (Hoboken, NJ: Wiley, 2000); Dorine C. Andrews, "Audience-Specific Online Community Design," *Communications of the ACM* 45, no. 4 (2002): 64–68; Rob Kling and Christina Courtright, "Group Behavior and Learning in Electronic Forums: A Sociotechnical Approach," *Information Society* 19, no. 3 (2003): 221–35; Arvind Malhotra, Sanjay Gosain, and Alexander Hars, "Evolution of a Virtual Community: Understanding Design Issues through a Longitudinal Study," *ICIS 1997 Proceedings* 4 (1997): 59–74; Etienne Wegner, Richard McDermott, and William Snyder, *Cultivating Communities of Practice: A Guide to Managing Knowledge* (Cambridge, MA: Harvard Business School Press, 2002). In the list here, we present the articulation of four stages only as a model to help leadership recognize how a community's needs change with maturity. Many smart people have listed differently named phases with different characteristics. In our humble opinion, other (differing) models can also help.
2. Iriberri and Leroy, "Life-Cycle."
3. Iriberri and Leroy, "Life-Cycle," 14.
4. Damon Centola, Joshua Becker, Devon Brackbill, and Andrea Baronchelli, "Experimental Evidence for Tipping Points in Social Convention," *Science* 360, no. 6393 (June 8, 2018): 1116–19.
5. "Fitbit Reports $571 Million Q4'18 Revenue and $1.51 Billion FY'18 Revenue," Fitbit, investor.fitbit.com/press/press-releases/press-release-details/2019/Fitbit -Reports-571-Million-Q418-Revenue-and-151-Billion-FY18-Revenue/.

Chapter 5

1. Caroline Aubé, Vincent Rousseau, and Sébastien Tremblay, "Team Size and Quality of Group Experience: The More the Merrier?" *Group Dynamics: Theory, Research, and Practice* 15, no. 4 (2011), doi:10.1037/a0025400.

2. Jon R. Katzenbach and Douglas K. Smith, *The Wisdom of Teams* (Boston: Harvard University Press, 2015), 42.

3. Katzenbach and Smith, *Wisdom*, 43.

4. Nick Bunkley, "Joseph Juran, 103, Pioneer in Quality Control, Dies," *New York Times*, March 3, 2008, https://www.nytimes.com/2008/03/03/business/03juran .html.

5. Jakob Nielsen, "The 90-9-1 Rule for Participation Inequality in Social Media and Online Communities," Nielsen Norman Group, October 9, 2006, https:// www.nngroup.com/articles/participation-inequality/.

6. Daniel Oberhaus, "Nearly All of Wikipedia Is Written by Just 1 Percent of Its Editors," *Vice*, November 7, 2017, www.vice.com/en_us/article/7x47bb /wikipedia-editors-elite-diversity-foundation.

7. Robert Steuteville, "The Missing Middle of Our Social Lives," *Public Square: A CNU Journal*, February 8, 2016, https://www.cnu.org/publicsquare/missing -middle-our-social-lives; E. J. Dionne Jr., "Where Goes the Neighborhood?" *Washington Post*, August 10, 2014, https://www.washingtonpost.com/opinions /ej-dionne-where-goes-the-neighborhood/2014/08/10/8a137cde-1f39-11e4 -ae54-0cfe1f974f8a_story.html.

8. Elinor Ostrom is a twenty-first-century Nobel Prize–winning political econo- mist who discusses managing common shared resources. We think that her deeply respected work can help leaders choose how best to manage their unique participants. (Please see appendix C for a list of some of her work.)

9. Andrei Hagiu and Julian Wright, "Multi-Sided Platforms" (Working Paper 15-037), Harvard Business School, March 16, 2015.

10. Wikipedia, s.v. "Two-Sided Market," last modified October 23, 2019, https://en .wikipedia.org/wiki/Two-sided_market.

Chapter 6

1. Dan Ariely, "When Are Our Decisions Made for Us?" *TED Radio Hour*, March 10, 2017, https://www.npr.org/2017/03/10/519270280/dan-ariely-when -are-our-decisions-made-for-us.

2. Kelsey Campbell-Dollaghan, "Why Ikea Shutting Down Its Most Popular Fan Site Is a Giant Mistake," *Gizmodo*, June 6, 2014, https://gizmodo.com/why-ikea -shutting-down-its-most-popular-fan-site-is-a-g-1591401344.

3. Simone Mitchell, "How IKEA Learned to Love IKEA hacks (Almost as Much as We Do)," news.com.au, January 21, 2016, https://www.news.com.au/lifestyle /home/interiors/how-ikea-learned-to-love-ikea-hacks-almost-as-much-as-we -do/news-story/8f03b2779d6807315763ef56b0cd6fda.

4. "Etsy Teams," Etsy, https://community.etsy.com/t5/Etsy-Teams/ct-p/teams.

5. Jen Yamato and Ben Collins, "Reddit Fired the Woman Trying to Save It," *Daily Beast*, July 4, 2015, www.thedailybeast.com/reddit-fired-the-woman-trying-to -save-it.

6. Yamato and Collins, "Reddit Fired."

7. Brian Lynch and Courtnie Swearingen, "Why We Shut Down Reddit's 'Ask Me Anything' Forum," *New York Times*, July 8, 2015, www.nytimes.com/2015/07/08 /opinion/why-we-shut-down-reddits-ask-me-anything-forum.html.

8. Davey Alba, "Ellen Pao Steps Down as CEO after Reddit Revolt," *Wired*, June 29, 2017, www.wired.com/2015/07/reddit-ceo-ellen-pao-steps-down -huffman-replacement/.

9. Alba, "Ellen Pao."

Chapter 7

1. Priya Parker, *The Art of Gathering: How We Meet and Why It Matters* (New York: Riverhead Books, 2018), 36.

2. Carrie Jones, "How to Create Your Community Commitment Curve," Gather, August 24, 2018, https://www.gathercommunityconsulting.com/blog/creating -your-community-commitment-curve.

3. Sarah Schulman, *Conflict Is Not Abuse* (Vancouver, BC: Arsenal Pulp Press, 2016), 14.

4. Michael Roth, "Don't Dismiss 'Safe Spaces,'" *New York Times*, August 29, 2019, https://www.nytimes.com/2019/08/29/opinion/safe-spaces-campus.html.

5. Michael Roth, "Don't Dismiss."

6. Patricia Hernandez, "Twitch Streamer Swatted while Playing Pokémon Go Outside," *Kotaku*, July 27, 2016, https://kotaku.com/twitch-streamer-swatted -while-playing-pokemon-go-outsid-1784309781; "10 Streamers Get Swatted Live," *YouTube*, https://www.youtube.com/watch?v=TiW-BVPCbZk.

7. Nathan Grayson, "Streamer Trihex Apologizes for Homophobic Slur after Twitch Suspends His Channel," *Kotaku*, October 8, 2018, https://kotaku.com /streamer-trihex-apologizes-for-homophobic-slur-after-tw-1829604490.

8. Grayson, "Streamer Trihex."

9. "Reddit.com Competitive Analysis, Marketing Mix and Traffic," *Alexa*, n.d., www.alexa.com/siteinfo/reddit.com.

10. Amjad Masad (@Amasad), Twitter post, June 6, 2018, https://twitter.com /amasad/status/1004173806787702784.

11. "Stack Overflow Reducing Headcount by 20%," *Hacker News*, November 3, 2017, news.ycombinator.com/item?id=15613101.

12. Ingrid Lunden, "Developer Community Stack Overflow Reportedly Lays Off 20% as It Refocusses Business," *TechCrunch*, November 3, 2017, techcrunch .com/2017/11/02/stack-overflow-lays-off-staff/.

Chapter 8

1. Zoe Weiner, "Sephora Is Hosting Its First-Ever Beauty Convention," *Glamour*, June 5, 2018, www.glamour.com/story/sephora-sephoria-house-of-beauty -convention.

2. Priya Parker, *The Art of Gathering: How We Meet and Why It Matters* (New York: Riverhead Books, 2018), 160.

3. Stuart Brown, with Christopher Vaughan, *Play: How It Shapes the Brain, Opens the Imagination, and Invigorates the Soul* (New York: Penguin, 2010), 66–69.

4. The hosts are part of the diaconate, as discussed in *The Art of Community*. In communities in general, the diaconate make events more special and maintain more authority over the community values and membership.

5. Michael Sailer, Jan Ulrich Hense, Sarah Katharina Mayr, and Heinz Mandl, "How Gamification Motivates: An Experimental Study of the Effects of Specific Game Design Elements on Psychological Need Satisfaction, *Computers in Human Behavior* 69 (April 2017): 371–80, www.sciencedirect.com/science /article/pii/S074756321630855X#bib23.

Chapter 9

1. Mary Kinney, "How to Throw a Great Event," Etsy, April 18, 2016, www.etsy .com/seller-handbook/article/how-to-throw-a-great-event/43929408125.

2. Julie Schneider, "Join the Party: Etsy Craft Party 2013," *Etsy News* (blog), Etsy, May 6, 2013, blog.etsy.com/news/2013/join-the-party-etsy-craft-party-2013/.

Chapter 10

1. Kenneth Thomas, "The Four Intrinsic Rewards That Drive Employee Engagement," *Ivey Business Journal*, November/December 2009, https:// iveybusinessjournal.com/publication/the-four-intrinsic-rewards-that-drive -employee-engagement/.

2. Susan Fowler, *Mastery of Motivation* (Oakland, CA: Berrett-Koehler, 2019).
3. Daniel Pink, "What Motivates Us?" *Harvard Business Review,* February 2010, https://hbr.org/2010/02/what-motivates-us.
4. Mark R. Lepper, David L. Green, and Richard E. Nisbett, "Undermining Children's Intrinsic Interest with Extrinsic Reward: A Test of the 'Overjustification' Hypothesis," *Journal of Personality and Social Psychology* 28, no. 1 (1973), 129–37, doi:10.1037/h0035519.
5. Michael Sailer, Jan Ulrich Hense, Sarah Katharina Mayr, and Heinz Mandl, "How Gamification Motivates: An Experimental Study of the Effects of Specific Game Design Elements on Psychological Need Satisfaction," *Computers in Human Behavior* 69 (April 2017): 371–80, www.sciencedirect.com/science/article/pii/S074756321630855X#bib23.
6. Amy Jo Kim, *Community Building on the Web: Secret Strategies for Successful Online Communities* (Boston: Addison-Wesley Longman), 2000.
7. "The Business of CrossFit: An Update on New Market Research" (blog post), Rally Fitness, March 13, 2017, https://rallyfitness.com/blogs/news/the-business -of-crossfit-an-update-on-new-market-research-2017.

Chapter 11

1. Juliana Stancampiano, *Radical Outcomes: How to Create Extraordinary Teams That Get Tangible Business Results* (Hoboken, NJ: Wiley, 2019), 15.
2. David Brooks, *The Second Mountain: The Quest for a Moral Life* (New York: Random House, 2019), 267.
3. Michael Harris and Bill Tayler, "Don't Let Metrics Undermine Your Business: An Obsession with Numbers Can Sink Your Strategy," *Harvard Business Review,* September–October 2019, 64.
4. Harris and Tayler, "Don't Let Metrics Undermine Your Business."
5. Amy Gallo, "The Value of Keeping the Right Customers," *Harvard Business Review,* November 2014, hbr.org/2014/10/the-value-of-keeping-the-right -customers.

Last Word

1. Margaret Mead, "Unique Possibilities of the Melting Pot: 1950," in *The World Ahead: An Anthropologist Anticipates the Future,* ed. Robert B. Textor (New York: Berghahn Books, 2005), 74.
2. Merton to Jim Forest, February 21, 1966; full text in *The Hidden Ground of Love,* ed. William H. Shannon (New York: Farrar Straus Giroux, 1985), 294–97; http://jimandnancyforest.com/2014/10/mertons-letter-to-a-young-activist/.

Appendix A

1. "Buzzfeed.com Competitive Analysis, Marketing Mix and Traffic," *Alexa*, n.d., www.alexa.com/siteinfo/buzzfeed.com.

2. Charles Bethea, "The BuzzFeed Layoffs and the Case of the Teen-Age Quiz-Maker," *New Yorker*, February 2, 2019, www.newyorker.com/news/news-desk/the-buzzfeed-layoffs-and-the-case-of-the-teen-age-quiz-maker.

3. Akanksha Rana, "Spotify Hits 100 Million Subscribers, Reports Revenue Jump," *Reuters*, April 29, 2019, www.reuters.com/article/us-spotify-tech-results-idUSKCN1S50TH.

4. Jeremy Heimans and Henry Timms, *New Power* (Sydney: Pan Macmillan Australia, 2018).

GLOSSARY

Acknowledgment: The act of specifically articulating the contribution a participant makes (or made), without judgment. Typically, this includes words that specify how the individual is making a difference.

Advocacy: Any organizational effort to motivate individuals outside the organization to enact change. In advocacy, work usually includes sharing a change message widely. With advocacy, an organization seeks to grow its influence, whether, for example, in the domain of political change, in the adoption of a for-profit company's technology, or in a nonprofit's involvement in promoting a social good.

Appreciation: A kind of acknowledgment that includes a judgment.

Belonging: People's experience of two feelings: (1) feeling valued (or needed) by the entire group or some part of it, and (2) feeling that they are a fit for what is needed in the community and in the environment that has been created.

Brand: Any identifiable organization that promises value. A brand can serve for-profit, nonprofit, political, social, artistic, faith-based, or other purposes.

Brand community: A community with an aspiration to serve both individuals and organizational goals. All brand communities have members who (1) care about one another, (2) share an identity founded on value(s) and goal(s), and (3) share experiences that reflect shared value(s) and goal(s).

Building community: Facilitating, accelerating, and supporting the individual relationships that together form a community.

Campfire events: Planned events in which participants can find an intimate experience.

Campfire principle: A principle that leaders adhere to when planning events to build participant relationships. At campfires, we have proximity, permission, and conditions to connect meaningfully with others. Most important, campfires are small enough that everyone can participate, if they choose, and feel seen.

Campfire space: An offered space where there is no planned event, but participants can use the available space for intimate conversations.

Coercion: The use of fear and threats to get people to do (or not do) something that the coercer wants done (or not done).

Community: A group of people who share mutual concern for one another.

Community activities: Experiences offered to members. These include programs, events, blog posts, trainings, celebrations, rituals, and so on.

Community health: Members' satisfaction that they feel supported, included, and accepted.

Critical mass stage: Critical mass stage is marked by additional members taking on leadership roles and upholding community guidelines on leadership's behalf. At this stage, resources come to the community without leadership needing to bring it all inside or specifically asking for it.

Establishment stage: The stage of community development that can be identified as the point at which the returning-participant rate reaches and then remains approximately 50–60 percent.

External motivation: A driver of action in order to get a reward or avoid punishment. Typically the reward is offered and/or given by other people. They decide whether, when, and how much is awarded or punished.

Founding members: The early members who shepherd the community from its beginnings to critical mass stage.

Gamification: Refers to using game mechanics to manage a group, usually by introducing competition between members. Gamification is designed to help motivate groups to do things—that is, get actions done.

Inception stage: The earliest stage of community development, when the founding members constitute the community.

Inner rings: Groups within a community that segment members by some criterion (geography, skills, interest, etc.). Mature communities offer members inner rings that provide a path to growth.

Insider (esoteric) understanding: Things insiders understand that outsiders do not or cannot.

Internal motivation: A driver that comes from inside us and feels like a natural part of ourselves. When we are internally motivated, no one else needs to provide anything more to inspire us to action. The (internal) joy we feel after an activity can be enough.

Intimate experience: The usually small-scale experience that makes participants feel connected because of the individual conversations, private moments, and vulnerability that they experience with other participants.

Meaningful community engagement: Any action by a participant that supports that participant in (1) caring about the welfare of other community members and/or (2) feeling connected to the community as a whole.

Member: Someone who returns to connect with members, considers themselves a regular participant, and ideally has experienced some kind of opt-in initiation, so that they have reason to identify themselves as a member. Without a recognized initiation, members are difficult to distinguish from visitors. Even if the initiation experience isn't dramatic, there should always be some discernible difference between members and visitors.

Mirage community: A group that aspires to form community, and may even call itself a community, but lacks fundamental elements that constitute a community. As a result, mirage communities fail to deliver positive community and organizational benefits.

Network effect: In a brand community context, the effect whereby the more people who use (or participate with) a resource, the more value it offers.

Norms: Common terms, behavior patterns, rules, and discussion topics.

Organization: People participating in an agreed order, including at least one element of membership, hierarchy, rules, monitoring, and sanctions. (This definition is from Göran Ahrne and Nils Brunsson, "Organization outside Organizations: The Significance of Partial Organization," *Organization* 18, no. 1 (2010): 83–104. https://doi.org/10.1177/1350508410376256.)

Organization outcomes: Behavior, skill, or resource that supports organizational goals.

Pareto principle: Also known as the 80-20 rule. It predicts that in many situations no less than 80 percent of success (or results and value) will come from no more than 20 percent of resources. This principle will show up in many areas in a community, including in membership involvement.

Participant: Anyone who takes an action to participate in your community in some way. Typically participants include both visitors and members.

Platform: The technology that allows participants to connect. As a tool, it is never enough, by itself, to form a community. Typically a platform enables members to communicate, share, and discover both one another and resources no matter where they are.

Rituals: Activities that have meaning. Appropriate rituals can be a great way to offer acknowledgments and appreciation. In mature communities, rituals acknowledge changes and milestones.

Segmentation stage: The stage at which a community branches off into subcommunities. These are a type of inner ring where not all members fit in all rings because of skills, interests, or maturity.

Shared experience: An event for a group or community that articulates, references, or reinforces the shared values of that group.

Shared space: A venue for meeting that allows participants to ask for help and deliver support. Whether they do or don't depends on several factors. In this book, *space* can mean a physical location or a digital location where participants can meet.

Surrogation: The tendency for people "to confuse what's being measured for the metric being used." (This definition is from Michael Harris and Bill Tayler, "Don't Let Metrics Undermine Your Business: An Obsession with Numbers Can Sink Your Strategy," *Harvard Business Review*, September-October 2019, 64.)

Two-sided market: An economic platform that brings together at least two distinct user groups that provide each other with network benefits. (It is also referred to as a *two-sided network*.) A platform that offers value primarily by supporting connection between at least two types of affiliated customers is called a *multisided platform*.

Visitor: Someone seeking to learn more about your community. Typically, the person reads about the community, discovers its website, watches a video about the community, or visits an event, and grows interested.

FURTHER READING

Brown, Stuart, and Christopher Vaughan. *Play: How It Shapes the Brain, Opens the Imagination, and Invigorates the Soul.* New York: Avery, 2010.

Caplan, Robyn. "Content or Context Moderation? Artisanal, Community-Reliant, and Industrial Approaches." Data & Society. 2018. datasociety .net/wp-content/uploads/2018/11/DS_Content_or_Context _Moderation.pdf.

CMX Community Industry Trends Report. CMX Hub. 2019. https://cmxhub .com/community-industry-trends-report-2020/.

Heimans, Jeremy, and Henry Timms. *New Power* (Sydney, Australia: Pan Macmillan, 2018).

Kalbag, Laura. *Accessibility for Everyone.* A Book Apart, 2017.

Kim, Amy Jo. *Community Building on the Web: Secret Strategies for Successful Online Communities.* Berkeley, CA: Peachpit Press, 2000.

McMillan, David W., and David M. Chavis. "Sense of Community: A Definition and Theory." *Journal of Community Psychology* 14 (January 1986), 6. https://pdfs.semanticscholar.org/e5fb/8ece108aec36714ee413876e61b0 510e7c80.pdf.

Ostrom, Elinor. *Governing the Commons: The Evolution of Institutions for Collective Action.* Cambridge, UK: Cambridge University Press, 1990.

Ostrom, Elinor. *Understanding Institutional Diversity.* Princeton, NJ: Princeton University Press, 2005.

Ostrom, Elinor, and James Walker. *Trust and Reciprocity: Interdisciplinary Lessons from Experimental Research.* New York: Russell Sage Foundation, 2003.

Ostrom, Elinor, James Walker, and Roy Gardner. *Rules, Games, and Common-Pool Resources.* Ann Arbor: University of Michigan Press, 1994.

Parker, Priya. *The Art of Gathering: How We Meet and Why It Matters.* New York: Riverhead Books, 2018.

Roberts, Sarah T. *Behind the Screen: Content Moderation in the Shadows of Social Media.* New Haven, CT: Yale University Press, 2019.

ACKNOWLEDGMENTS

Projects that take a year and a half and then get shared around the world come out of a community. So much appreciation to the people who shared, listened, lent time, insight, trust and wisdom.

Melissa Allen

Samantha Altán

Erin Anacker

Will Bachman

Irina Banciu

Louise Beryl

Dianna Brosius

Traci Cappiello

Teddy Carroll

Newton Cheng

Liz Crampton

Andrea Dehlendorf

Heidi Dezell

Elena

Aram Fischer

Trish Fontanilla

Scott Forgey

Marcus Graham

Gabriel Grant

Evan Hamilton

Rosemary Hitchens

Thibaud Jobert

Kurt Johnson

Martha Jones

Robert Jones

Sarah Judd Welch

Fred Keller

Anand Kishore

Erica Kuhl

Emily Lakin

Allison Leahy

Emily Levada

Shira Levine

Sally Mahe

Allie Mahler

Neal Maillet

Jessica Malnik

Marianne Manilov

Danielle Maveal

Megan McNally

Guy Michlin

Rose-Anne Moore

Gil Morris

Nish Nadaraja

Ana Noemi

Julie O'Mara

Alastair Ong

Eric Paul

Paras Pundir

Sister Sabina Rifat

Casey Rosengren

Jeremy Ross

Carlos Saba

Jennifer Sacks

Dona Sarkar

Bobby Scarnewman

Sahiba Sethi

Ruby Somera

Rochelle Sonnenberg

Adrian Speyer

David Spinks

Danny Spitzberg

Juliana Stancampiano

Vincent Stanley

Arielle Tannenbaum

Hannah Talbot

Casper ter Kuile

Erin Wayne

Sandra Weng

Mara Zepeda

Joshua Zerkel

Appreciation also goes to the generous people who helped with insight and prefer anonymity.

From Charles

Thank you Socheata for supporting this adventure we call a life together and the many days squirreled away alone.

Rev. Dale Peterson, who role-modeled the most extraordinary community leadership I've experienced.

The patient people at a particular Emeryville cafe on 40th St. with the banquet that hosted me for yet another book.

From Carrie

A special thank you to Dominick Garrett. Your unending support makes my work possible and keeps me in high spirits.

The lovely folks of Seattle's Queen Bee Cafe and Squirrel Chops Cafe.

My ongoing community and business confidantes and friends Sarah Judd Welch and David Spinks.

Tanya Geisler, who modeled for me true and life-changing online community leadership.

INDEX

ABOUT THE AUTHORS

Photo by Ruby Somera

CARRIE MELISSA JONES is a community leader, entrepreneur, and community consultant who has been creating community online since the early 2000s.

Her work influences the world's leading brand communities, including the American Medical Association, Brainly, Buffer, Google, and Nerdwallet. In 2016, Salesforce's Mathew Sweezey named Jones one of three experts to follow on community management.

As the founder of Gather Community Consulting, she consults brands to build robust new communities and audit existing communities, and trains brands to lead their own communities. She has worked with organizations including Brainly (the world's largest social learning network), the American Medical Association, and nonprofits including DoSomething.org and Canada's PovNet. Together these brands connect well over one hundred million people worldwide.

In 2014, Jones joined CMX and served as COO and founding partner until 2017. CMX (acquired by Bevy Labs in 2019) provides training, events, and programs for community builders around the world. It now boasts a twenty-thousand-person and growing membership. With CMX, Jones trained teams at Google and Facebook, and community leaders within Salesforce, Airbnb, ADP, Discovery Channel, and other firms.

Her writing has appeared in *Venture Beat, The Next Web, First Round Review,* and *CMS Wire.*

Jones continues to volunteer with Seattle-based organizations, including Young Women Empowered and Empower Washington. She has a BA from

UCLA in both English and mass communication. She is pursuing an MA in communication at the University of Wisconsin–Milwaukee.

carriemelissa.com

CHARLES H. VOGL supports leaders in for-profit, nonprofit, and civic organizations to grow in alignment with their core values. He draws from the realm of spiritual traditions to understand how individuals build loyalty, strengthen identity, and live out shared values. These principles apply to both secular and spiritual leadership.

Photo by Tony Deifell

Vogl teaches how to build critical connections that change lives and global organizations, and impact generations. He believes that every effective leader relies on a community of stakeholders on which their success depends. Several of the world's most well-known companies use his work worldwide to connect the people most important for their success.

His book *The Art of Community* distills concepts from three thousand years of spiritual traditions so that leaders can use them to create a culture of belonging in any organization, field, or movement. The book won a Nautilus Silver Award for business and leadership writing.

His book *Storytelling for Leadership* draws on his experience as both an American PBS documentary filmmaker and a human rights advocate to teach leaders to share the truth with emotional resonance.

After conducting his own work in human rights advocacy on three continents, he went on to study leaders in social movements, business, and spiritual traditions at Yale University. He earned a master of divinity degree as a Jesse Ball DuPont foundation scholar and continues as a regular guest lecturer at Yale.

He lives in beautiful Oakland, California, where on good days he sits with his best friends without talking, because they don't have to.

CharlesVogl.com

Also by Charles Vogl
The Art of Community
Seven Principles for Belonging

"A useful field guide to create durable and profound connections . . . An important undertaking, as isolation and loneliness are a root cause of the breakdowns all around us, including extreme violence."

—**Peter Block, author of Community and Flawless Consulting**

Strong communities help people support one another, share their passions, and achieve big goals. And such communities aren't just happy accidents—they can be purposefully cultivated, whether they're in a company, in a faith institution, or among friends and enthusiasts. Drawing on 3,000 years of history and his personal experience, Charles Vogl lays out seven time-tested principles for growing enduring, effective, and connected communities.

Print, paperback, ISBN 978-1-62656-841-9
Digital PDF, ISBN 978-1-62656-842-6
Digital epub, ISBN 978-1-62656-843-3
Digital audio, ISBN 978-1-62656-850-1

BK Berrett–Koehler Publishers, Inc.
www.bkconnection.com   800.929.2929

Berrett–Koehler
BK Publishers

Berrett-Koehler is an independent publisher dedicated to an ambitious mission: *Connecting people and ideas to create a world that works for all.*

Our publications span many formats, including print, digital, audio, and video. We also offer online resources, training, and gatherings. And we will continue expanding our products and services to advance our mission.

We believe that the solutions to the world's problems will come from all of us, working at all levels: in our society, in our organizations, and in our own lives. Our publications and resources offer pathways to creating a more just, equitable, and sustainable society. They help people make their organizations more humane, democratic, diverse, and effective (and we don't think there's any contradiction there). And they guide people in creating positive change in their own lives and aligning their personal practices with their aspirations for a better world.

And we strive to practice what we preach through what we call "The BK Way." At the core of this approach is *stewardship,* a deep sense of responsibility to administer the company for the benefit of all of our stakeholder groups, including authors, customers, employees, investors, service providers, sales partners, and the communities and environment around us. Everything we do is built around stewardship and our other core values of *quality, partnership, inclusion,* and *sustainability.*

This is why Berrett-Koehler is the first book publishing company to be both a B Corporation (a rigorous certification) and a benefit corporation (a for-profit legal status), which together require us to adhere to the highest standards for corporate, social, and environmental performance. And it is why we have instituted many pioneering practices (which you can learn about at www.bkconnection.com), including the Berrett-Koehler Constitution, the Bill of Rights and Responsibilities for BK Authors, and our unique Author Days.

We are grateful to our readers, authors, and other friends who are supporting our mission. We ask you to share with us examples of how BK publications and resources are making a difference in your lives, organizations, and communities at www.bkconnection.com/impact.

Dear reader,

Thank you for picking up this book and welcome to the worldwide BK community! You're joining a special group of people who have come together to create positive change in their lives, organizations, and communities.

What's BK all about?

Our mission is to connect people and ideas to create a world that works for all.

Why? Our communities, organizations, and lives get bogged down by old paradigms of self-interest, exclusion, hierarchy, and privilege. But we believe that can change. That's why we seek the leading experts on these challenges—and share their actionable ideas with you.

A welcome gift

To help you get started, we'd like to offer you a **free copy** of one of our bestselling ebooks:

www.bkconnection.com/welcome

When you claim your **free ebook**, you'll also be subscribed to our blog.

Our freshest insights

Access the best new tools and ideas for leaders at all levels on our blog at ideas.bkconnection.com.

Sincerely,   pt rule

Your friends at Berrett-Koehler

Certified

Corporation